DEHUMANISATION

A TRUE STORY OF ORGANISED
CHILD ABUSE

JEN

and

SAMUEL GRACE

First published in Great Britain in 2023 through Amazon self-publishing service Kindle Direct Publishing.

ISBN: 978-1-3999-4941-5

Produced by samanthahoughton.co.uk

DEDICATION

My incredible son has suffered so much because of my past.

I want you to know that my love for you is unconditional. My admiration grows each day for you, from the baby boy to the strong, kind, intelligent young man you are. I'm so proud of you, Samuel James Grace (SAMUEL MEANING "GOD HEARD").

TABLE OF CONTENTS

ACKNOWLEDGEMENTS

Sam Grace, Nancy Borrret, Christine Shortman, Kwans, Dr Brown, and Kate Blewett.

Plus, all of us who have suffered through any abuse, you are perfect the way you are. All of you are heroes.

Thanks to Samantha Houghton for editing and bringing the book to life - her expertise has been so valued. She has been a saint amongst the story.

AUTHOR BIO

Hi, my name is Jennie.

My ethnicity is African/ Caribbean. I live near London and am a proud mum of two. I'm a self-taught artist, Giftsmadewithzazzle on Etsy.

As a public speaker and published author of two biographies, Nowhere to Belong and this follow-up, I needed to write about my life experiences. My passion is to support those marginalised and speak out against injustice. I want to see people prepared to help others who have experienced child rape and to recognise dissociative disorder as a real illness resulting from traumatic events as babies while not receiving love and nurturing. We deserve the right support to help us live with our trauma without it living for us.

FOREWORD

I have learned a great deal making television documentary films over thirty years, covering global issues such as slavery, trafficking, racism, exploitation, abandonment, neglect and child abuse, particularly child sex abuse. Sadly, Jen's life embraces all of these issues. I have never met anyone like Jen before; she is extraordinary on so many levels. She taught herself to read and write and has written *Dehumanisation* about her life of extreme abuse. The only way she could survive the horrific pain inflicted upon her as a child was to 'dissociate' - where her mind fragmented into 'many parts' for her survival. The parts that Jen calls her 'me's' carry different memories of the multiple and relentless abuses she suffered throughout her childhood. How amazing is that? The mind dissociates as a natural response to the trauma while it's happening, and that's how Jen and many other abused children survive. Yet the condition is called Dissociative Identity Disorder. Well, it is not a disorder; it's surely ordered and an amazing survival tool of the human mind. Something to celebrate because without dissociation, I believe Jen would not be alive today.

Jen is a woman of strength and warmth, so caring, bright and addictive to be with. She shares her life story in her book with dignity. This is actually Jen's second book. When she presented her first book to the publisher, they told her to remove the "darker" material; otherwise, they would not publish it. So after a great deal of thought, she removed 'that' material to get her voice out there and to no longer be an invisible, silent person in society. But now, we have a new Jen, a Jen with confidence and a life in front of her that she's looking forward to. Why? Because she's voicing her full life story in this book so that others can know and understand and be informed. Jen wants to help survivors who have suffered and continue to suffer the hideous injuries caused by child abuse, particularly child sex abuse.

Though Jen was broken, she still manages to be a wonderful mother to Sam, a caring, intelligent young man who witnessed some of his mother's abuse and was abused by the same perpetrators when he was just a child. Together Jen and Sam have grown. Together they take life one day at a time. It's not easy.

I am making a documentary about Dissociative Identity Disorder. With my hand on my heart, I can say that Jen is unquestionably one of the most glorious human beings I have had the privilege to film with. And that big laugh of hers is utterly infectious, despite her horrific childhood years. *Dehumanisation* needs to be read to understand why.

I love you, Jen.

Kate xx

Kate Blewett
Television Producer and Director
Global Documentaries

PROLOGUE

The traffic is whizzing past on the dual carriageway below at a sickening speed. It's a stifling hot July afternoon, and the stench of car fumes fills my nose. I look down again at the roaring vehicles below: red car, juggernaut, white car, motorbike; whizz, whizz, whizz. Everyone is whizzing off somewhere. Where are they all going? Why are they all in such a hurry? It's time to go home. I guess they're all going home. To families. To loved ones. Home.

Then it hits me again. I feel a pang. I have nowhere to go home to, nowhere to belong, and I decide it's time to heave myself over the edge of the bridge. After making my way to the centre of the red brick bridge, I peered over the parapet for God knows how long. The afternoon heat, coupled with the smell and sound of the traffic, makes my head swim. In my right hand, the photo looks crumpled. I daren't look. I've only just stopped crying, and I don't want to start again. In a flash, I decided - this is it. No more battling, no more struggle. I am weary. All I must do is climb over and drop. It's that simple. But would it be better to drop onto a car or the road? For a minute,

I hesitated. If I get hit by a car, I might hurt someone. I don't want to do that. The desperation inside of me wells up at the thought of hurting someone. I know all too well what it's like to be hurt. I want the clean, hard satisfaction of smashing myself into something, of dropping like a stone. I need to throw myself at something because the pain inside threatens to engulf and destroy me. It almost has already. Why not finish the job?

Okay. I just need to land between the cars. Hit the road. Then they can run me over. Over, over and over. It's all over. I don't want to feel any more. I can't think. Won't think. I have to do it now - this minute. I can't breathe. I can't go on. I'm sick of it all. I can still feel the photograph stuck fast in my gripped hand. I won't let it go. With all my effort and attention focused on this moment, I pull myself up onto the brick parapet. All I have to do is get to the top and drop. Simple as that. I'm a bit heavy for all this, although I used to be able to run so fast. I can't run now, but I can fall. Okay. One, two, three. Heave...

A strong hand lands firmly on my shoulder. Shit! I look sideways, to the right, where the hand is. It's a big, white hand against my black skin. There are black hairs on the back, like a giant spider. All I want to do is to brush it off. Further up from the hand is a hairy arm in a white shirt, with a stocky man attached. He's looking at me with what seems to be a concern. I've seen that look before. Shit. I pull hard against his hand, but it holds fast.

'Wait a moment,' the man's voice says urgently. 'Think about it'.

Wait a moment! What the hell does he mean? Think about it? I've thought about it. I thought and thought and thought 'til it's made me ill. What does he know? I look away from his worried face, back over the bridge to the road below. It's so inviting, so seductive, that hard concrete and that endless stinking drone beneath me. It's beckoning me with its siren call: Come on, jump. Do it. Now. Get it over with. I can't look at the man. If I do, it will be over. I've got this far, and I can't turn back.

'Nothing's worth that. Life's worth living,' his calm voice says.

Ha! He doesn't understand. No-one does. How could he? I bet he has a family, children, and a home. Someone who loves him, who cares and who has somewhere to belong. God, who's that with him? Underneath my lashes, I can see a woman's anxious face peeking from behind the man. She's standing by their blue car, which has drawn up to the curb. Her face scrunched up with worry – or is it fear? I can't decide. She's biting her lip with her arms crossed. Other people are gathering around us now. Shit. Okay. It's now or never. I've got to go. I pull hard against the man, trying to wriggle from his iron grasp to hoist myself up onto the parapet further. Just a few inches more, and I'll be gone. I'm nearly there. I can let go. I'll be free. I'll fly like a bird in the sky. Get away, you stupid, interfering man.

Leave me alone, and let me be. But the hand is holding firm. The voice is droning on and on too.

'You have something to live for.'

Suddenly I am angry. Furious. Stupid man, what does he know?

'No, I don't!' I shout. 'No, I don't – there's nothing left.'

'You're wrong,' he says quietly in my ear, 'I can't let you do this.'

'Let me go!'

I want to smack him. How dare he stop me? What does he know or care? Why can't he just let me go? I try to kick at his legs, but I miss. Everything I had has been taken from me by others. I've nothing left to live for. At twenty-five, I've had enough of this life.

Out of the corner of my eye, I see some figures running. Oh no - the bridge. I know what they'll do. They can fuck off too. I struggle harder.

The man is still holding on and talking in a patronising tone, 'come away from the edge; it will be okay. You will go on. We all have to.'

"I can't,' I shout, the hot tears coming again.

I don't cry but can't stop the tears from forming. The pain in my inner being is overwhelming, and I can't continue; it's too much for anyone to carry. There's nothing to live for now. I've lost her. They've taken her.

'You don't understand.'

Suddenly, the photo in my hand drops to the pavement. Oh, God. I panic. The woman steps forward, picks it up and uncrumples it. I see a sweet little face, black curls, and dark eyes. It's too much. She can't have her. I try to snatch the photo back, but the man's arms pin me. I'm trapped in a life sentence!

'Come on,' coaxes the man. 'Come down, now. Nothing's that bad, believe me.'

But it is - they've taken her. They fucking won. Suddenly, my legs are jelly. There's another hand on my shoulder. I turn and see the familiar face of a male nurse I know, and he is helping the other man pull me down. Behind them are more people. They've got me, the bastards. I'm trapped. Why can't they let me do what I want?

'Come on, Jennie,' says the male nurse. 'Come on now.'

I've heard it all before. I know that voice, and I know that tone. They talk to me like I'm dumb - a stupid, crazy person. In answer, I struggle and fight. I put all my effort into trying to wrench free. I wrestle, but the two hands restraining me are strong, and I feel their fingers digging into my arms. I'm bruising as I pull away from them with all my might, but I don't care. I like the pain; it relieves the anger and grief. My clenched teeth part as I let out a humongous roar of despair and frustration.

'Let me go. Let me go!'

I try to bite and scratch whatever flesh I can find. I've nowhere to go or nowhere to belong. I have nothing to live for. This is the end, and I want it to come. Right now. Hard and fast. Moments later, I feel a sharp prick in my buttock. Then darkness.

*   *   *

Imagine if I had been given the right support and taught the basics of being a mother with someone by my side. Instead of fighting to be heard, even then falling on deliberate deaf ears, people took over instead of guiding me. What if I could have kept her if someone had listened and wanted to help? Would I have been given the proper support instead of behaving like a wild beast trying to wrestle the world? I could have been a mothering bear nurturing my child, becoming free of the wildlife they put us through. Then my secondborn wouldn't have had to go through such a horrific childhood due to my past. He would have been safe from the horrors of this world

1

DID IT BEGIN WITH DADDIES' SIN?

'...the whereabouts of the father is not known... mother lives somewhere in London, but doesn't seem to be interested in the right of having any contact with her daughter...the children appear well cared for by their foster parents and are not unduly disturbed by the lack of contact with their own mother...'

(Social worker's report) 1969

Right from the start, I had nowhere to belong. I was homeless from day one. I truly believe every child should be wanted and have loving parents, a safe home and a strong sense of belonging. Even one loving parent is better than none. That's every child's natural birthright. Unfortunately, I had none of these things. The truth is – I don't know, but I can imagine outside influences forced my mum to give me up.

Because of my scandalous background, there seems to be a scant record of the beginning of my life. I don't know how much I weighed or if I had hair. There are no proud baby photos or baby albums - nothing at all to note about my coming into the world. In a way, this set up a pattern that would be repeated over and over for the rest of my life; hidden, unseen. I was an embarrassment - something to be forgotten, lost, or even hated. From my very first moments, I was an object of shame. As such, others blamed me for anything bad that happened.

It seems from my NHS records, which I eventually managed to procure, that I spent my first couple of weeks in a nursing home. The notes are very brief and impersonal. Nobody writes anything much about me as an individual. After that, authorities handed me to a temporary foster carer, a GP and her family, who took pity on my situation while social services found a longer-term solution. Although the records are poor, it seems social services placed me desperately as soon as possible.

The temporary foster home I was in terminated very quickly when, sadly, my foster mother suddenly had a heart attack and died. There must have been a lot of confusion and upset, and the adults around me would have handed me around again, a bit like an unwanted package. A series of strangers – nurses, social workers, GPs, midwives-indeed anyone around must have bottle-fed me.

Finally, a local white couple stepped forward to foster me. Social services must have looked at their files and noticed this pair had fostered before and that there were no apparent complaints. Plus, they were willing to take a 'coloured' child (as people would have called me back then), something most people in my home community would have thought twice about. It was an era when newspapers were crammed full of stories about the imminent swamping of the UK by a flood of black immigrants. There was a real sense of fear about what might happen to (literally) change the complexion of English life, and our town seemed to be doing its best to resist that change.

The Stabards, a middle-aged couple, had three children who had already grown up and left home by the time I entered their household around the Easter of 1969. When the social workers brought me in my regulation social services carrycot, with no clothes or toys of my own, the only other child in the house was another foster daughter. She was also black and three years older than me. The services thought her to be a 'difficult' child to place with a family since she was sickly, with a drooping right eyelid. Also, they believed her to be somewhat 'educationally subnormal' (the term used at the time for 'learning difficulties'). She had absolutely no family, so it was a permanent placement with the Stabards.

The house the social workers entered had a neat, magnolia-painted hall and lounge. There was an orangey, chintzy sofa, two armchairs, floral wallpaper and curtains, white paint, and burgundy-coloured, patterned carpet. The overall effect would have been of a family home, lived-in but tidy. Mr and Mrs Stabard would have seemed a dowdy but solid middle-aged couple. Sat on their comfy 'best' sofa, with me gurgling in my carrycot sandwiched in between, they would have probably seemed the perfect pair to take care of a waif and stray with murky beginnings. The social worker might well have left the house feeling satisfied that, at last, they had placed another 'difficult' child with people the local authority could trust to put a child's interests first. After all, another child lived there, probably dressed in a neat pale blue dress and white cardigan, with a big white bow in her short curly hair - her Sunday best. She was a testament to how well looked after a black foster child could be. Although shy and a little slow, she would have looked like a sweet little 'piccaninny' to an outsider with her shiny black patent shoes and clean white socks. She would probably have watched the proceedings quietly, with wide eyes and may have sucked her two fingers for comfort. She would not have made a fuss or spoken unless the adults had spoken to her. She would not have shown any feelings – she knew better.

Social services would probably have made an official report noting that she was clean and well cared for, just as they usually did about the children in our house. They didn't know that the neat living room and the Sunday best was a show to distract them from delving into the mess beyond.

Memory is a strange thing. Most people can remember faces and places, time and dates, whereas my earliest memories are of smells, feelings, looks and strange visual images. When I think back to my early childhood, my main memory is of fear, darkness and immense feelings of claustrophobia and dread. My memories are like a string of snapshots – like flashed-up images on a screen – and it is often difficult to remember all the bits between them. My flashes of memory have many horrible feelings attached, which make me shiver. In fact, they're so painful I've tried to shut them out, or shut them down, for most of my life - I am lying in wait.

...I remember it's cold and dark, and I'm hungry and wet. I just know I've been waiting a long time, and there's a horrible feeling that no one will ever come. A small brown face appears above me and disappears. It happens several times. I think I'm in a small dark room with another girl. I can hear crying. No one comes, and the room gets darker, light, and then dark again. As well as hungry, cold and wet - I am scared. I cry till I cannot cry anymore, but no one comes except the little brown face, which looks at me and goes away again. I am on a cold floor in a very dark, scary place. It smells of wood and dampness, and there are lots of spiders. I feel things running over my legs and arms, and I'm hungrier, wetter, colder and more frightened. Although it's so dark, I can hear the other girl there again, and she comes over, and I see her brown face in the shadows as she gets closer. She hauls me up by my arms, which hurts and then

I'm on her lap, sitting on something softer, which feels nice. I'm warm and comforted. I put two fingers in my mouth and suck them, which taste warm. She's humming in my ear, holding me tight, and I feel a little calmer, although she smells of wee and poo. I forget I feel so hungry as she strokes my hair and hums. She rocks me back and forth, and I feel less afraid, although I somehow know we can't get out of where we are...

...Back in the small, dark, boxy bedroom, I'm in a cot with wooden bars crying – I don't know why. Suddenly a white-haired man's ruddy face appears above mine with stinky breath, and a hairy arm grabs me by the hair while another arm pulls me out of my cot by my arm. I scream, and I feel a slap from a big hand sting my face. I'm half-pulled, half-carried on the man's shoulder, and he's pongy. My eyes sting, my face is burning, and I'm still crying. I can feel he's very angry. He's shouting something, and I feel the force of his strength as he quickly goes from my room to the next one, opens a door in the corner and suddenly throws me on the floor in the dark. Slam...

...He shut the door tight, and it's stifling and pitch black. I scream my head off, terrified. I want to get out - right now. But I can't. I'm next to something big and padded, which is hard and boiling hot. I put my fingers through the padding and scream in pain when I touch something which burns my fingers. I hear the man shouting outside and telling me to 'shut up and stay there till I tell you.' I know I can't move. I'm crying and shaking, and my wee leaks out, and *the floor is wet when I touch the puddle underneath me with my fingers. Then I put my hands up, and there's something hard and wooden over my head – a shelf. The crack of light under the door gradually goes dark as the hours go by.*

I'm starving and now cold and wet, but I know I can't get out, or the man will shout at me and slap me even more. I feel terrified, lost and completely alone... I am walking along the road, dressed in my Sunday best, holding the hand of Mrs Stabard. I like walking while holding her hand, but she walks fast and doesn't look down at me. She has tightly curled my hair, and I have a big bow on the side – it hurts where it's clipped in. My shoes are too tight, and she said I mustn't get my white socks and cardigan dirty. I am aware that people are stopping and staring at us...

We were a show for them.

The Stabards' bedroom wallpaper was green with big orange flowers, and they had fitted carpet and wardrobes. It looked like a palace to us at the time, although we were not allowed in. There wasn't any central heating in the house, and the Stabard's bedroom had the only bar fire – a necessity on cold winter nights. Next to their bedroom was a bathroom with black and white lino tiles and a separate, old-fashioned chain-pull toilet with a dirty grey floor. Between our front box room and their bedroom at the back was a large bedroom with pale blue walls, three single divans, and more fitted carpet. This was the Stabard's own children's room, and as they'd left home, it was now kept for when their grandchildren came to stay. Each bed, (there were four, I believe), had soft white sheets, several thick blankets and a fancy candlewick cover. The room was much nicer and cosier than ours. There were fitted cupboards, a dressing table with a heart-shaped mirror and flowery curtains. This room was bright and clean and felt like a proper bedroom.

However, the other little girl I discovered was Faith, and we were completely forbidden from entering the luxurious room, even though it lay empty most of the time because it wasn't ours. The Stabards didn't think we deserved a room like that. Our home wasn't in the house but in the garden shed. Looking out the back kitchen window to the left, next to the neighbour's fence and high hedge, there was a concrete ugly-looking shed with a plastic see-through corrugated roof. It was about five feet tall and six feet long and rectangular. There was a narrow slit of a window, about a foot long and six inches deep, along the underside of the roof, facing the lawn. It had a slanting roof, higher at the fence side, like a lean-to. We accessed the shed through a high, black wrought iron gate with a big padlock. There was a small, paved courtyard about three square feet deep between the shed door and the gate. The shed might have been a coal bunker in earlier times, with a wooden roof or covered chute where people would pour the coal. I remember a coalman selling sacks of potatoes, so there must have been a coal round in the area not too long ago. The Stabards put us in the shed because we weren't supposed to be in the house. After all, it wasn't 'ours'.

It was where we girls, there had been the arrival of a younger child called Hope a while later, and the other part-time children had to live every day, come rain or shine, except on Sundays when the Stabards dressed us in our best Sunday clothes and took us to church. And, indeed, we called the shed 'our home'. The shed was the home of any black or disabled foster child passing through the house. From as far back as I remember, the Stabards took us out of the house in the morning and told us, coldly and firmly, to stay in the shed, behave and be quiet. Then the outer wrought iron gate was locked with the padlock – clunk. The shed was dark and smelly, which we hated. It had no lighting except the sunlight through the slit window and the dingy corrugated roof. It had big spiders, which absolutely terrified me. Since there was no heating, it was freezing in winter. Of course, it had no toilet – which probably explains why they kept us in nappies. We didn't have anyone to change us, so we weed and pooped all day into the same nappy, which became sodden and heavy by bedtime. When we were too old for nappies, we simply went to the toilet on the floor in the corner of the shed, as there was no way we could get out of there without being let out by one of the Stabards. Since we couldn't wash, we were always filthy, and I expect we stank.

The shed had a rickety, falling-apart table, a ripped, smelly, brown armchair and a peeling, upright kitchen chair. We would cuddle on the armchair together for warmth or stand around. Sometimes we'd sit or lie on the concrete floor, but it could be ice-cold, especially in winter. There was no food in the shed, but there was water. They put an old white plastic water bottle in there with us, and we could swig out of it when we were thirsty. But if it ran out, which it often did when it was hot, there was absolutely nothing we could do about it. We could shout and call Mrs Stabard, but if she heard us, she usually ignored us. If we were especially 'good' and didn't make too much noise in the shed, Mrs Stabard would come and open the shed door and let us go out in the little paved courtyard. This was our reward. But sometimes, we'd get a bit too bold and start shaking the iron gate bars. It was so tempting being only inches from the lawn. We could see all that space to run around in and beyond the garden. The freedom of the hills seemed to beckon us. Sometimes it was just too hard to control ourselves. When we needed the loo, we would shake the bars, and the padlock rattled. Sometimes we'd jump up and down with our fingers in our mouths, shouting, 'Ya, ya! Ya, ya!' as a kind of protest.

I think we just felt very fed up with being caged, and sometimes it all boiled over, especially on summer afternoons when the sun was out, and the sky was blue. We just wanted fresh air, exercise and freedom. And as we were hungry all the time, we wanted some food too. But whenever we made a noise, Mrs Stabard would be furious with us. She'd come marching out with an expressionless face and push us back into the shed, slamming the door shut. When night came, and we were allowed back into the house, we were exhausted, cold and shut down. Without a word, we'd head straight to our dark, cramped home for rejects.

We learnt how to survive in the shed as best as we could, sometimes in total silence listening for footsteps of either of them coming to open the door. Even if they were to shout at us, those moments, regardless of how long, let light in and gave us hope that things would get better. I would hum quietly and tell stories of wonderful, funny things in a distant land of hope and peace to comfort other children staying temporarily with the Stabards. We were all together in that tiny shed, and sometimes they were scared, hungry or cold. We always laughed in silence at the end of the stories as each child would add something to the story.

I wonder if neighbours knew we were in that shed against their perfectly trimmed hedges. If so, why didn't they rescue us? Why didn't they see us as worthy of being saved? They must have seen the men come in and take me away in the army jeeps during the night, carrying my drugged, limp body out. They didn't seem to miss much, so why didn't they notice? I am aware that the bigger ring involved some of the neighbours. They were the druggers and runners, gathering us up for the men to take and steal our innocence. I prefer to believe the other neighbours didn't know.

The Stabards were a part of everything. Was the plan for me to be the bait for powerful men to use my body to violate and batter whenever they liked? To fill my belly with a child and deliver them on the top of a field in front of a party with many people attending. Some were very powerful; of course, you didn't know their names or even who they were at the time. All you knew was their rank in society and at these murderous sex parties. Fire, sex, murder and the torture of babies. And savage dogs that ate the remains of the corpse, whether the dead were children or adult women. They engraved cloaks and daggers symbols on the cave walls. Evil prevailed in these places, yet the silence from the neighbours was just as deadening. Someone must have known why there were no questions or why there were no police. Some of the parties involved police. I was taken all around to these rituals of sex and the killing of children and women, especially women carrying babies.

I realised at a young age they would never kill me. They would use me as an experiment like they did in the Nazi camp, choosing just a few to be experimented on. They were intrigued by my resilience because I managed to get up each time. I was a toddler when I was taken to the infamous hospital and was suspended and stretched with ropes attached to my legs and arms. They pulled me so hard that I could have snapped. I learnt to blank out after a while. I allowed myself to pass through the pain by numbing it out and drift into a daydream of being loved by my birth mum. She would come and rescue us once she knew, but it was just a silly dream. I allowed myself to fracture. This hospital was the same place a notorious rapist was. He took great joy in his satanic games, one being the 'wizard's train'. It is where he would have me at the front, and the boys behind were joined by their genitals. The rapist and a consultant doctor would encourage us to run around. If one of the children's privates fell out of the back of one of us, he would burn us with his cigar and tell us to run again – 'faster and faster' he would bellow with laughter.

They took everything about me as a baby, a child and a human being. I was a reject that most people thought they could treat me as one - throwing me out of normal worldly life to a dark, painful obscure existence. I always ask myself why on earth didn't those social workers, who were not involved in the abuse ring, speak out. Or, look around that house; they would have come across the signs of abuse within the home, the torture room in the shed, the cold bedroom with floorboard nails stuck up in case we tried to escape. But no, they took the word of the abusers.

2

OPEN DOOR FOR MISFITS

'...they appear well cared for by their foster parents...they seem very happy in their present home...'

(Social worker report 1972)

'They are very lucky to have a family who accepts them for being coloured.'

(Social worker report 1972)

The Stabards were a well-respected, highly religious, local couple with a track record of fostering children, especially those who were difficult to place: black, Asian or disabled. They had been married just after the Second World War when they met in the forces and were now in their fifties. During the week, Leonard Stabard worked full-time as a maintenance engineer in a local factory. His wife, Mavis, ran their 1940s council house and looked after their three children, Bernard, Gemma and Carla, before they moved out when they were of age.

Their town was an old farming community with old-fashioned values and traditions. The Stabards lived in a quiet cul-de-sac on the edge of town, overlooking a small circular green. The surrounding council houses around 97 Forestlane Way were respectable red-brick homes with trimmed hedges and neat lawns. There were few cars, as most people used the buses, walked, or cycled into town. By the time I went to live with them in their end-of-terrace semi, they were already very set in their ways.

Despite being devoted churchgoers, the Stabards were a very odd couple. Although we passed the neighbours when we went to a religious church that preached more about the devil than anything or saw them through the hedge in the back garden, we never spoke to them. Mr and Mrs Stabard would say 'hello' and seem friendly enough, but they never invited the neighbours in, so they were unknown to us. We didn't go to nursery, pre-school, or other children's houses or parties. We never went swimming, to the park, or any local shops or cinemas. Our world was tiny: our shed, our room and whatever we saw on the weekly ten-minute walk to the Baptist church.

I don't ever remember seeing the Stabards kiss, hug, or show warmth or affection towards each other. I don't know if she was happy with him or if they loved each other. She seemed a bit trapped and down sometimes, like she just had to make the best of things. They didn't seem like a married couple but more like a brother and sister living in the same house. She seemed to keep him at arm's length physically and was a little scared of him. I saw them row only once when he raised his hand and hit her across the face. I was shocked, but all she did was turn and scuttle off without a word. I never saw him hit her again after that, but he was the dominant partner.

Mrs Stabard was a short, round woman who seldom smiled. She had long, grey hair pulled into a severe bun and wore very plain, conservative clothes. Most days, she wore either a grey or navy top and skirt or a white blouse and grey skirt. She'd always wear one of those old-fashioned housewives' pinnies with little flowers and a big pocket at the front. She never wore makeup or perfume and rarely sported jewellery. The only exception would be a simple silver or gold brooch pinned to the lapel of her navy Sunday suit. On her feet, she usually wore school-type black brogues and pinkish stockings. I remember her legs always being 'bad' and her wearing bandages around them. She was a cold, odd woman who always kept her distance – even from her husband – and stayed inside most of the time.

Mr Stabard was about six inches taller, with a florid complexion and cold blue eyes. He had white hair and a streak of grey through the top. Mr Stabard was quite a strong man, with muscled arms and was stocky, yet had clearly been quite fit in his military years. He wore old-fashioned dark tweedy trousers with braces and a white shirt with rolled-up sleeves. His one personal luxury was Brut aftershave, which he splashed on liberally. He was often out of breath and wheezed, although he didn't smoke. However, he did drink a great deal, especially Guinness, whisky and gin, and I was used to the heady smell of alcohol when he got close. The outside world was completely alien to the smell of his breath mixed with the Brut aftershave. He often went out to the local British Legion club to drink with ex-forces mates after work, leaving his wife at home alone with us.

I never saw Mrs Stabard drink herself, although she didn't seem to mind it when her husband came home drunk. Instead, she liked her tea and cakes, which she consumed in great quantities. The Stabards prided themselves on being good with children. Mavis had worked as a nanny before she married and had her brood. Their blood children, now adults, also hated us and treated us like vermin. Thus, several small grandchildren would visit the house twice a week and have lots of fun with all the toys and games their parents had hidden away in the cupboard under the stairs.

They had both worked as volunteers in a notorious residential children's home in the area. They were very friendly with the chief officer. Later this children's home was closed, and the chief officer was convicted of crimes against children, including sexual abuse and child cruelty. I'm not sure what they learned or taught from working there, but it certainly didn't improve their fostering skills. At the time, of course, I had no clear idea of what foster parents were supposed to be like. I'd never been in anyone else's home, and I suppose I thought what I was experiencing was normal.

However, it hurt seeing Mrs Stabard warm and friendly to her children and grandchildren. It was the only time I ever saw her round, bland face breaking into a smile

...I'm standing in the penned-in area in front of our shed. It's a warm day, and I'm watching the cats fight on the lawn. I hear voices and see Mrs Stabard with a little boy in the kitchen. I'm looking through the side metal gate bars door, and I feel pain in my tummy as I watch her give him a big hug and ruffle his hair. Mrs Stabard goes to a kitchen cupboard, gets a lollipop, and gives it to the little boy, bending over towards him and smiling. I feel tears sting my eyes...

Later, Mrs Stabard is bent over, doing up my buckle shoes. My legs are dangling over the chair's sides, and she roughly drops my foot with the shoe on, snatches up the other one and pushes on the shoe. I look at the top of her grey head and long for a hug. I want her to look at me warmly and smile as she did to the little boy.

'Sit still!' she snaps or something down those lines in a voice full of hate towards me.

She's so cold and distant that I feel like crying. Why doesn't she like me? When she finishes the job, she straightens up and turns away. No smile. No hugs. I put my fingers in my mouth and suck. I start swinging my legs to make myself feel happier.

Mrs Stabard turns round and says sharply, 'Stop that. Sit still and be quiet.'

I sit there sucking my fingers, feeling very lonely and less. She talks to me like I'm the poo that's got under her shoes. It's not fair.

As I got older, I noticed that my foster mother had two sides to her personality: a strict, cold one that she'd show me and the other rejects, but the warm, tender side she saved for her real family. And those in church and social workers. Even so, I still felt very attached to her and desperately wanted her to love me. I hoped that if I tried hard enough to get everything right, she would treat me like her grandchildren one day. If I did whatever she and her husband wanted, she might finally give me a safe, loving hug. Or be kind and warm and say 'I love you'. Oh, to hear those words that she or someone did love me was like a knife digging into my heart, waiting in anticipation of three little words that never ever came. It was unbearable to think that her coldness would go on and on forever, so I did everything I could to win her approval.

They really hated us foster kids. Until I left that home, I always thought I knew how much involvement Mrs Stabard had in grooming us foster children. He was much more aggressive than she was, who may have been cold but wasn't as cruel. She seemed under his thumb most of the time. She barely spoke to us; instead, she'd point with her arm to tell us to go upstairs or out to the shed. I don't know if she thought it was beneath her to talk to us or whether she thought we were so thick we couldn't understand English. Mr Stabard, on the other hand, would bark orders. He was quite militaristic and would shout at us to get tea or supper and then come and check we had done it. If we hadn't cut the bread right or peeled the onions correctly, he would bark at us like a sergeant major (like some of the men that paid him for their bit of me). We'd have to stand to attention until he'd finished and then do it all again until he was satisfied. He liked it when he made us jump with fear. It would make him laugh. He had a dry, nasty, sarcastic laugh, which we'd come at first to loathe and then later, utterly fear and detest.

The uncomfortable truth was that Mr and Mrs Stabard hated black and disabled people and children. For them, fostering was simply an easy way of earning money. From the start, they said that we should be very grateful that they fostered us. We were obviously very lucky. Not everybody would take in the likes of us, and clearly, nobody else wanted us. The Stabards told us repeatedly that they put us in the shed because we were 'bad, dirty evil children'. In their twisted minds, black skin and disabled children equated evil and filth. We were not, therefore, worthy of going into all the areas of the house that the little white grandchildren could go into, such as the lounge or the nice bedroom upstairs. We would only spoil them.

Since we were not allowed to play in the garden, we could only watch the grandchildren kicking a ball about as we peered through the slit window in the shed wall. When they left their toys scattered carelessly on the lawn, we had to tread past them, careful not to touch them in case we contaminated them with our evil. It was all very confusing and upsetting. What was wrong with us?

Strangely, the Stabards loved animals (certainly more than little black disabled children) and had a small menagerie of pets. They had cats of various colours and varieties, four dogs and four rabbits, hamsters and guinea pigs in wooden hutches. There was also an aviary sporting zebra finches, quails, cockatiels, budgies and canaries. Geese and ducks sat on the small, stagnant pond in the back garden near the rockery and old greenhouse. They even had three brown, fluffy chickens and a tethered white goat. I really loved one of the geese and used to tell her all my worries. She was white and waddled around after me, and unlike her human owners, she didn't care about my skin colour. It was important to the Stabards that they try to purify our souls because we were black or disabled and, therefore, evil.

The Stabards marched the three of us, me, Hope and Faith, to church every week. It was full of quotes and strange pictures, such as one-eyed people on the cross. Some were very frightening such as the eyes on the walls that followed us. We were always dressed up smartly in our Sunday best. They'd do our hair, pulling it taut in big white ribbons, Minnie-Mouse-style. Our pale blue dresses with matching blue jackets or little white cardigans would come out. We'd wear our too-tight black patent squeaky shoes, little white socks, or tights in winter. Hand in hand, we'd walk along the road in complete silence, following Mrs Stabard like three little black ducklings bobbing along behind a big white mamma duck. Since there were virtually no black faces in our neighbourhood, we three, in our silly white ribbons, were a total oddity. People trimming their hedges would stop mid-clip to gawp at us in our church finery. Mrs Stabard would be in her plain navy suit and a navy hat, and Mr Stabard would be in his dark tweedy suit and shiny black shoes.

We'd look very respectable, but people would still stare at us as we passed. I felt so self-conscious and awkward and aware that having black skin made us different. It was drummed in at home when Mrs Stabard would tell us sharply to come away from the window in case someone saw us. It was like she felt embarrassed to have the likes of us seen in her house. Even when we were walking to church, looking very prim and sweet but unmistakably black-skinned, I could sense Mrs Stabard's tension as she met other people. The Stabards were a different couple once they were out of the house together. He became friendly and chatty, and she smiled at people and talked to them - like they were with their family. I looked at her, wondering, 'why doesn't she talk to us like that?' and 'why doesn't she smile at me that way?' At home, Mr Stabard was a very silent, secretive man (except when he was drunk or lost his temper), so it was weird to see him all jolly and talking to other churchgoers. It was like a different man had emerged into the daylight. He'd even take our hands to cross the road, and part of me would think: 'Ooh, maybe he's changed. Maybe he likes us now. Maybe they'll love us when we get home?' Then we would go home, and the minute we crossed the threshold, he would revert instantly to the old regime.

Then one day, something happened that was very strange indeed. It was a weekday, and we expected to go into the shed as usual. However, Mrs Stabard came up to our box room.

She stood in the doorway awkwardly, gestured to the wardrobe and said, 'Put on your Sunday outfits.'

It was a Wednesday, but we did as she told us, although we were very confused about what was happening.

Mrs Stabard pointed to the stairs and said, 'Front room, now.'

Since she seldom spoke to us, it was all very unusual. We filed downstairs and stood in a little row at the bottom. Mrs Stabard walked past us and opened the lounge door. The lounge. I had never been in that room, to my knowledge, since arriving in the house. When we walked in, we saw a pile of bright objects gleaming on the burgundy carpet. Toys! We looked up at Mrs Stabard's flat, emotionless face, and she pointed at the toys. Amazed, we three girls looked at each other for reassurance and then back at her, but when nothing untoward happened, we shot towards the toys and started playing. I chose a big pink dolly and began brushing her hair and moving her long eyelashes up and down. She made a 'waaa' sound when I tilted her. I couldn't believe it. I'd seen the grandchildren playing with her before, and it had always been my wildest dream to hold her myself – and now I really was. It was a fantastic feeling, something I'd never experienced before.

Suddenly, the doorbell went ding-dong. We never had visitors. All three of us looked up with wide eyes open, curious and alert, just in time to see Mrs Stabard disappear and come back in with a tall, fair woman in a dark suit. She sat in one of the chintzy chairs, and Mrs Stabard sat in the other. The visitor got out a clipboard and started writing something. The two women talked in whispers, so we couldn't really hear.

We were sitting on the floor, each so engrossed in the toys, we didn't really care, and every so often, we would look up at each other and grin secretively. We were having the time of our lives and were completely ecstatic, and little Hope was sitting on her bottom, putting toy after toy in her mouth. Suddenly, we heard the door click. We looked up, and the visitor was gone - so absorbed we hadn't noticed. Mrs Stabard rushed towards us, a strange look on her face, yanked us up and pulled us out of the room. The toys went flying, and I had to drop my dolly, which made me distraught, and I strained to pick her up again. I started crying loudly, which I knew my foster mother hated. Hope and Faith joined in. 'She's my dolly now,' I thought. I didn't want to let her go. Mrs Stabard kicked the doll out of reach and pulled me out of the room. Then she pushed us upstairs, as we sobbed loudly and ordered us to take off our best clothes.

After that, we were frog-marched outside to the shed and briskly locked in, with absolutely no explanation whatsoever. It was only much later after this scenario was repeated and again over the years, that I realised that this had been one of our first visits from Social Services. The authorities would write to the Stabards, giving them two weeks' warning, so they had time to stage-manage the whole event. Mrs Stabard knew they never looked beyond the front hall and the lounge, so she felt safe. I guess the officials assumed it was as nice everywhere else and took the Stabards at face value. The scene of us playing happily with toys, dressed in our Sunday best, was entirely staged for their visit. At no other time did we ever have access to the grandchildren's toys. Social Services never came upstairs to see where we slept, and they never went out to the kitchen and had absolutely no idea about the shed.

What's more, they didn't ever come near us. They never spoke to us or examined us. They observed us from across the room as the social worker ticked the boxes on her clipboard, sipping tea with Mrs Stabard, who was almost nice to us for once. The officials would talk to her about us over our heads but never ask us anything directly. If they looked at our bodies, they did so with our clothes on, so they never found anything untoward. Of course, the social worker did not know that something was happening beneath the surface at the Stabards, which was far from savoury or normal, despite appearances to the contrary. It was something so profound that it would shape my life – and that of every other foster child who entered their house over the next twenty-three years. It was something that no visitor would have picked up on sitting in the neat, cosy living room, sipping tea with Mrs Stabard, or even sharing a glass of Guinness with Mr Stabard. However, once the act for the social worker was over, life returned to 'normal'. And that 'normal' was the most abnormal life anyone could possibly imagine for three small children, supposedly 'in care' – especially as we three kids were the Stabard's domestic house slaves.

> ..."*Please look at previous allegations made against these foster parents of child abuse in 1962, where they had been excused from abusing looked after children.*"
>
> Social care records (1972)

After many years of trying to get hold of my social care records, I finally obtained a few records after being passed on to me. My care records were drip fed to me. Why were they hell-bent on playing these twisted games? Couldn't they see that learning who we were was just as important as oxygen to survive? I still believe there are more because of significant gaps and lots of contradictions. But the most harrowing of all is that social services knew the Stabards were abusing us. Why the hell did they make me feel I was a liar? Why the treatment in psychiatric wards for years, the heavy sedation and the brain-numbing head-emptying ECT? I felt angry again and knew I had to put these emotions away as the punishment would be too heavy. There was no way I was giving them any more of my life or my children's life. I am and will continue to speak the truth.

3

LABOUR CAMP

Jennie enjoys the company of her sister and the other child at the foster home. She has normal interests for a girl of her age . . . and continues to enjoy good health...'

(Social worker's report)

We three foster children had to 'earn' our place in the house, and we had to do that by doing all the chores. Behind the 'respectable' façade of the house was a different world altogether. While the hallway and the front lounge were presentable public areas, clean and tidy, the rear of the house was a completely different story. The kitchen was filthy, the red-tiled floor permanently grimy and covered with animal faeces. The cats, dogs, geese and ducks could wander in and out at will and deposit their droppings wherever they wanted.

The kitchen was large, cold and old-fashioned, with tatty, brown-painted cupboard units and a huge wooden table down the centre of the room with eight wooden chairs. The kitchen windows looked out over a hundred feet of scrubby garden to the aviary and the brick wall at the back. The kitchen was primitive, low on mod-cons, and always greasy. The Stabards expected us foster kids to prepare all the meals for them.

...I'm being picked up roughly under the armpits by Mr Stabard and made to stand on a chair at the sink. He puts a thing in my hand and, with his hand over mine, makes me pull off the skin of a potato. I can feel my legs wobbling on the chair, and the water is cold, but he makes me take all the skin off and start on the next potato. There is a whole pot of potatoes by the sink.

'Do that lot now,' he barks. 'Cut them like this.'

He cuts the potato in half, and although I try, I can't do it and the potato skids off the sink onto the floor. Now he's angry, and he makes me get down to get the potato, then up again. I'm scared I'll get it wrong, and the more scared I become, the worse it gets. Then the carrots must be cut in a special way, getting it just right. I cut the carrots in half instead of in slices (they're too hard and slippery), and suddenly I feel a sharp jab in my stomach. I look down, and there's a knife. Mr Stabard is poking me in the side and laughing his dry 'ha ha ha' laugh. Then he chucks some carrots on the floor and makes me jump down and pick them up for him – it seems to amuse him to see me scrabbling about for them. Afterwards, when I look, there are red marks on my body, like little slashes...

Although they taught us to prepare the meals, we weren't allowed to eat with the Stabards. The deal was this: we got their breakfast, lunch or tea, then went to the shed and waited. We had to get up before them every morning, whether the week or the weekend, go down, put the kettle on for tea, and lay out the breakfast. When we were older and going to school, we had to cut the bread for toast or make a fry-up, which Mr Stabard liked a lot. However, on no account were we allowed to eat anything ourselves. He would punch us if we did or slap us around the face. Our job – it was made absolutely clear – was to prepare the food as quickly and quietly as possible. We had to do this every day before we went to school and after we came home from school – no excuses. Back in 'Our Home' (the shed), we'd peer out of our slit window, watching them eat the food through the house's kitchen window. Of course, we'd be starving by then, drooling with hunger. Our bellies would ache, and our empty tummies would rattle, but we'd have to be patient - and silent. It did us no good to complain. We'd suck our fingers in a vain attempt to assuage the pain in our bellies. When I was younger, I remember us shouting, crying, screaming, stamping our feet, and even swearing (copying Mr Stabard, whose language was often colourful). Mrs Stabard appeared at the shed door at these times and would look furious with us and tell us to be quiet. The neighbours also complained because we made a noise, and they would come round to the front door and tell Mr and Mrs Stabard to make us quieten down. We had to skip a meal on these occasions, even if we'd been up very early or at night preparing it all. So, we learned to be quiet, to wait and control our hunger.

We couldn't eat until the Stabards finished, and they would take all the time they wanted to and eat as much as they wished to in silence until they were ready for us to eat their leftovers. Then one of them would come to the iron gate, unlock the padlock, and the shed door would swing open. We'd be allowed to go from the shed, across the paved area, through the iron gate and into the kitchen, where the half-chewed leftovers would be on the floor on the Stabard's plates or in dog bowls. We had to go on all fours on the floor and eat the leftover food, like dogs. Mr and Mrs Stabard would sit at the table and watch, silently amused by our plight, or go out of the room and leave us to it. They would lock away any quality food so we couldn't get to it.

The food we ate was disgusting. Even worse, sometimes, was when Mrs Stabard's eldest daughter, Gemma, was there. It amused her to walk through the plate of food I was trying to eat on the floor with her shoes on. She would put her foot right in it and walk past, then turn and smirk, watching to see if I would go on eating. She seemed to like to see me get upset – and I often felt very angry with her, although I tried my best to suppress it. I had to learn to control my emotions, to bottle them up. I didn't want to give her the satisfaction of seeing me upset, so I'd eat the disgusting, trodden-on leftovers. I was outraged, but more than that, I was hungry, and I knew that if I didn't eat this slop, there wouldn't be anything else. So, I ate it all; I swallowed my pride and, with it, the food, footprints and all.

After we'd eaten whatever we could scrounge, we had to clear up and do the washing up. Sometimes we were made to wash up before eating, which was torture. We'd have to stand on chairs at the sink and scrub the pans, knowing our food was cold. Then after our chores, we had to go back to the shed. There was no playtime in the garden, no watching TV in the lounge, no drawing on paper with coloured pens at the kitchen table or playing with toys – all the things we saw the grandchildren do when they came around. No, they'd march us back to 'Our Home' and lock the three of us in until bedtime. The Stabard's kids and grandkids really hated us, and I think it gave them immense pleasure to ridicule and humiliate us whenever they could. Gemma's behaviour signalled her children to mistreat us, and I even saw one of them spit in my food once before they handed it to me on the floor. I had no option but to eat it. I couldn't complain, as this was all I knew, and there was no one to tell. There were more of them than us, and they knew it. I was so hungry that I'd eat what they dished out, whether it was disgusting or not.

Another horrible aspect of everyday kitchen life was the leashes on the doors. The Stabards had dog leads hanging from the door handles; from time to time, they would chain us up to one of them. They would put the leather collar bit around our wrists, and we would be tethered like a dog, having to watch them eat when we were starving hungry. They did this particularly when they had parties for their grandchildren. Of course, it goes without saying that they didn't celebrate our birthdays – none of us ever had a birthday cake, a present or a card. But when it was any of their grandchildren's birthdays, there would be a party – and we, their house slaves, had to prepare the food as usual. There were trifles, jellies, cakes, sandwiches, little sausages and crisps. And cheese and pineapple on sticks, Twiglets and peanuts - all those amazing, yummy things we'd never eaten.

As we got older, we sometimes tried to sneak a bit of something and put it in our mouths or pockets while no one was looking. But they usually were, so we had to prepare their birthday feast while trying not to drool and our tummies rumbling with hunger before being tied up to the door and made to watch the other little children have fun. It was part of the grandkids' birthday party to throw food at us to see if we could catch it. We were so hungry that we really tried hard to catch it with our mouths, but we often missed, causing even more laughter from our 'audience'. Sometimes it was just one of us in the room being humiliated while the other two were in the shed, watching vigilantly through the window, sniffed at on the floor, or even licked by passing dogs and cats if outside.

I used to chuckle to myself; if only they knew I loved cooking. The heat from the large old cooker was like a warm hug. I loved how my sisters and I looked at each other and knew exactly what extras we could add to their meal - dog poo, mud or worms. The menu had a secret ingredient added each time. Sometimes if they were extremely horrible (which was most of the time), there would be a couple of secret ingredients added to the meal as we gleefully stirred the pot. I used to think, 'you think we are thick, but...' Even though life was hard, we had fun getting our own back. We would hold our bodies stiff as we tried not to laugh when we imagined them each, lapping up our made-up recipes of disgusting delights.

4

DELUDED NARRATIVE

'...the foster parents are well-established and experienced, especially with handling difficult placements...I believe the foster parents wish to give the children their full support...'

(Social worker's report 1978)

Right from the start Mr Stabard was rough with us. Apart from the incident with the vegetables and the kitchen knife, he always seemed to manhandle us somehow. There was definitely no tenderness or care in his encounters with us. Mr Stabard never missed any opportunity to call me 'ugly', 'fat', or 'hideous'. He hated how I looked and always referred to me as 'wog' or 'nigger'.

My hair was wiry and would sit on my head in tight, thick curls when it grew. Mr Stabard used to coil his finger around a curl in my hair and pull me along by it – it felt like he was pulling my brain out, and my head hurt and ached for days afterwards. He would use this method to yank me upstairs, into another room, or to get me wherever he wanted me to go. I felt like a dog pulled on a lead. He did it to all of us, making my blood boil. He'd laugh his sinister little laugh, amused that he'd hurt us. Having yanked us into place, he would stand me on a chair to cut my hair fiercely with a pair of kitchen scissors. Chop, chop, chop. Since he had no idea how to cut black hair, he'd hack at it randomly, sometimes digging into my scalp and cutting me. Of course, he never would have taken us to a hairdresser because it would have meant spending money on us, and we clearly weren't worth it.

I doubt whether our town would have had someone who knew what to do with black hair at that time. Even if there were a specialist salon, he wouldn't have wanted to go there – he would have hated being surrounded by black people. However, he liked my hair short, so short it was. He'd grab us all by the head, one by one and shear us like sheep, making sure he left just enough hair to tie a big Minnie Mouse bow to when we were paraded at church on Sunday like prize piccaninnies. In our household, violence was normal: Mr Stabard sometimes whacked us (and that's putting it mildly) across the legs or arms or face. It hurt like hell. He'd suddenly lash out, just like I'd seen him do to Mrs Stabard that once. But at times, he could also be oddly playful with us. He liked to act out a particular 'game' with us.

...Two hands were pulling me up high onto his knee. I want to sit there; it's nice as it feels like a cuddle - like I'm getting a hug. I want to go on his knee first because it's my treat. I want to be the one today. I want a hug, a kiss, a cuddle, anything. I like it when he smiles and looks pleased with me. I want him to smile, and I want to make him pleased. I like the warm feeling of being up there, special. He's nice now, not shouty. I don't like his angry, red face. Now he's smiling, and his eyes are looking nicely at me...then I am sitting on his lap (the other one, or two, are standing or sitting on the floor, watching, wide-eyed), and he's pulled my legs on either side of his legs, moving my legs around his body like they're round his waist. Then he bounces me up and down, up and down, on his lap. It's fun, and I get giggly. It feels nice to giggle. The other two watch and giggle, too – we don't often laugh, so it's nice. We feel it's fun. We go 'ha, ha', and so does he. Then he tickles me on his lap, his fingers on my legs, under my arms, around my tummy, and we all laugh more. We all laugh because it's fun. All the while, I'm bouncing up and down, up and down, up and down. Then it begins to feel strange. His eyes glaze, and he starts panting, and I can feel something hard, like a lump, in his lap, under his trousers, just under me. I don't know what it is, but it makes me feel strange and unsafe. Then he holds on to me very tight, squeezing the breath out of me and pushing me down harder and harder onto his lap and the hard thing there, with both his strong hands. Being close feels nice, but I also feel very uncomfortable, like

something's wrong and he's out of control. He's gripping me harder now. I can hardly breathe as he's squeezing me, pushing me down so tight. He's now wide-eyed and glazed over, pushing his lumpy bit hard into my bum as he moans and groans.

His cold blue-grey eyes stare through me in a trance. Then it stops. Suddenly. Just like that. He pushes me off, and I fall in a heap on the floor. He stands up, adjusts his trousers and then barks at us to stand up. I sit on the ground, looking up, very confused. He doesn't like us again now, and I feel like crying. Then I'm marched through the lounge, down the hall, through the kitchen, out to the garden, through the iron gate and thrown into the shed. Slam. He's distant and cold now and bangs the door shut, and that's that. Game over, the fun has all gone, and I feel so sad, so confused, so numb...

We didn't understand exactly what the 'game' was, but we knew it was 'our secret'. When it happened, he would draw the curtains, Mrs Stabard would be out, and we instinctively knew it was just between Mr Stabard and ourselves. There was a strange kind of rivalry for his attention, and it made us feel uncomfortable with each other if he seemed to have a 'favourite' – which was often me. Even between us girls, we never talked about it. We felt it was too weird to talk about, that there was too much to lose if we fell out with each other.

One of my foster sisters/children, who was older than me but often very poorly, was diagnosed with Leukemia, which I didn't understand. It meant that she was off for long periods in the hospital, and we wouldn't see her for weeks. When she came home, she would be very pale and weak. However, she continued to be part of the shed regime and had no special treatment. Despite being ill, there was no lying in bed or watching TV on the sofa for her. Hard times continued. Her illness did nothing to alter the Stabard's conviction that we were completely 'evil' and that they had to 'purify' us. We soon found out that Mr Stabard had his special method of trying to purify our souls that would leave us totally terrified and hurt in body and mind. From as early as I can remember, Mr Stabard talked to us seriously about our 'sin'. I don't know whether he felt that because we were black, we were more tainted and sinful than anyone else, or if we were unwanted (due to our shameful origins), he felt something about us needed purifying. Either way, he came up with his own bizarre way of cleansing our sins, which involved a further extension of the 'game' he played with us on his lap whenever Mrs Stabard was out of the house.

...It's early evening, getting dark when he suddenly appears in the doorway of 'Our Home' with a brown canvas holdall in his hand. We're sitting on the floor in a daze – bored and shut down, as we often are – when we're startled by him. We're very scared of our foster father, as we never know whether he will be nice or nasty. Rather than take any chances, all three of us girls run over to the battered armchair in the corner of the shed, fling ourselves on it and

cling onto each other, peeking out at him. Usually, he comes to punish us in some way – which could just be shouting but can also be a slap or a beating – but today, he obviously has something else in mind. He can hardly stand up in the shed, as it's so low. He comes in, plonks down his holdall on the shelf that runs along the back wall, and then unzips the bag. We watch him carefully as he rummages in the bag, and then he brings out something strange: a purple and silver long thing. We sit together, wide-eyed, staring as he takes the object out of the bag and puts it in his pocket. Mr Stabard says nothing but points at me. I don't move, just huddle closer to the girls. I'm in the middle of them, holding on tight to them both. With Faith sick and Hope so little, I feel it's up to me to protect them.

Since I don't move, Mr Stabard comes over, winds his finger into a curl on my head, and pulls me over to the rickety table in the middle of the shed. He puts his big hands on either side of my waist, lifts me, and plonks me back down, so I'm sitting on the table, facing him, my legs hanging down over the edge. My heart's racing, and my mouth's dry – I've no idea what he's going to do next. Suddenly, he pushes me backwards, and I end up flat on my back with a whack to the back of my head. My knees are still over the table's edge, legs hanging down. He stares intently as he bends over me, and I can smell a beery, stinky breath. I get a waft of his pungent aftershave, and I'm only inches from his cold blue eyes, which bore into mine. His knee comes up, and suddenly, I can feel the heavy weight of it on my chest. I panic and wriggle, trying to push him off, but he holds me down. All the time, the other two girls are watching this. I can hear one of them begin to whimper quietly. It's probably best if she stops, or things might get worse. They do. Suddenly, with a swift movement, Mr Stabard rips off my nappy. Something long and brown appears. I recognise the smell of chocolate. Is he going to give us a treat?

'If you make a noise, I'll hurt you.'

I'm terrified now, and my heart flutters wildly with fear. What's he doing? I stare at his glinting blue eyes, which are dead and empty.

'This is to purify you, to let the evil spirits out...'

Then I feel a searing, ripping pain between my legs. I gasp, shriek, and try to sit up and wriggle away. But his knees are still on my chest, and his other hand is now clamped over my mouth, pushing my head back hard on the table. I can't breathe. All I can feel is a burning, stabbing pain where my wee comes out. Mr Stabard's other hand begins to move in and out between my legs, and I feel something hard stabbing into my body down there.

'I'm going to make you pure...this is to make you clean.'

His eyes bore into me – the pain is agonising. Tears run down my cheeks, but his hand is over my mouth, and I can hardly breathe or cry out. I can't move or get away, and he works the brown thing roughly in and out, ripping the flesh in my wee place for what seems like hours but for what is maybe a few minutes. All the time, he's hoarsely whispering that he's purifying me, that I needed cleansing.

'I'm doing God's work,' he hisses through his teeth. 'Otherwise, you'll have to be locked up – in prison, or a home somewhere... you're that evil...'

Then he stops for a second and partly stands up. I try to scramble away, but he grabs me with his free hand and flattens me down again, whispering a prayer we hear in church each week, which begins:

'Fathers above all heavens, beseech the devil from these evil dark children...'

As he mumbled the prayer, it wasn't Christian; it was a prayer they used in the vile rituals full of evil; he continued to push and pull the thing in and out of my raw flesh. His voice begins to rise in a fever as he does it. My head is swimming, and I can't see properly now. I feel split open and sick with pain. Suddenly he stops. He rips the brown thing out of me as fast as he's pushed it in, and I scream under his hand. He goes to the holdall and drops it inside. I lay there blinking, confused, agonised, my legs akimbo on the table, tears running down my cheeks. Suddenly, his face appears two inches above mine, and he holds me down with his hand.

'If you tell anyone about this,' he spits, 'you'll be locked up, I'll be sad, and then I'll have to kill myself. Do you understand?'

I blink. I can't speak. I can't cry and I'm shocked. And then he's gone. Slam. It's dark. I feel numb, wet, and confused. I feel I'm peeing and pooping uncontrollably. I lie there until the other two come over and help me put on my nappy again. It's the old one, filthy and stinking. I hurt *between my legs. When I look later, there's red stuff in the nappy. What is it? Mr Stabard said I mustn't tell anybody, so I can't show Mrs Stabard, can I? There's no one else to tell. Afterwards, I hurt badly, can hardly walk or sit down, and it burns terribly to wee. If I sleep, I have nightmares. We girls never talk about it. It's happened in front of them, and yet we all pretend it hasn't really happened...*

What I didn't know the first time my foster father 'purified' me was that this would become a regular evening ritual training ready for the bigger games and would happen more frequently. Mr Stabard would appear once or twice a week at the shed door. He always had the same brown holdall, which I understood eventually was full of sweets and chocolate bars. Sometimes we'd thought that he would just give us some and leave. We even thought we might be rewarded with some of the sweets in the holdall after being 'cleansed'. Not so. He always did the same thing. He chose a different one of us each time, so the other two had to sit in the chair or hide behind it, trying not to witness his sickening chocolate bar ritual with that evening's chosen victim.

Sometimes he would insert the chocolate bar into my poo hole, which hurt like hell. I could feel myself rip open, and for hours, even days, afterwards, I would have red stuff in my nappy. As I got older, I realised it was blood. I bled every time I pooped, and I would lie awake wondering if he had broken something inside my bottom. Mostly he inserted it into the front hole, which he seemed to prefer. He would always chant religious verses, even praying, saying he was 'driving out the devil' and making me 'pure'.

Sometimes he would come into the shed and say, 'we're nearly there, girls; you're nearly pure. Just one more time.'

For a split second, I would believe him and think if we went through the humiliating, painful ritual just once more, we might be 'cured' of being so evil. I sometimes volunteered to save my sisters from the pain and because I felt it might get me purified quicker, I offered myself. In a twisted way, he made me believe that the more I did it, the more I would get better. That was the trick of his mind games with us. But, of course, it didn't work. Mr Stabard just kept doing it, and we never seemed to get any nearer to being purified.

It went on until I was four or five, I think. I learned not to fidget and not to fight him once on the table. At first, because it was agony, I would wriggle and twist, trying to get away, and tears would spring to my eyes. But I could sense he relished my pain, so I began to shut down. I learned to lie very still and blank out my feelings. That way, I could get through it. I looked at the ceiling and counted plastic ridges. I learned to suffer and to put up with it in silence, hoping that it would be over soon and I would be pure. When he saw that he'd made us bleed – he could hardly miss it – he told us that the blood was a sign he was purifying us. The bleeding was a cleansing thing, he said. He never cleaned us up afterwards and always left us naked and battered on the table. We had to sort ourselves out and put the dirty nappies back on without washing or cleaning up the mess. It was totally and utterly humiliating, leaving us battered and bruised, shocked and degraded. Sometimes my nappy wouldn't do up again.

Sometimes he would come to us in the shed to purify us after church on a Sunday. It might be after lunch or later in the day, and he'd often be drunk. He was much more violent than before. I don't know whether going to church had worked him up into some kind of frenzy or whether having a few drinks got him going. But he would grab one of us and throw us violently on the table, pull off our nappy and...this would hurt much more than the chocolate bar.

'See, there's evil coming out of you. You're being purified.'

The chocolate bar in the shed routine continued for what seemed like years. Every evening we would begin to get agitated, sensing that he might soon descend on us. But what could we do? We were locked in there, unable to escape. He just came and hurt us, and we were powerless to stop him.

This is how they used us; to us children, this was normal. In our minds, it was our hugs and his showing love. I don't think I thought it was wrong until he started to share me with his friends. You feel it's too late then to tell anyone because it was your fault you liked it; 'Jenny, you fought with your sibling for that special love, and now you must live with it.'

Children deserve the right to be loved and to be taught by their adults that raping a child is wrong and it's not the child's fault; it's the adult's. We need classes in that adults teach children about wrong love as that's what you feel it is as a child. Most of the time, it starts with grooming, not touching. Making you feel special, playing you against your sibling/or peers. Noticing you by watching you and commenting on changes, taking notes of your likes and dislikes, and using their findings to groom you. And then the sexual abuse starts. I had so many questions to ask these apparently good people; who were they to think they could use the word of God to beat, rape and steal our breath from us? Who were they to be able to sleep restfully in their beds at night, knowing full well what wicked things they had put upon us, poor innocent children? What he said to us about being evil, he was speaking the words that portrayed him and his fellow paedophiles.

5

GETTING ME READY

'I view Mr and Mrs Stabard as a safe pair of hands, with years of experience, which Jennie can benefit from...'

(Social worker's report)

One vivid memory stands out for me: my fifth birthday. Although we never celebrated our birthdays or had any fuss, I remember this one – probably because it was the opposite of what any child would ever want their birthday to be like. I was allowed a bath that day, which was a rare treat. I remember sitting in the bath, with about six inches of warm water; I knew hot baths were expensive and a luxury – when Mr Stabard came in. I froze. I'd been expecting Mrs Stabard, not her husband. But he was in the bathroom, leaning over me, being very nice. For the first time, he seemed to care about me, and I remember thinking: 'It's my birthday, so maybe he's decided to love me after all.'

Then he whispered hoarsely, 'Stand up.'

I stood up, dripping and started shivering in the cold bathroom. The water was only up to my mid-calves and was rapidly cooling down.

'I'm sorry I have to do this,' he said mysteriously. 'Be very quiet.'

With a quick movement, he had a chocolate bar between my legs and inside me. I gasped as he ripped into me. He looked very fierce, but I grasped onto him involuntarily, feeling my head swim and knees buckle.

'Ssh! I have to do this, to purify you... you wicked girl.'

My feet were slipping in the water, and I felt giddy and sick, as though I was going to fall under the water and drown. Suddenly I was down on my bottom, the water splashing around my waist, but he still stooped over me, thrusting the chocolate bar in and out of me with a crazed look. My head was going round and round, and I saw stars, feeling nauseous and terrified. I felt ripped apart and wanted to get away, but his grip on my upper arm was like a vice, his fingers digging into me, still holding me half-upright. Then the blood came. It flowed into the water. I wanted to cry, but he pressed his face right up to mine.

'Don't cry, don't say a word. This is the evil coming out...'

He moved the chocolate up and down, up and down, as I slipped in and out of consciousness. I felt like I was dying, but I just stared at him, which he hated. I stared and stared. I felt I was just an object in the bath, not a girl, not human, just a thing.

'All that dirty stuff is coming out of you,' he hissed, 'see!'

He started chanting one of his favourite prayers, and I wanted to slip under the water and sink without a trace. Please make it stop. Everything was going black when he suddenly pulled the bar out very abruptly. It was over. He let out his dry, harsh laugh – the filthy old man's chuckle he always used. At that moment, I absolutely hated him with all my being. But I was too weak to do anything, and now the bath was streaky red. Suddenly, Faith's head popped around the bathroom door. Her eyes widened.

'Why's the bath red?' she asked.

None of us ever spoke without being spoken to, but she was often bolder and braver than me and would say things we'd only think. I'd hate her for it sometimes because I feared he'd punish us even more.

'It's the evil stuff coming out, Lord be praised,' whispered Mr Stabard.

Then he flung open the door, knocking Faith sideways and disappeared, leaving me appalled in my red-streaked bath. Faith helped me creep to our box room, and I snuck into my bunk bed – something I was never allowed to do usually. I preferred the top bunk, but I just crawled to the bottom, wrapped in an old towel and lay there. I didn't move for a very long time. I must be very evil, I thought, for him to do that to me. Luckily, Mr and Mrs Stabard didn't come, and I got time to lie down, close my eyes, and wish it would all go away forever and ever. There was a bottle of rat poison on the shelf in our shed, and I had a fantasy about putting this in Mr Stabard's food or beer – he'd never notice. I comforted myself by 'magicking' him away in my fantasies and eventually drifted off to sleep. What a happy birthday present he'd given me – I certainly never forgot the day I turned five. The bath treatment also began to be an occasional part of his gruesome purifying routine from then on.

When Mr Stabard hurt me as he did in the shed and now in the bath, I felt he absolutely hated me and hated my blackness. I used to stare him in the eyes at these times because I also despised him for what he was doing to me and my sisters. It was my only weapon. If I was on the table and stared at him, it unnerved him, and he would slap my face to stop me from looking. I concentrated all my hate on my stare, and eventually, he'd have to look away. I would lay still, telling him with my eyes how much I loathed him and how much pain he was causing me. My sisters didn't meet his eyes, but I always did. I wanted him to know that I was watching him while he hurt my child's body.

Meanwhile, the rest of my body would be on shutdown, and when it got so bad, I would black out. I controlled my emotions while he did whatever nasty thing he felt he had the right to do in God's name. What

I didn't know was that Mr Stabard had plans to 'purify' us evil black children in ways which would be even more frightening and painful. Not long after the bath incident, Mr Stabard began to want to play a new game at night. It especially seemed to happen when he'd drunk a lot that evening. After work, he would go to his club, the British Legion, or he'd come home and open a beer, then have whisky or gin. As the years went by, he seemed to drink more and more, sometimes even having a drink in the morning. This was never good news for us.

...The first time he comes into us at night, he's drunk. We three now sleep together in a bunk bed meant for two and take turns for us to sleep together on the bottom bunk, top to toe, with the other on the top bunk. The best place is on your own on the top, so we rotate who can sleep there, to be fair. I'm on top this night, and the other two are on the bottom, fast asleep. The room's pitch black as it's late at night – probably midnight or the early hours. I suddenly become aware that someone is in the room. I'm awake, bolt upright, sitting up in my bed. I'm scared, hearing our foster father's unmistakable heavy breathing, and I can instantly smell his horrible breath and aftershave. Suddenly the light goes on.

Mr Stabard has come upstairs with a light bulb and has put it in. The other two wake up then, and we all jump out of bed and stand to attention. It's very strange to think how much he has trained us by then, but we knew if he came up to our room, which he often does when he wants a fry-up or cup of tea late at night, then we have to jump to it. He's like a sergeant major commanding his troops – even if we're three young children and it's the middle of a dark winter's night. It's absolutely freezing cold. Our nighties are thin, and the windows draughty as we stand barefoot, waiting for his orders. He's swaying a bit and looks quite bleary, so we know not to move or say anything until he's ready.

I'm shivering like a leaf; my heart's racing, and I know we'll have to obey him, whatever he wants us to do. The chocolate game is being played a lot in the shed and bath these days, and it crosses my mind he might want that, but he doesn't have the brown holdall with him. Every time he comes to us in the shed or pulls us by the hair into the lounge for a lap game, I hope with all my being that he'll tell me I'm now pure, and it is all over. But he never does. Purification seems further away than ever, especially on this bitterly cold night. Mr Stabard stands there momentarily, scrutinising us woozily like he's sizing us up.

'You're evil; you know that, don't you?' he slurs in a hoarse whisper. 'You're sick...sick and evil...'

Instinctively we crowd closer together and hold hands, sensing a new threat. I feel something awful is about to happen, and I want to protect the other two at all costs. Hope starts whimpering, and I squeeze her hand hard, willing her to stop. He hates crying or any sign of weakness, and it makes him lash out even more.

'It's God's job to purify your souls. It's His will to make you pure...'

He sounds like he is working up to something.

'...and he wants me to continue His great work. He wants me to purify your evil, wicked ways...'

My knees are shaking as he takes a big, lurching step forward. He's towering over us (like a monster in those horrible places he takes me sometimes) looking dishevelled and red-faced. We look up at him, blinking against the light bulb that swings just above his head, casting a weird halo of light around his white hair. Mr Stabard bends over us even closer, and I get a whiff of sickening boozy breath as he points with his thick sausage-like finger to each of us in turn:

'Eeny, meeny, miny moe, catch a n.....r by his toe...or if wiggles let him go, Eeny, meeny, miny, moe... '

'Ha, ha, ha' goes his dry little laugh as he amuses himself with his ditty. He grabs me roughly by the shoulder and pulls me towards him. The other two hang onto my hands for a second, but he jerks me away, so they must let go. Without a word, he rolls up my nightie and looks at my body. His eyes look hungry, and he licks his lips. I feel shy as the other two scuttle up the bunk bed ladder and hide on top, holding each other. I whimper as Mr Stabard grabs me to him hard with both hands. I glance quickly at the door he's closed behind him, calculating whether I can push past and escape – no way. Hope's snivelling gets louder, and Mr Stabard shouts up at the top bunk with a fierce look.

'Shut that noise up and get down here you two.'

Obediently, they crawl down the ladder again and stand just behind him. I can see them shaking, with their arms around each other. Oh my God, what's he going to do this time? My mouth's dry, and I feel sick. I want to cry, but I bite my lip – I must control myself. Roughly, he pushes me backwards, and I fall hard across the bottom bunk. He moves swiftly towards me and pulls my arms down by my sides. I stare at him, which I know he hates, but he just looks over my head. Then, he's on top of me. I can't breathe - a fifty-year-old man on top of a five-year-old child. His whole weight is on my chest, and my body's squished. I'm frightened as he is crushing me to death. Brut, mixed with sweat and alcohol, fills my nose as he puffs and blows on top of me. My throat's closing, and I can't get air, so I wriggle, trying to get free, breathe, and to get him off.

'Lie still,' he snaps, 'or it'll get worse.'

He lifts himself off me slightly, and I can breathe a bit better. There's some fumbling and a zipping sound while he moves my legs apart with his free hand. All the time, my heart's racing, and I'm thinking: I've got to get away. Get me away! My mind whirls. I hold my breath in sheer terror. Help me. Ignoring my struggles, he yanks my legs back open and pulls himself back on top of me again, his full weight pinning me down to the bed.

Somewhere behind him are the girls, but I can't see them over his hulk. I will help them to get help. Go and tell! But Mr Stabard is entirely focused on what he wants. It seems like I'm dying - like I'll be flattened out and crushed under him. I have pins and needles in my legs. Are my bones snapping? I want to scream out. What's happening? His whole weight is heavy and sweaty on me. He starts moving on top of me, grunting. This is much worse than ever before. Then it's over, and he leaves.

The other two, I now see, are sitting crouched against the wall, arms around their heads and faces turned away from the bed. The door flings open, and he's back. My heart stops, and I play dead. He shuffles over to the light bulb and takes it out; then, I hear him go out the door again. I wait for ages, and I hardly dare breathe until I'm sure he's really gone this time. Even when I know he's not coming back, I just lie still in the cold, dark room. Sweat is like ice on my body, and I'm half-naked, spread out on the bed.

I can't move. I can't cry. I feel something. I lie there completely still for what seems like hours, not moving. I don't sleep, and I'm in total shock. I don't understand what has just happened. I know it was utterly horrible, like nothing I ever imagined was possible. I expect to see a hole in my body, with my insides spilling out. I don't look. Eventually, I somehow roll sideways and pull the sheet and blanket over me, hardly breathing. The other two girls are back on the top bunk. I can hear them rhythmically breathing like they're asleep, but I'm sure I'll never sleep again. I can't take my eyes off the door.

Finally, it's the grey morning light. Maybe being black and disabled is bad, after all? Perhaps he's right? It must all be our fault - black ugly evil children. He's gone to work *already when I get up, and I feel relieved not to see him. I'm still shocked as I try to go and make breakfast with the other two. It hurts to walk, sit, stand, and wee, and my legs are like jelly. I'm bending down to bandage Mrs Stabard's stinky legs, just as always, and I wonder if I can say something to her. There's no 'hello' or 'good morning', and she doesn't look at me. I give up; I don't exist. I don't speak to the other two. I don't look at anyone's face. I don't cry.*

I'm locked in the shed all day as usual, but I'm not playing or singing. In the armchair, I hold myself and rock backwards and forwards, over and over, humming quietly. I don't want to feel what he has done to me. I can tell that the other two don't know what to do. We don't talk about anything; we never do. I can't talk about it anyway. There's no one else to tell, no one to go to get help from.

From that first night onwards, from when I was just a little girl until I was twenty-three, Mr Stabard came and played his 'eeny, meeny, miny, moe' game with us three girls regularly. It was always late at night and always after he had been drinking. Because Faith was often in the hospital, the choice was usually between Hope and me, and he alternated between us. Whoever his chosen girl was for the night, the others had to watch. It was part of his sick game. He hated if we cried and would start slapping us about until we stopped. Hope often cried more, and I willed her to be quiet. I learned to bite my lip and clench my teeth. I knew how to pinch myself and dig my nails into my flesh to shut down my feelings. Mr

Stabard would chant a prayer from the ritual book, or so he proclaimed it was. It would say we were 'wicked' and needed 'purifying' before every sordid ordeal began. I wanted to protect the other two from him, so as time went on, I actually volunteered when he came into the room to save the others from pain and humiliation. I said, 'I'll be your special girl tonight,' which made me feel sick. His constant brainwashing was working. But no matter what we did, he kept coming back.

Only very occasionally, when the other two or how many were in the box room at the time were asleep, and the house was quiet, did I cry. Even then I'd keep it brief because I was always vigilant; I was bottling up oceans of pain and masses of bad feelings, and there was nowhere to put them. I took on a mothering role for the other two and other children who entered via the authority wagon, so I had to be strong for them. It felt like a great responsibility, but in some ways, it kept me alive, forcing me to be stronger and braver for them. Of course, I didn't always feel it, but I knew I couldn't give up. Only much later did my feelings begin to come out. When they did, it was like unleashing a torrent of pent-up fury stored over those years and years of horrendous abuse.

Once Mr Stabard had got the taste for us at night, there was no stopping him. I wondered for a long time if Mrs Stabard had any idea what her husband was up to. Did she know what he was doing to us? Surely, she noticed when he got out of bed in the middle of the night. I fantasised about telling her everything and throwing myself at her mercy, begging her to make it better, requesting her to ask that he stop hurting us.

One night, she came into our room very late and went over to where I was sleeping. Without a word, she made me sit up, took off my nightie and laid me back down on the bottom bunk. My foster mother spread my legs apart; seconds later, her husband entered the room. I lay there, horrified, not knowing what to do. Mrs Stabard silently turned and went out of the room, leaving her husband to unzip himself and then throw his heavy bulk on top of me. This pattern of behaviour continued until well into my late teens. Mrs Stabard would come in and lay one of us out for him. She'd stand there in her bulky dressing gown and slippers, not speaking or making eye contact with us until her husband arrived, and then she would leave him to his nasty night work. At first, this happened once a week, but as I got older, it happened twice or three times, sometimes more. Mrs Stabard not only knew what he was doing to us, but she was part of it. She helped him; in fact, she seemed to endorse it. It shocked me to the core and meant there was no one I could turn to. Sometimes it also made me feel like I was crazy, like what was going on was a nightmare, and I would wake up one day and find out that it was all a bad dream. Unfortunately, it wasn't. It was our reality – one that no one could have guessed at by looking at the God-fearing Stabards or at the respectable white front door of 97 Forestlane Way.

That's where it went wrong, or so I thought. As soon as social services thought these people were good caring people, they backed off from ensuring they treated us well. So, they allowed the torture to continue.

I remember when I did the Stabard's washing once, and as his white y fronts were dried, I rubbed pepper into the crutch. And my heart smiled as I looked over at my foster sibling. We knew each of us was laughing inside... but this could never be expressed as our torture would be far worse than it was. So, we silently planned revenge and silently laughed, chuckled, and giggled as we held our beings still.

6

REPRESSED

'...Jennie is lucky to have such caring, experienced foster parents as she is such a moody, difficult child to deal with. This family have been excused from allegations of sexual abuse against previous foster children during the early 60s.' (1974)

(Social worker's report)

Even though Mr Stabard was 'purifying' what seemed like every day, the housekeeping continued as if nothing had happened. We still had to do all the household chores and be locked in the shed while the Stabards and their family lived a seemingly 'normal' life.

I suffered from chest infections a great deal, which the damp shed and freezing box bedroom didn't help. They took us to a local doctor and dentist when necessary and scrubbed us up for visits, so we didn't look as dirty and smelly as usual. I had to see the doctor quite a lot, as I often couldn't breathe properly. However, even then, I didn't speak to the doctor directly, and sometimes Mrs Stabard sent me out of the room. I had no idea what the doctor and Mrs Stabard were really saying about me. Sometimes she took us to a local hospital, where we had to exercise without ever knowing why. We had to hold onto wall bars and stretch, perhaps to make us breathe better or stand straighter – we didn't get much exercise in the shed all day. Again, we never spoke to the medical staff about anything; we just quietly got on with whatever they told us to do. Even if we were ill, we weren't allowed to rest; we were still shoved out into the shed all day, and we'd still have to do the chores, regardless.

We girls had a little bit of cloth we used as a comforter – a scrap from an old dress – and we used to sniff it under our noses and cuddle it, especially when we were sick. We'd also suck our middle and index fingers and stroke our hair. I think we did this to comfort ourselves. After all, no one else hugged or snuggled us up when we were poorly. We just had to do what we could for ourselves, without parents or teddy bears to keep us happy.

Another strange thing was that the Stabards always gave us pills to take. I had no idea what they were, but they would hand out the little white and pink tablets daily. They weren't multivitamins since they came in brown medicine bottles. Every day we would be lined up and made to take our pills. As we got older, the number of pills increased – sometimes, we took ten or more a day each. I didn't know if the doctor prescribed them for us, but looking back, I wonder if they were giving us tranquillisers to keep us quiet in the shed. We always had to take them, and they got furious if we didn't. Apart from keeping us docile, the most important thing to the Stabards, I believe, was not to leave us alone with anyone. We might have started talking about what was going on at home, and they did not want us to give the game away. Mr Stabard was never there when social services came or when we went to the doctor – I felt he hid from the authorities. However, he'd already frightened us so much that we wouldn't have said anything, even if someone had asked us directly. I think we were too scared of the consequences. Mr Stabard had told us repeatedly that if we told anyone about his nocturnal activities, he would have to kill himself. As much as we hated him and hated what he did to us, we didn't want to be responsible for his death. Also, if he did die, where would we go? Who would look after us? Not only did we have no idea what was 'out there' beyond the Stabards' house, but we didn't feel we belonged anywhere else. We desperately wanted to stay together as the three of us had become a real family by then.

However, something we began to do to keep us sane and make ourselves feel a bit better in a less situation was to get our own back. We only did fairly little things, but it made us laugh and feel more powerful, even if just for a few moments. We often acted out a scene in the shed about giving Mr Stabard rat poison we found on the shelf.

Me (playing it up as Mr Stabard): 'Gulp. Oh, I've swallowed something . . . aaagh, I feel so ill. I'm dying. Help me!' (the other two watching, smiling from the chair as I fall to the ground, writhing, clutching my stomach and groaning).

Innocently, as me: 'Oh dear, Mr Stabard, you look very sick. What's wrong?'

Me: 'I drank something. I think it's poison! I'm dying . . . Help me, please help me! I need help . . .Aaaaaagh!' (Stepping over his writhing body).

'Oh, dear. Sorry, I can't help. No way. Never. Bye.'

We'd all fall apart giggling at this point, and then we'd re-enact it. We loved getting to the bit where we said 'NO' to him, which would reduce us to fits of helpless laughter. The very thought of leaving him in agony made us feel a whole lot better about our plight.

Mr Stabard was our main focus. There were times when he was paralytically drunk when he rolled home from the British Legion and drank beer from the crate in the larder. In our forbidden territory, the front lounge, he would fall asleep in his favourite armchair. It would be late at night and very quiet in the house, except for his drunken snoring. We would muster up all our courage, tiptoe barefooted downstairs into the lounge and tie his shoelaces together. Later we'd hear an enormous thud, followed by incoherent shouting, and we'd be back up in our box room bunks, giggling helplessly under our thin covers. It was a brilliant moment; to think of him falling over and banging his head, completely confused because he was too out of his skull to know what was happening. We tied his shoelaces together many times, and it always gave us a thrill. These moments made us stronger, made us laugh and feel happier and allowed us to develop a sense of humour together, which I believe was one of the things that kept me going. We were naughty little girls, but in a tiny way, we were also managing to fight back.

We didn't get our own back on Mrs Stabard very often, as we felt she probably had no choice but to help her husband hurt us. However, we knew she was terrified of mice, so one day, we nicked her grandson's toy mouse and put it in her slipper. We were preparing tea that evening, and there was suddenly an enormous shriek behind us. Mrs Stabard had put her slipper on, found the mouse and, thinking it was a real one, had thrown the shoe across the room and nearly fainted with shock. We were helpless with silent laughter but just had to carry on peeling spuds and carrots at the sink. She didn't say anything, but I know she was angry as she sulked for ages with us afterwards.

Of course, we were still creative with our cooking and adding some 'interesting' extras to their food. Every time we did this, it would be a thrill. We'd been waiting for adverse reactions to worms in their spaghetti or dog poo in their casserole, but it gave us a sense of victory to visualise them scoffing it all down, and we'd giggle together in the dark. Also, when Mr Stabard was drunk at night and got us up to make him food, we'd take our revenge by making KiteKat sandwiches or adding laxatives to his food. It felt like we were getting one over on him at last, especially when he was up in the toilet all night and complained of a tummy ache the next day. We also put wee in the roast potatoes and enjoyed seeing them eat them with relish, even though we knew we'd be dishing up the remains in our dog bowls later.

However, the place where we showed our greatest revenge was against the grandchildren's toys. It seemed so unfair that they had loads of toys stuffed under the stairs, and we had none. Christmas was the worst time, as they would unwrap masses of lovely, brightly coloured things. While preparing the Christmas lunch, we'd hear the kids ripping open their toys and shrieking with delight at what they found. The Stabards left us out of the celebrations: no stockings, no decorations in our room, nothing. So, one year, while they went in to eat the Christmas lunch we had prepared, we snuck into the lounge, where all the grandchildren's presents lay carelessly strewn amongst the ripped Christmas paper. There was an amazing wooden train set and boxes of Lego, but my favourite thing was a baby doll with a mouth that opened and eyes that fluttered. The tummy button made noises to ensure the nappy was clean, the bottle was never empty, and the child had fed the doll! I was fascinated that you could feed her with a bottle made of gluey stuff, and she would wee in her nappy, and you'd have to change her. I wonder if I was more drawn to this doll because it seemed a toy had more essential properties than we had.

The three of us secretly played quickly with the toys, and then a look passed between us. Without a word, we started ripping things up. I remember smashing the boxes, ripping the train set apart, and damaging as much as possible, as quickly as possible. It felt absolutely wonderful, especially as the grandchildren taunted us so much and behaved like they were superior to us. We all worked hard and fast and then ran upstairs to the box room. After lunch, the grandchildren went back into the living room, and we waited at the bedroom door, holding our breath and waiting for their reaction. When we heard the shrieks and screams of upset, we hugged each other. Triumph! There was a sense of victory, of momentary joy, because, as we saw it, we had got our own back on the spoiled little brats who made our lives a living hell. Inevitably, we were dragged out of our room, beaten and slapped and shoved into the airing cupboard as punishment, without even having our Christmas leftovers. But whatever they did to us, the shrieks of the grandkids were still ringing in our ears, and I have to say, we savoured the sense of revenge. Of course, the Stabards bought them mountains of replacement toys, but we realised that we could always sneak under the stairs and smash them up again. It was war.

I'm sure our revenge-filled antics convinced the Stabards that the devil was at work in the house. If anything, our behaviour justified their mistreatment of us even more – we were clearly wicked black children who needed to be purified. Since what they had done to us so far was not working, they had to find another way to 'teach us a proper lesson'. They were grown-ups with all the power, but we felt we were fighting for our freedom and lives, so we weren't going to give up. Most weekends were interminably boring for us. We'd be locked in 'Our Home' in the shed and listen to the grandchildren playing tag or hide-and-seek outside on the lawn. We'd hear the neighbours talking and cutting their hedges next to the shed, but inside, the hours seemed to drag on and on.

Then one Saturday, when I must have been about seven or eight, something different happened. Mrs Stabard appeared at the wrought iron gate while it was still light and unlocked the padlock. It wasn't time to prepare supper yet, so we looked at each other, a bit confused. We crowded to the slit window to see what was up. The door was flung open, and she pointed for us to come out and follow her; as usual, she said nothing to us. Did she think we were too stupid to understand words? Or did she think we were mere animals to herd? Like the mute, dumb creatures she thought we were, without a word, we did as she indicated and trotted obediently out of the shed, stretching and yawning in the dimming light and then through the hall and, amazingly, into the lounge.

The lounge was usually so out-of-bounds that I couldn't figure out why we were going there. Was it a visit from a social worker? If so, she would have scrubbed us up for it. It wasn't Christmas . . . that had just passed. It wasn't a lap game with Mr Stabard, as he only did that when his wife was out of the house. And then we saw them. It was a total shock. We recognised four people from church standing and sitting in the lounge, waiting for us, with weird expressions on their faces. What was going on? Our immediate reaction was to shrink back towards the door and cling to each other, as they seemed far from friendly. One was the man with thick white hair who always smoked a cigar. The atmosphere was tense, and I felt a real tingle of fear rush up my spine. It didn't look at all good. The assembled people were quite old, and all white; one had a woolly hat. There were two women and two men. Mr Stabard was standing by the ceramic fireplace with the fierce expression I recognised so well. Mrs Stabard stood between us and the door. I suddenly felt very trapped, like something really bad was about to happen.

Without a word, Mrs Stabard pushed me in the back, and I stumbled forward a little. I looked round at her, and she pointed to the centre of the room, to the dark red carpet, between the sofa and the two armchairs. Mr Stabard snapped at us in his usual military tone:

'Come here. On the carpet. Here. All of you. Now.'

The three of us shuffled over to the spot where his fat finger indicated. The other adults stood up and surrounded us. Oh my God, what's going on? We girls darted looks of sheer panic at each other. What were they going to do? What was going to happen now? Were they going to kill us? As they approached, all I felt was dread. One of the grown-ups got out a piece of paper and showed it to Mr Stabard, who nodded.

He said to the people there, 'We're here to drive out the devil, as you know,' and then said something that sounded like 'xisms'.

I was utterly terrified as the man holding up the paper started chanting the words out loud in an eerie voice like he was half-shouting:

'Oh most Glorious Prince of the Heavenly Armies, St Michael the Archangel, defend us in the battle...and in our wrestling against principalities and powers, against the rulers of the world of this darkness, against the spirits of wickedness in high places...'

We three girls held each other tightly, shaking, while the grown-ups moved in on us. We didn't understand the words or what was going on. The adults started walking around us in a circle, with their left arms raised over our heads, like they were playing some bizarre adult game. Mr and Mrs Stabard joined in, looking very solemn. We soon had six adults circling us, their hands joined above our heads, and we were dizzy and terrified in the middle. The voice continued to boom out, getting wilder and scarier:

'...Beseech the God of Peace to crush Satan under our feet...cast into hell Satan and all the other evil spirits who prowl throughout the world seeking the ruin of souls...'

The man went on and on, getting louder and more urgent until one of the older women suddenly fell on the floor and started shaking and screaming. It looked like she was having a fit – she was writhing and moaning and practically frothing at the mouth. We girls hid our faces and clung on even tighter to each other, but the old woman continued to scream and shout, and as I peeked out, I could see her arms and legs thrashing about. It was completely bizarre and very frightening since I still had no idea what was going on. While the woman was rolling about on the carpet, the man was still repeating the chant. His voice was getting louder and louder, and stranger and stranger, like it was reaching a frenzied pitch. I wondered again, for a moment, if they would kill us in some ritual. The woman's legs were still kicking out and she just kept screaming. It was terrifying.

Then all of a sudden, the man stopped chanting, and the woman quietened down. She lay on her back panting at first, then closed her eyes and lay still, and I wondered if she was asleep or even unconscious. One of the men bent over and pulled her up to her feet. She was flushed and sweaty and looked very dazed, so the others fussed over her. Meanwhile, nobody said a word to us about what had just happened. Then Mrs Stabard came up to us and pointed to the door, and, just like that, we were shunted back out to the shed. Once there, we huddled on the dirty old armchair and cuddled each other. We did not utter a word to each other; it all seemed too scary to mention.

This spooky ritual happened several times over the years. I eventually understood that the Stabards were 'casting out the devil' that they thought resided in us through an exorcism. It was another kind of purification they must have believed was necessary to cleanse our blackened souls or whiten our skins. Our wrecking of toys and naughty tricks around the house must have exasperated them to the point where they thought they had to teach us a lesson we would never, ever forget. They were right, we wouldn't forget, but it wouldn't make us give up fighting back, either. These were adults there to nurture us, yet they instilled fear during these episodes.

I know God's love, and his love is gentle, and I've met him in my darkest days, and he has loved and nurtured me. He didn't command demons out of me for what man had done. The religious folk have these man-made tools that are damaging. God is with me, and if he shows me that I need to get rid of stuff or change, then that will be his call, not man's.

7

MISFITS

'Jennie is of low average rather retarded with low intelligence, appears emotionally immature, but gets on well with most of the girls at school... Appears that jennie has been abused...but if we were to look into this, who would care for these misfits in society?'

(Social worker's report 1972-1974)

The Stabards sent me to primary school at five and three quarters (I am not sure if this was the right age as I never knew my age, but my little me says she was five and three quarters), and it was a total shock. I'd never really been out of the house, except to go to church or the doctor and then only with the Stabards in tow, so I had no idea what life outside was all about. Not surprisingly, Mrs Stabard didn't prepare me for it. I simply walked to an enormous reddish-grey stone building with loads of children running around in the playground outside, who all stopped and stared at me, open-mouthed. Everybody else was white, and my arrival was the source of much amazement and amusement. It was as if the alien had landed: I was an alien come to earth, and it was a bumpy ride.

After the silence of the shed, the school seemed wild to me. Children ran around screaming, playing, and shouting, and I'd jump when they passed. I used to think to myself; they think I'm the animal. I feared other children and parents, especially after the horrible church people had come to our home to 'purify' us, so I didn't really understand where I was. The kids sensed how terrified I was because they started picking on me from day one. They would shout 'wog' or 'blackie' right in my face or say I was a 'fat, ugly or a black bitch'. I felt like a misfit from the start, especially as the parents of the children weren't happy that I was there either. We three were some of the first black children to ever come to the school, as we were a minority in our village. When the parents saw me coming in through the school gate, they would put their heads down and hurry past, pulling their children behind them. Or they'd cross the road, so they didn't have to look at me or talk to Mrs Stabard, who took me there at first. Was I so alien? Obviously, to them, I was.

Three things stick out in my mind about first going to school. Right from the beginning, there were objections to me using the same things as the other children

– simply because I was black. The parents pressured the headmaster, Mr Harrow, not to let me use the same facilities as their children because they believed we would contaminate them somehow. Unbelievably, we had to bring our own cutlery, plastic beaker and plate in a plastic bag for mealtimes and sit at a separate table. Faith was already at the school by then, although she was away a lot through illness and wasn't there the day I started. Hope joined the year after, and we three eventually ended up sitting together at a small table to the side of the dining hall – again, a little isolated group of three. As I got older, I began to feel Mr Harrow should have stood up for us and let us use the cutlery and eat at the same table as the other kids. I became fearful about eating in front of white people after that. Secondly, I wasn't allowed to drink out of the water fountains in the playground. A playground rumour was that if I – or any of us three – drank from the fountain, the other kids would catch something. I did sneak a drink a few times as I was thirsty and got rapped over the knuckles with a ruler by my strict form teacher, Mrs Brookfield, which I thought was very unfair. The third thing that really hurt was that I was not allowed to swim with the other children.

There was actually a swimming pool on the school grounds, which all the kids learned to swim in – except us three. The school would not allow us to go swimming. Maybe it was the parents bringing pressure on the school to keep us out of the water. There was this great fear that we were carrying some awful disease or would contaminate the children. Nobody wanted to be near us, let alone allow us to share the swimming pool water with them. It really upset me, especially on hot summer days when everybody excitedly went off to swim. Of course, the Stabards didn't fight for us – since we didn't confide in them, they probably didn't even know. Moreover, given that they were keeping us in the shed at home, they probably would have agreed with the parents that we would be kept separate from everybody else. After all, they were doing it too. I actually think the headmaster, Mr Harrow, felt quite bad about what he was doing. He was quite nice to me personally – and to the other two – and he would say things like, 'I'm sorry, but my hands are tied,' whenever he told us we couldn't go swimming or use the water fountain. He was probably the first adult who had been warm towards me, which meant a lot, even though the outcome was unpleasant. What was important was that he talked to me like a person, something I had seldom experienced before. I think the parents were scared of us because not only were we black, but we were also quite dirty. There was no way we were as clean as the other kids, and we must have smelled quite badly because the Stabards didn't properly look after us.

One really embarrassing incident sticks out in my mind. Just after starting primary school, I was bleeding heavily from a nasty night attack by Mr Stabard. I remember it so well: my knickers were full of blood from where he had 'hurt' me (I always thought of it as 'hurt', it was the only way I could describe it), and I was supposed to do PE. I didn't have any PE kit, so I had to borrow a pair of shorts from the teacher, who kept some spare shorts at the back of the class in case any kids forgot them. Of course, the shorts were also covered with blood after the lesson, and I was terrified. I didn't know what to do or how to manage the situation, so I stuck them in my bag and took them home. I hid them at home and hoped they'd disappear somehow and she'd forget about it. About a week later, the PE teacher called me to the front and asked me about the shorts. I didn't know what to say. How could I explain it? I couldn't. What did I have to say for myself? I had nothing to say. She told me, in front of everyone, that she was very disappointed in me. I felt so humiliated, but even more so when a girl piped up:

'That black girl, over there, she's stolen the shorts. She's a thief.'

I couldn't say, 'Actually, I've hidden the shorts because they're covered with blood,' or explain how that blood got to be there in the first place. So, I said nothing, and they thought the worst of me. I was labelled 'dishonest'. But what did they expect from black foster kids, after all? In their eyes, I was obviously behaving true to form. What made things worse was that the Stabards never acted as proper parents or supported us at school. They never sat down with us and helped us with our homework (to be honest, I can't remember doing homework) or talked to us about what had happened at school that day – they simply weren't interested. Instead, I spoke to my favourite goose, who roamed the garden and the house, if I needed to confide in someone. I told her all my worries and wildest dreams. However, I'm convinced Mr Stabard wrung her neck pretty quickly once he saw she was my favourite confidante. The Stabards had no real idea what went on with us once we left the house. Although we walked to school unsupervised, it never occurred to us to run away. Even though I desperately wanted to get away, the world 'out there' seemed just as hostile and unwelcoming as the world 'in there' at home.

When there were school trips, we didn't go on them. I don't know whether that was because no one invited us or whether the Stabards refused to fork out the money for us to go. I remember the rest of my class going to the zoo, and we were left out. There was another big trip to an ice rink I really wanted to go to, but again, we were left behind. I was probably six by then, going on seven. The Stabards didn't attend parents' evenings. Mrs Stabard usually made an excuse, and I had to take a note for the teacher. I think we simply were not important enough. The irony was that although the school didn't like me because of my skin colour, I liked school. Not the environment, particularly, or the other children, but I loved the lessons, and I loved learning.

My favourite thing was reading. At home, I managed to sneak the odd Daily Mirror newspaper, which Mr

Stabard read daily and then dumped in the waste bin. I'd fish it out of the bin and smuggle it into the shed to read by the streetlight at night to pass the time. I still remember the thrill of first beginning to make out letters and then some words; it felt so exciting to be able to read. Neither of them had ever sat down with us, read a book, or even pointed out letters. So, reading at school was a fantastic experience. I adored the books, and I loved beginning to learn some French. I also liked maths and found I had quite a facility for it. But being able to read especially fascinated me. I wanted to know what signs meant at school or in church or on advertising hoardings on the way to school and wanted to be able to understand all the things around me. Now I was at school, there were things to read everywhere, and I started to pick it up fast. I continued to fish out the old Daily Mirror at home and practise and even began to make out whole stories, which was very satisfying. In time, I could piece together the outraged letters to the local paper's editor about the influx of black children lowering standards at the local primary school. Given it was such a tight, rural community, I wondered if Mr and Mrs Stabard were getting letters and phone calls from parents who objected to us going to school altogether. The local community felt that we were somehow invading and taking over the school and should be sent back to whatever planet we came from. People shouted things at us on the street while walking to church together. I'd hear, 'Go home, wog!' or 'Dirty black bastards!' and the Stabards wouldn't react. I also remember a parent coming to our front door complaining about us playing with their children at school, and Mrs Stabard just saying meekly:

'Oh, I'm very sorry, it won't happen again.'

She didn't stand up for us; she just seemed to agree that we shouldn't be mixing with the local white children – and I guess it suited her to keep us isolated. Even though we were at school during the day, our lives didn't improve at home. Mr Stabard continued to come into us at night, and his wife continued to make us do the chores – and if we didn't do them well enough, we'd have to start again from scratch.

Meanwhile, back at school, I discovered I was very good at running. I think all that time pent-up in the shed, not running around like other kids, meant I was utterly thrilled when I was finally allowed to stretch my legs. I was a good athlete and even went on to represent the school in athletic races. It was really the only thing I was allowed to do, and I excelled at it. The PE teachers pushed me, and I enjoyed winning all sorts of medals and trophies for the school. It was the only place I was allowed to succeed. I guess they thought it was okay for black kids to be sporty, as it was acceptable for us to be good at that in a racist society. However, I didn't get any praise from the Stabards, who never commented on my success. The one aspect of PE I didn't like was when the teacher told me to take the skipping ropes back to the PE cupboard, which meant I had to cross the playground, holding a huge bundle of ropes. Once, a gang of white kids and a PE teacher cornered me, stripped me down to my underwear and then tied me to the football goalposts. I was there for ages until a teacher came and untied me. When they asked who had done it, I didn't give the names away. I knew it would only make things worse if I told them. They told me to go and get dressed and never told anyone off.

From the start, I was very isolated at school. I didn't really make friends with the white kids, and everyone left us three black children (or two when Faith was away in the hospital) very much to ourselves. Later, there were more ethnic minority children at school – when the Stabards fostered more black and Asian children themselves, and some more families arrived in the area – but we all had a hard time. The school didn't integrate us well at all. The main thing was parental opposition to our being there. I remember when I did very well in a reading test and came top of the class; one of the parents made a big fuss and said I couldn't possibly read better than her daughter, who had always been top until then. I was embarrassed and upset as I'd really tried hard to improve my reading by myself. This parent made such a big hoo-ha with the headmaster that I was eventually marked down to keep the peace. That really hurt, although I kept it to myself, as always. There wasn't even the goose to go home and talk to anymore, so I had to bottle things up.

Of course, I did try to make friends. Sometimes I made myself into a playground donkey, giving other kids piggyback rides. I wanted to please them, to buy their friendship. I was quite a bit bigger than other children my age, and I tried to make them laugh and give them a good time. It would work to some extent, in that they would play with me at playtimes, but only if I remained their donkey. I made myself useful in a clownish way. I wanted them to like me, I needed to join in, and it was all I could think of doing. Other times I could be disruptive and not sit down or get on with anything. Teachers told me off, and I would want to sulk or misbehave to get my own back. I didn't take it too far, but the teachers weren't as scary as Mr Stabard, so I think I was trying them out.

Few of the other children wanted to talk to me or for others to see them talking to me. However, one girl, Tanya, did invite me to her house one day for a play. I was very excited about this, as it was the first time it had happened. I must have been about eight by then, but I had never been inside anyone else's house before, and I had no idea how other people lived. I must have thought everyone lived as we did. When I got to Tanya's house, we'd just taken our coats off – her mum was quite friendly, although I was painfully shy – and we were beginning to play when Mr Stabard arrived at the door. Within ten minutes, he pulled me out of her house. He literally grabbed me without explaining anything and dragged me home. It was very embarrassing. After that, Tanya avoided me and never invited me back again. Looking back, I guess he was terrified that either I would spill the beans or I would see how a 'normal' family lived, and it would make me rebel. Instead, he nipped my flowering friendship well and truly in the bud.

Christmas at primary school was fun as we had parties for the first time. The staff would give us sweets and presents, and Santa would come and visit, which was utterly wonderful. When we got our sweets and stuff, we'd gobble them all up on the way home; else, the Stabards would confiscate them the minute we got back. One trick we learned over the years was to hide anything we wanted to keep under one of the wonky floorboards in our bedroom. If we got a bit of cake or a book, we'd hide them there and then bring them out on Christmas Day – which would be our Christmas presents to ourselves. Even if the cake were stale, we'd eat it, as it was like precious buried treasure. A couple of times, however, Mr Stabard found things I had hidden – a book and some sweets – and he ripped the book up in front of me and threw away the sweets. One thing about Christmas at school was that I was never picked for any of the main parts in the nativity play, even though I liked acting things out and had plenty of practice, thanks to the endless imaginary games we played to keep ourselves sane in the shed. Even so, I was backstage, or I'd be a tree or the end of a donkey or something hidden well out of sight. The same was true of Faith, who was much more outgoing and mouthier than me and Hope, who was shy but could play-act and sing. Everyone at school pushed us to the back, and they never picked us for anything important.

However, even if we had been, neither of our foster parents would have come to see us perform, as they never appeared at a single school concert or play. We never had someone in the audience to look out for, smile, and wave at. It obviously hurt like hell to see other parents looking proud or cooing over their kids in the play while ours were absent as usual – but that's just the way it was. I loved doing woodwork in primary school, and one day, I brought back a little table I'd made in class. I'd spent all my time working on it, and although it was crude and simple, I was very proud of it and thought it was the 'bee's knees'. It was childish, but I was so pleased to be able to show Mr Stabard because I knew he liked doing woodwork himself. When he came over to the shed eventually at bedtime, I couldn't wait to show him and blurted out:

'Look, I made this.'

When he saw it, he had an odd look on his face but said nothing; he just turned around and disappeared. A few minutes later, he returned with a hammer and smashed it to pieces in front of me. I couldn't believe it, but I didn't cry – I knew better than to cry, as he would lay into me and call me weak. I saved my tears for much later, when I was finally alone in bed, and everyone was asleep. All this time at school, Mr Stabard was still playing his purification games with us at home. I never thought for a moment that I could tell anyone about it, and it felt like I was living in two completely different worlds at home and school.

During the visits from social services or the surgery check-ins, they never picked up on what Mr Stabard was doing to us at night. When I did urine tests, Mrs Stabard came to the toilet with me. She peered at my sample, probably checking it was clear of streaks and then took the bottle back to the doctor, making sure I didn't get a chance to say a word. Despite my many urinary infections, they went unnoticed. I might have had blood in my pants, but the doctor wouldn't have known as he didn't look, and I couldn't have told him. Anyway, I don't think doctors thought about those things back then, and the Stabards had convinced me that if I said anything, they would have thought I was making all those horrible things up. And always, the Stabards would be with us, watching us carefully.

It seemed like things might be getting better when the Stabards took us to join the Brownies (what a fitting name for us!) when I was about seven. Most of the girls in my class were in the Brownies, and for some reason, Mrs Stabard agreed to take us to a meeting. The three of us were standing in a queue amid the white children. The Brown Owl was sitting there with a register, and she let in the three white girls before us in the line. But when she got to us, she looked at Mrs Stabard, then at us, very po-faced and looked down at her register and tutted.

Then she simply said she was sorry, but there was no more room for new kids. Mrs Stabard just accepted it at face value, and we walked away, crushed, although as I looked back, I saw the white girls behind us in the queue being let in, no question. I never said a word to the other two, but we knew deep down, without saying anything, that unfairness was the score. The most painful aspect of it was Mrs Stabard not standing up for us – she wouldn't have thrown water over us if we'd been on fire.

8

OUR LIFE SUPPORT

'Mrs Stabard is concerned about Jennie's fits of temper and wants help in controlling these – but otherwise, Jennie seems to cope fairly well with the foster home...'

(Social worker's report)

One night Mr Stabard was particularly brutal with me. He was in a very bad mood and quite drunk when he came to our room late that night. He shouted at us all to get up – Mrs Stabard must have heard it – and he put the light bulb in, swaying on his feet. Faith wasn't well then, and I pleaded with him to leave her alone, but he started on his 'eeny, meeny, miny, moe' thing and then chose her.

I found my voice somehow and said, 'No, leave her alone.'

He turned on me, furious. You never, ever answered him back: that was the rule. He grabbed me, threw me down on the bottom bunk bed, and barked at the other two to watch – he nearly always said this. I was fuming with a mixture of fear and rage, and I glared at him. I seldom spoke – I knew what I had said meant I had already gone too far. He kept cursing me, saying I was evil and needed to teach me a lesson, as he prepared to throw himself on top of me for the usual degradation. All the while, I was glaring at him, trying to make him feel the fury I felt inside, channelling it through my eyes. They were my only weapons in this sordid war.

Suddenly, he fumbled in his trouser pocket and out came a roll of something. I only had a moment to try and work out what it was before I heard a ripping sound, and suddenly, he was pulling Sellotape across my eyes. I put my hands up instinctively to pull it off, but he slapped them away and then wound the tape around my head very roughly a couple of times. The pressure on my face felt unbearable. Satisfied, I wouldn't glare at him anymore; he pushed himself into me very brutally, and I just switched off and lay there, totally inert and numb, eyes stuck closed, Sellotape cutting into my face, counting the minutes in my head until it was over. It seemed even more revolting now I couldn't see a thing or stare my protest at him. Then he pulled out roughly – job done – and I could hear him stumbling around the room, fumbling with the light bulb, and it all went dark again. I lay there for some time until my sisters crept over and helped me get the tape off my head, taking with it clumps of my hair and pulling out loads of eyelashes. After this ordeal, we didn't say anything to each other, but I felt desperate that night. What had happened felt like a step further into something horribly dark and violent. I sometimes wondered if Mr Stabard would suddenly produce a knife and kill me one day. I think he was capable of it because when he was drunk and full of hatred towards me, I felt I was just an object to him, just a piece of meat for him to skewer on the spit.

In the silence of the early hours, I made my way over to the window. There were old grey nets and some dark material curtains hanging there. I pulled them to one side and looked up through the smudgy glass at the wonder of the stars. It was something I had done several times late at night. I just loved looking up at the space in the sky, looking at the inky black and the twinkling lights and imagining the vast space out there. It was magical to me, so fabulous that it made me relax. I felt so utterly trapped in our room, in the shed, in the house and at school, but the sky offered something fantastic, far beyond things made by the humans who always seemed to hurt me. I imagined flying up to a star and sitting on it, looking down at all the little people going about their daily business and feeling they were not that important anymore. I'd love to be able to fly like a bird, or like a fairy, up to the heavens. To be free, to have wings, to fly. While I looked out in my reverie, the other two had crept to my side and were looking out too. I have no idea why I did what I did next, but it would change our lives forever. I must have been only around six and a half or seven, but I opened the window. We could smell the sweet night air rush into our stifling, soulless room, and it felt good. Beneath our window was a small grey flat roof, the porch over the front door. I looked down at it for a few minutes, and for the first time, I realised that on either side of the porch was a trellis with shrubs.

Without further ado, I got up onto the window ledge and popped my legs over the sill and onto the cold, gritty flat roof. I had to drop down a couple of feet, but suddenly I was standing on the roof in my bare feet and nightie. I looked back, and the other two were hanging out of the window with huge eyes, looking terrified. I don't know what made me do it, but an urge to escape filled me. The Sellotape over the eyes was like the last degrading straw, and now I needed to break free. I turned and started climbing down the trellis on the right side of the porch. I stopped, looked up at the other two, and beckoned them to follow. Without a word, Hope hopped over the windowsill, crept to the edge of the porch roof and anxiously watched me go down. I hit the floor and grinned – it was fun climbing down. I beckoned to her furiously, and she started to follow. However, much weaker than us, Faith was still half hanging out the window, looking scared. I wildly gestured for her to follow, but she shook her head.

'Come on!' I hissed and beckoned again.

Hope was now nearly at the bottom of the trellis by then. Suddenly Faith decided, and she was out the window, on the roof and feeling her way carefully down the trellis.

She was clearly scared she would fall but probably more scared of being left behind, so she gathered all her courage and joined in. What a trooper! When all three of us were at the bottom, we stood for a moment in the front garden, wondering what to do next. All we had on was our nighties, and with bare feet, it was chilly. I was hurting a lot between my legs, and I must have been bleeding, but I didn't care. The fresh air was like nectar, and the night breeze felt fantastic, so, without a word, we turned right, crept past the house and then padded through the alleyway, past the shed and up to the tall back fence. The sky was clear shades of indigo with clouds scudding by, and we could still see the stars sparkling like diamonds above. We never spoke to each other or discussed what we were doing, but I started climbing the back fence, and the other two quickly followed. Suddenly I dropped down – what seemed like a very long way – onto a gravelly path that was actually a narrow back lane running behind the house. The other two dropped down beside me.

If Mr Stabard had woken up and put on a light in his bedroom or shone a torch out onto the back fence, he would have seen three ghostly little bare-footed figures making a bid for freedom. He would have discovered our antics and ruin our one chance of escape. However, luckily, he didn't wake up. No doubt he was snoring away, deep in his drunken sleep, worn out from hurting me. Faith was shaking with fear, but I could see her eyes were shining with excitement too. Free, for once, we padded happily down the lane in the dark, which led out into some fields. We could hear animals snuffling in the darkness, but we weren't frightened. The wind was rustling in the trees overhead, and we could hear an owl hooting nearby. But still, we weren't scared. It felt fantastic to be outside, free, alone and untethered; just going where we wanted to go. We came to cornfields, and we started walking along them, then through them, past bungalows and the backs of houses, where I imagined families were fast asleep, with no idea that we were trotting past outside. I could feel my lungs expanding – for once, I could breathe good fresh night air. I could hear cicadas making their night noises and felt light-hearted. We picked up stalks of corn each and chewed them, which was fun. We walked along, not talking but chewing on our corn, feeling the hard, dried mud between our toes and the wind on our faces.

Next, we came to a narrow path leading upwards through some woods. We all looked at each other – not in fear, but in a sort of question – but I was determined to go on. I wanted to know where the path led, so I started walking, pushing aside the brambles. The woods got denser and denser, and the tree branches met in an arch over our heads. It was pitch black in places, the darkest we had ever experienced, even in the shed or airing cupboard. We clutched each other's bramble-scratched hands and walked in a little crocodile, scrambling our way up an incline on a narrow, woody path. The smells and sounds were amazing; we could hear all sorts of rustlings, buzzing, and even the odd bird. We didn't know much about nature, but we felt like we were right in the middle of it, and it felt like it was protecting us somehow. Eventually, we came to the top of a hill. We had a view of the valley below, of yellow streetlights and dotted house lights. The stars were burning bright overhead, and we could see clumps of trees on the top of the hill and then sweeping, rolling curves, with bushes and hedges lining the surrounding fields. It was utterly glorious, and I started running downhill as fast as possible. From top to bottom, in the open space, I could feel the soft dewy grass between my toes, and I could smell those wonderful, damp, new-mown smells as they wafted up to me as I ran. At the bottom, we found a dip covered with fallen leaves. We worked out it was some kind of bunker or hideaway that ivy and branches had grown over. We chased each other around the base of the huge trees, giggling quietly. We played catch like we'd seen the kids do at school. We mimicked people we knew – the Stabards, their grandchildren (particularly the ones who swore at us), nasty parents we'd met, the teachers, church people – and fell about laughing until our sides ached.

Up until this moment, we had never been free. We'd never had the experience of running around with the wind in our hair, free to choose what we did next. We'd never climbed trees or explored our neighbourhood. We'd never been allowed to dig the garden or ride bikes. This was our very first taste of being out in nature and enjoying its beauty entirely for ourselves. To my amazement, I wasn't scared of the dark here like I would have been at home. It didn't feel menacing; it didn't feel like it was out to get me and do me harm. It wasn't stifling or demeaning. I felt I could be myself and that I belonged to, finally, the world. We looked up at the sky between the gaps in the branches, spotted stars and gave them names between the spaces in the bushes. We could see the moon as it rose, a honey-coloured wonder. We could make out the face of the man on the moon, who looked very kind and calm. The moon seemed to follow us as we explored the undergrowth, putting our toes into all sorts of squishy wet things. It didn't matter; we just laughed and giggled, ran and breathed deeply, jumped, and whooped for joy. We looked to see if the moon was peeking out over the branches at us like a wise old thing. We hid behind ivy-clad trees and played hide-and-seek with each other. We made up songs and dances and 'looked' around. It was wonderful. We jumped off rocks and rolled around in the dirt. We had fun.

Eventually, when the light began to change, we realised that dawn was breaking. Without saying a word, we turned together and started walking home. I could remember how we got there, although it was about half an hour's walk. We walked back in total silence. We were exhausted but very happy. The birdies were tweeting wildly around us, and I had no idea how much they sang in the early hours until that moment as the day came up. Once we got to the house, it was quite light, and we managed to get up the trellis again fairly easily (although we struggled a bit) and then fell through the window back into our room. After pulling it shut, we collapsed into bed. It was a school day, and we had to get up only a couple of hours later, but oddly I felt energised. I was very tired, but I felt something very special had happened to us. The three of us made our way down to make breakfast and then on to school with lighter hearts. That place, Wildflower Woods, was our great, secret escape. From then on, we went to the woods as often as possible. We always went after he had hurt us at night, usually once or twice a week. It was our special place. We called it 'Wildflower Woods' because there were loads of wonderful wildflowers that we didn't know the names of. We had no idea the names of trees, animals, or plants, so we made them up.

Over the next few years, our trips to Wildflower saved our sanity. It became our real home, where we celebrated our lives and performed wonderful rituals. For instance, on birthdays, we never had presents from the Stabards. It used to upset us deeply. Now we had a place to celebrate, and we would use leaves, twigs and stones to create cakes and presents for each other. We'd sing 'Happy Birthday' and have all sorts of birthday ceremonies for each other. As we got older, we got clever at stealing some food to bring with us. I remember we sometimes filled a sock with the dog's Winlot biscuits, and we'd eat them for a treat. They weren't that bad – very crunchy – and at least we weren't starving like we were most of the time at home.

If we were lucky, we would get some cheese or bread and have a real party. If we had anything left, we'd hide it under a stone, wrapped in paper or foil. We even managed to take a tablecloth, a red and white checked one, which we'd spread on the floor for our picnics and parties. It was brilliant. We would have imaginary toys, or a baby, which we'd feed. At Christmas, we'd nick some Christmas cake and have a Christmas party. Sometimes we'd argue about whose turn it was to have a birthday party. One of us would say, 'Oh, she had hers last time,' and then we'd giggle because it didn't matter who had it last time, as we all enjoyed it. We acted out all those things we'd never ever had at home. And also, all those things that we'd seen the grandchildren have, which we knew we weren't allowed. We would sometimes have a tea party, where we had to talk in very posh voices (like those men who hurt us) to each other and stick our little fingers out while we pretended to drink tea. We'd ask to pass the sauce or the potatoes, and we'd giggle at being so refined. Sometimes we'd even have real potatoes or a piece of pie we'd squirrelled away. It was a real picnic then, and we revelled in it.

Sometimes we'd play swapping roles and pretend we were the Stabards, and they were the slaves, and we were the bosses – we particularly liked that game, as we got to tell them what to do all the time. I would point at my feet, playing Mrs Stabard and command 'lick my boots', and she'd have to do it. We'd point to everything, issue commands to each other and fall about laughing endlessly as it seemed absurd. We never played out the 'eeny meeny' game, as we didn't ever mention that to each other. We avoided that completely; it felt too dangerous to go near, too painful and humiliating. Instead, we danced, sang and frolicked to our hearts' content. Sometimes we'd lie on our backs, hands under our heads and gaze at the stars and moon, watching the clouds wander past and call out what shapes we thought they were: animals, cakes, anything that caught our fancy. It was our earthly paradise out there in the woods and utterly fantastic.

We went whatever the weather; in the wind, rain, snow, sun and storms. We didn't care. One time I burnt my foot on snow when it was freezing cold. I guess it was some sort of frostbite. Luckily Mrs Stabard didn't notice; she never paid much attention to me. It was really painful and still hurts to this day, but I don't mind. It was worth every inch of pain to have the freedom that going out to the woods gave us. It was our reward for being hurt – the release from the pain and constant humiliation, mistreatment and slavery. The only problem was we would be very tired in the daytime. As we went more and more, we got increasingly tired, and I'm sure it affected my ability to concentrate at school.

I was the pack's leader when going up to Wildflower. Over time, I helped develop other ideas, such as taking a black bin bag with us and a watering can full of water. We would climb carefully to the top of the hill, wet the underside of a bin bag and slide down on one of the long chalk markings. It was an amazing instant slide. Sometimes we would burn the back of our nighties or legs, but it didn't matter. We did the washing and ironing so we could hide any holes and scrub off any marks ourselves. We even went to the woods while other foster children lived in the box room with us. We would simply wait until Mr Stabard had played his 'game' and the other children were asleep. We'd silently signal to each other before setting off to the woods. I don't know if any of the other children found out we'd gone, but if they did, they never said anything.

When we went to Wildflower, we were desperate. When we trotted back, exhausted and spent, we always felt better. We still knew that we were evil and had to be purified further, but somehow the long journey to purification seemed more bearable if we could escape at night and be free to be children, far away from the constant, critical gaze of the Stabards. We were different people up there; we were like real children, not vigilant, silent slaves like at home. We were sometimes vicious to each other at the Stabards, hitting each other out of sheer frustration or getting jealous of each other over something trivial. But up in the woods, we felt united again. I could be generous, loving and kind. We would put our arms around each other and dance a happy, carefree dance, the likes of which we could never, ever do in the prison that was 97 Forestland Way.

9

THAT PILL WAS TO BE
MY COMFORT

...'We believe these girls are being abused by foster parents; the problem we have if we looked into this is who would care for these misfits.'

(Social workers report 1976)

One night, without a word, I went downstairs, into the kitchen and inside the walk-in larder where I knew the Stabards kept our pills. There were painkillers there, too, and I found a bottle and started taking tablets. I was only nine years old, standing barefoot in the dark, desperately trying to swallow down tablet after tablet with the help of a mug of water. Although they were hard to get down, I swallowed the bitter pills until the bottle was half empty – I was like a little robot. Then, to my horror, Mr Stabard was suddenly there behind me, breathing heavily, smelling of drink and looking furious. I thought he would beat the living daylights out of me. He started swearing at me, saying I was an ungrateful bitch and that I was evil and deserved to die. He grabbed the bottle of pills from me, poured some into his huge hand and started stuffing the pills down my throat. I gagged. He kept pushing them into my mouth, one after the other, until I retched. He had a hold of me by the back of the neck and was towering over me, forcing me to swallow pill after pill until I could hardly breathe. His hand hurt my neck, and I could see him staring at me with hate-filled eyes and snarling as he crammed more tablets into me with his fat fingers.

The next thing I knew, I was coming around in a hospital. I was in a bed which had clean, crisp white sheets. I thought I'd died and gone to heaven at first, especially when I saw the walls were light and bright. The staff seemed to float by on clouds and were very kind to me, just like I imagined angels would be. A nurse came and stood by me, took my right wrist and looked at her watch. She bent over me and stroked my head, and said I had had my stomach pumped. I didn't understand what that meant at all. She asked me how I felt, and I didn't know what to say. My throat felt very sore, so I just nodded. I was amazed by the day or two I spent in the hospital. The nurses came and plumped my pillows, fed me hot food and helped me wash. They talked to me and smiled and even stroked my hair. I didn't have to go out in the cold;

I could stay nice and warm, and I slept a lot in my warm, clean, comfy bed. The nurses smoothed the sheets and tidied things up.

People spoke kindly to me, and no one was angry. I thought I'd get into big trouble for taking pills, but I didn't. I didn't tell anyone what Mr Stabard had done with the tablets; I didn't dare. At the end of the first day in the hospital, the nurse said my parents were outside. For a moment, I didn't know who they meant. Then she said, 'your foster parents,' and I understood.

She leant towards me and said, 'They were really devastated they might lose you.'

I felt really confused. Surely, she didn't mean the Stabards, who were only too keen to get rid of me – especially Mr Stabard, who had just tried to kill me with the tablets? However, the door opened, and they came in together. I saw them walk down the ward towards me, looking very concerned. They both came to one side of my bed, and in front of the nurse, Mrs Stabard took my hand and looked softly at me. Usually, she was an ice-cold lady, but now she seemed to care for me. Then her husband leant forward and kissed me on the forehead.

I didn't know what to make of it. What on earth was going on? The nurse watched all this and smiled, and the Stabards stood by my bedside, making me feel that I was a little princess and that they genuinely cared about me. Despite everything, I couldn't help thinking: 'Maybe they've changed? Maybe they see how miserable I've been, and now they'll really love me?' I felt that things might change for the better. I decided they had finally seen the light, and I actually slept peacefully that night for the first time in years.

The next day they took me home. Everything reverted to how it always was the moment we got in through the front door. We were back to the old routine: out to the shed, then up to the box room after cooking supper and doing the cleaning. Nothing had changed. Faith and Hope were glad to see me and hugged me close to them. Faith looked weaker than ever and was soon back in the hospital. That night, however, Mr Stabard came to our room, and he was more vicious with me than I could ever remember him being before. He even slapped me around before 'purifying' me, so I ended up with bruises and cuts. Absolutely nothing had changed - not a single thing.

When I was nine going on ten, the Stabards had quite a few other foster children to stay. Some were very short-term – just a few weeks or so. They expected that we three girls would look after them at night and during the day at the weekends. The babies would be in a cot in our room, and we'd have to get them up, feed them, change their nappies and give them their bottles. It was hard not to resent them crowding into the small space with us. We were short of sleep as it was. The room next door still stood empty most of the time, with three nice divans and clean bedding, but it was out of bounds to the likes of us. At one time, there were ten of us in that room, and I had to sleep on the bare floor to let the little ones have the bunks. There were three children in each bunk, sometimes four – it was ridiculous. They would also be in the shed with us, which was very overcrowded. When it was hot, it was unbearable. I don't know how the Stabards got away with it.

As well as the babies, our foster parents took on a couple of Asian children, Raj and Prathi, who lived with us for three and a half years. Mr Stabard took a particular liking to the young boy, and he would hurt him at night – usually in the early hours – and get him to do things to him in front of us. Raj absolutely hated it and would choke and cry, but Mr Stabard would beat him, calling him an 'evil ungrateful brat.' It was disgusting. I would feel completely sick and powerless to help Raj, who was only about four or five at the time. I would feel so revolted afterwards I wouldn't be able to sleep. Instead, Hope, Faith and I would climb out the window to Wildflower Woods and try to run, sing and dance it out of our systems in the fresh early morning air.

During this time, things were not going too well at school. The horrors of home meant that I was getting to school exhausted and found it hard to concentrate. To make matters worse, the Stabards had zero expectations of me. As I was nearing eleven, the school decided that I was not fit to go to the local comprehensive along with the other children, but that I should go to a special school for the 'educationally subnormal' – the nice term they used to use for kids with learning difficulties. Amazingly the same decision was made for Faith, who had missed a lot of school through her sickness and also for bright, bubbly Hope. All three of us black foster children ended up labelled ESN.

Meanwhile, the white kids – even the very naughty ones who got up to no good and never did their homework – went to the local comprehensive. I had no idea what 'ESN' was at the time, but I knew it sounded bad. However, just before I was to leave and start this new 'special' education, something else happened that would take my mind off school altogether.

This was the next step in the tangled web of abuse and ritual cleansing. Mr Stabard gave me to other men who smelled of money and gold - men who thought they were bigger than God. Men who had other men running after them but nothing like we had to do for the Stabards. They would hurt me, drug me with a drink like the one foster father drank and then force me to do things I didn't want to, raping me sometimes in front of other men in big posh homes or outside at army barracks, some well-known, at what I would see as evil torture parties. Not all the men had English voices; some were American, and then the tea towel men (one, in particular, was at most of these bigger parties). Sometimes I was dressed in nice clothes, makeup, and styled hair - I was tidied up neatly like the hedges and lawns in our street.

I would be allowed in posh places with heavy and polished floors. The walls in some of these places were also wooden, with hard chairs covered with rich material; I even touched them sometimes to see how they felt; it was nice. Some of the fabric was a little rough, but I had never seen such grand items as this solid furniture in a home before. The places had a smell of air to them. Sparseness was vast in some of these houses. The rooms were big and decorated with bland colours and very similar in each room, unlike the Stabards, whose many colours in one room had you feeling like you were in the middle of one of those trifles they made for their wanted children's parties.

They were well-known places of leaders and their wicked friends. I was allowed in these places not because I was one of their posh friends but to continue the mixed cold, violent abuse. At times there were other children, not just me, others who I saw at times again, and some I would never see again. Local men, who were social workers, ferried me to different places, driven from the town I live in and accompanied by my foster father at times too. Sometimes the drive seemed miles and miles away; other times, it wasn't far.

One guy who abused some of the boys was silent but deadly; one swipe and he could knock a child out. He was like the king and had the first pick of us. He then took us to the hell place, dark yet light, with fire and water deep under the grassy hillside in a farming town. I thought the fire was a barbecue because I'd seen the Stabards having barbecues, but the smell was stomach-churning. I saw the flames roaring from stakes, some held by people in white, red or purple cloaks and what I presumed was the most powerful one in black with a gold roped hood. I recognised their voices from other places I'd been, even though the hoods were so big you never saw their faces. You knew who they were. Like at the Stabards, there was chanting, calling out the devil, and torturing children and babies. The hell as you witnessed pain of children being cut and burned alive became the norm at these venues, especially the tunnel games they played. This involved marking some of us with sharp objects, and for some time, you belonged to two men, then you had more men that had the rights to our bodies.

10

ANOTHER SECRET

'...Mrs Stabard cares for this difficult child very well...She was sectioned into St John's hospital care. Her behaviour is out of control, and her anger is towards Mrs Stabard for no apparent reason, especially after all the Stabards have done for these difficult-to-place children.'

(Social worker report 1980)

I had just started at my new ESN school – which I didn't like very much. A special minibus picked us up from around the corner that the local kids used to jeer and spit at. Once we arrived, the teacher usually put me in a classroom with children with all sorts of disabilities and problems to build towers of bricks. That's all we seemed to do, day after day: build bricks, sort bricks, play with bricks and stack bricks. They liked bricks there a lot.

Meanwhile, I longed for a book to read, and the boredom drove me mad. I was now just eleven and wondering if schooling would ever get any better. The only good thing was Faith was out of the hospital and at the same school as me. There were quite a few other black and Asian children at the school, too, so we didn't feel as alien as we had at our primary school.

I had started to bleed every month between my legs, and I didn't really know what it meant and hadn't taken much notice when I missed a month. I was too busy settling into my new school and getting used to the new teachers and endless brick building. If anything, I'd been relieved that the blood hadn't come as I found it very unpleasant to deal with each month. It was nice to have a break. Then one morning, after I had made breakfast with my sisters and cleared away the dishes, Mrs Stabard pointed for me to go upstairs to my room. The other two went to school as normal, and I headed to the box room, wondering what was happening. Mrs Stabard walked in, went to the wardrobe and pointed to my Sunday clothes. She told me to put them on and left the room again. I did as she said, and when I came downstairs, she was waiting for me with a small navy holdall. She handed me the holdall, but I didn't look in it – I knew better than to do something like that without being told.

We sat in the kitchen, and she didn't say anything to me. It was very unusual for us to sit together like this, and I couldn't understand what was going on. Suddenly the doorbell went, and Mrs Stabard stood up and pointed to me to get up and go down the hall. At this point, Mr Stabard arrived at the front door from upstairs, and my heart sank; I'd thought he'd gone to work already. I hated being in the same room as him, and I didn't fancy going anywhere with him, that was for sure. However, I had no choice in the matter, and I went out the door, sandwiched between my foster parents. Where were we going? What on earth was going on? Of course, they didn't tell me; they never did.

The Stabards had a car, but we weren't allowed in it. Outside there was a taxi waiting. We got in the cab, and I sat beside Mrs Stabard in the back in total silence while Mr Stabard got in the front seat and spoke to the driver. Mrs Stabard didn't open her lips for the whole half hour's journey. Once Mr Stabard had given directions to the driver, he fell silent too.

I just looked out the window and wondered at this new, fascinating experience. It felt very luxurious to glide along in the back of a big, silver car. Maybe they were going to take me for a treat? I didn't understand why I was getting special treatment. After all these years of allowing him to hurt me, was I purified? I now knew what it was like to sit in a big car like this, and I imagined I was a royal princess going to the palace for tea instead of for other reasons.

My daydream broke when we finally arrived at a big old house. It wasn't a fairy tale palace, however. It was one of those gothic Victorian houses, more like something out of a horror film than a daydream. Mr Stabard paid the taxi driver while his wife pulled me to the front door. I didn't like the look of the place at all. We stood on the step, and the big black door opened. Standing before us was a plump middle-aged woman, quite official looking, in a green suit, with her dark brown hair in a bun. She didn't smile.

Instead, she shook Mr Stabard's hand and asked, 'is this her?' nodding at me curtly.

'Yes', he replied sharply, not looking at me.

I thought, by now, that they were sending me away because I was evil. The Stabards had often threatened it when we misbehaved. This was clearly a new stepmother or a care home for naughty children; my new carer looked very cruel and nasty. Mr Stabard had frightened me many times by saying about putting me away somewhere – like a dungeon or a prison – where I'd have to stay until I rotted because I was so bad. Maybe it was a kind of prison, and I would be locked up? As I was thinking this, he turned to me and said, in front of the woman:

'We're here because you've been naughty. You know you've been evil, don't you? Well, there will be punishment for what you've done.'

I was now utterly terrified. I was hardly breathing or able to stand. The Stabards half-pulled me in through the front door, and we were in a large, cold hallway. It was clean but had an echo and a black and white tiled floor and felt very sterile, like a clinic. There was a medical smell to the place, like disinfectant. I was ushered into a side room and told to get undressed. I didn't know what on earth was going on. Maybe they were going to kill me like the babies? Mrs Stabard came in with me as I undressed, so I looked to her for reassurance. I pleaded with her with my eyes, feeling desperate and shaky, but she just turned away. She pointed to my holdall, and to my surprise, there was a new nightie inside, not my old shredded one. I put the nightie on and then a white towelling gown I found draped on a chair in the room. My knees were shaking, and I was panting with fear.

The woman came back in and looked at me sternly. She suddenly moved forwards and pulled open my dressing gown. I shrank back, but Mrs Stabard pushed me forward. Then the woman pulled up my nightie and saw that I still had my knickers on underneath.

'You must take those off, "she said in a very strict voice.

I stood transfixed. I couldn't move, barely breathing, so she leaned forward and yanked my pants down with both hands. I stepped out of them, dazed. The woman then told me to follow her, and very reluctantly, I went with her into another room while Mrs Stabard stayed behind in the changing room. The room had a long bench covered in a white paper towel and a small table with silver equipment next to it. I wondered if she was some kind of dentist, as I'd seen similar things in the dentist's room. There was a big bright light over the bed. The woman put on a white coat and told me to lie down. She said nothing to me, but leant over, picked up my wrist and looked at her watch, just like the nurse had done in the hospital. I lay there, blinking in the blinding light. I couldn't understand what was happening at all. Then, without a word, the woman turned around and fiddled with something. I heard a loud hissing sound, and then she turned back with a big black rubbery thing in her hand connected to a long metal tube going to a big bottle. She clamped the rubber thing hard over my face. It filled my nose and mouth with this hissy, terrible-smelling gas, and I thought I would choke. I tried to struggle, but my legs and arms felt like they were made of lead. I didn't want to breathe in, but I had to, and suddenly my mind whooshed off uncontrollably down a long dark tunnel.

The next thing I knew was waking up in severe pain. My tummy felt like someone had scooped out the insides with a vegetable peeler. I was back home, inside the airing cupboard, in a heap in the dark. When I felt myself 'down there,' I realised I had a sanitary towel on, although I hadn't been bleeding before I went to see the horrible woman in the big house. I felt completely bewildered. As I sat there, crouched over in pain, I had flashbacks of coming out of the big house, held up between Mr and Mrs Stabard, half-awake, half-asleep. As far as I remember, they'd half-dragged, half-pulled me to a car and bundled me into the back. There was now lots and lots of blood, and it started to seep out and down my legs and into a pool on the floor. I could feel it trickling down the inside of my thighs. I felt giddy and sick and worried that I might die. I was in absolute agony. I'd never felt pain like it: huge, engulfing cramps. Even when Mr Stabard was vicious with me and hurt me a lot, it was never like this. I cried and cried, just wanting to get out but knowing I couldn't. I was also starving and very thirsty. I was used to going without food, but this hunger was unbearable. I was utterly miserable and deeply in pain, and I didn't know how to get through it. When they finally opened the door two days later, there were no explanations. Mrs Stabard pointed to the mess on the floor, and I had to scrub and mop as usual before I could clean myself up. I was absolutely ravenous, but I still had to wait until after their meal before I had anything to eat or drink. All the time, I felt utterly mixed up.

Back in our room, I insisted on going to Wildflower that very night. I needed to get away – to get out and feel the fresh air on my face – even though I was weak and still bleeding. Out in the freedom of the woods, Faith, Hope and I played games and danced and sang, and I didn't ever tell them what had happened. We never really went into the gory details of what the Stabards did to us. However, we spoke more to each other outside than ever in the house, where we were mostly silent. I just needed to see the stars and moon and be reassured that they were still there. They were my friends, like the wood, with all its wild night sounds, movements, and smells. I was soothed by feeling the wind on my face and seeing the clouds flitting by. I had no idea what had just happened to me. All I knew was that it was the worst experience of my life so far, and it felt like the blue touch paper had been lit and was about to go off. I bled heavily for days afterwards.

At about this time, a new TV show called Roots started. It was about how the slaves had come to America, and it was on during the week, in the evening. Strangely, the Stabards sat us three children in the lounge and watched the show with us. We had never been allowed to watch TV in the past, and we'd never done anything recreational with the Stabards before. If they watched TV in the evening, we were either in the shed or the box room, so it took me aback that we were watching the show together. Were they now including us in their family life at last? Maybe they were changing their ways? I soon understood why they wanted us to watch the show. It told the story of how the Africans were taken forcibly from their homeland and transported as slaves to America. The Stabards were trying to tell us something: we were slaves; this was our heritage. One of their daughters – Carla, who particularly hated us – sometimes came and watched the show with us. Although it seemed like a treat at first, I found watching the programme very painful. It was hard to see others treating black people brutally as slaves; I hated seeing them stolen, chained, whipped and horribly mistreated.

It wasn't just the programme that was disturbing. After the show finished, the Stabards would make us get on all fours and go around the armchairs in a circle, just like in the chain gang. They thought it was very funny. They would laugh and tell us to speed up, so we would, and then we'd fall over each other, just like the slaves on the telly, and then they'd laugh even harder. Mr Stabard would take off his belt and start whipping us with it, laughing his dry, little cackle, then Carla would kick us as we passed, and they would all laugh like hyenas. Mrs Stabard would sit and watch, not saying a word. I don't know what she thought, but she didn't stop them from doing it. I got kicked in the stomach and whacked on the legs and arms. We three went round and round on our hands and knees until they had had enough fun getting us to re-enact scenes from the show. They thought it was hysterical, nudging each other and saying:

'Look at 'em go!'

The Stabards took the real meaning of the programme and twisted it around completely so they could use it against us. Instead of seeing it as a way of telling the terrible story of the enslavement of black people from Africa, they saw it as a prompt to treat us like slaves – worse than animals. I felt ashamed watching the show but even more ashamed of being kicked and punched without being able to fight back. We were bruised everywhere under our clothes. By this time, I was furious: beyond anger, beyond rage. Everything was getting mixed up, and I was reaching the point where it was all going to boil over, and I would no longer be able to hold my anger back. I was angrier than I could possibly express or than I could ever explain. My feelings were off the scale. I knew how they treated us was utterly appalling and inhuman, and I wasn't sure how much more I could take. The accumulation of nearly twelve years of being treated like slaves – being starved, beaten, shut in the shed, humiliated, deprived of food and love, 'purified' at night – was building up inside me into a massive ball of unstoppable rage. After years of suffering, I was poised on the brink of rebellion – whatever the consequences.

11

CRAZY

'Jennie is helpful, but still a very difficult teenager to live with...The Stabards want to foster more children as Jennie is upset when they leave.'

(Social worker's report)

I was eleven years old, and without warning, I found myself wanting to trash everything and anything I could get my hands on. I was tired of being a silent, obedient slave. The Stabards had hauled me along to that strange medical woman in the big house, gassed me and then locked me up in the airing cupboard for days as punishment. I didn't understand what I'd been through, but I knew it was abuse too far. When I was older, I realised that I must have been pregnant with Mr Stabard's baby – or at least Mrs Stabard must have been scared that my body would reveal his sordid secrets since I'd missed my monthly bleed. I'd only just found out from an older girl at the ESN school that my monthly bleeding was a 'period', which meant I could have babies. It was evident that Mrs Stabard knew exactly when I was bleeding and kept track of it. If I missed a period, she knew full well what it meant. She laid us out ready for her husband, after all, so she knew exactly what was at stake; I also believe she knew he had sold me to the posh men. It was as if I had been sitting on a mountain of anger all my life, which was now growing into a huge volcano threatening to blow any second. I didn't feel I could hold on anymore. I felt out of control. I was angry all the time, and because of that, destructive, manipulative and rude. I didn't care.

For a start, I was in a school I hated. The Stabards had moved Hope to another school in the year below me, and I felt extremely isolated. There was no one there I connected with, no one to talk to, and I missed my sisters. Many of the kids around me at school were severely disabled – unable to talk or walk or do much – and I felt like we were all treated like lesser a person. The teachers acted like I was stupid – like I was a freak of nature who wasn't worth bothering with.

Mr Stabard was still coming in at night and was getting more violent. I think he sensed I was beginning to resist. After the forced pill-swallowing incident, which had scared me witless, I had begun to be more rebellious, especially when I realised their show of affection in the hospital was just that – a show. They were still play-acting Roots with us; now, not only the Stabard's kids but the grandchildren also joined in the abusive game. They all taunted us and called us 'wog' and 'nigger' and kicked us about – anything to ridicule us. It was beginning to rile me all the time. It was like a sport to them; they seemed to enjoy goading me to the point I lost my temper, just like I'd seen the slaves do on screen.

I'd seen one of the slave girls in Roots being 'hurt' by a slave master like Mr Stabard hurt me, and it was called 'rape'. I often remembered her crying and him beating her. And I began to see that Mr Stabard thought he had us for himself; that he owned us, like the imprisoned slaves on the plantations, and he could rape us whenever he wanted to. All these years, that's exactly what he had been doing – imprisoning and raping us – and he was getting away with it. I found it unbearable as I began to understand more about what had really been happening to us. How was he allowed to do that? Why didn't somebody do something about it? How could the Stabards call themselves good foster parents? And how could they be proper church members when they treated us worse than their household animals?

There were days when we didn't even bother going to school. School became meaningless for children like us. After a night with no sleep, we'd be exhausted. I would lie there all night in pitch black, waiting for the noise of him coming into our room. I'd keep myself awake, fearful he might arrive, without me knowing in advance. I was on watch, so I could cope with him when he lurched into the room stinking of drink. Of course, he didn't come every night, so I had many nights of broken sleep, listening out fearfully for the creak of a floorboard or the toilet flush. If I dropped off, I would snap awake terrified that he was there. It was like being alert for the Bogey Man who wanted to come and get me. It was very stressful all the time.

Then, when he did come in, the whole ghastly ritual would begin. Afterwards, we'd rush to the window in silence, climb out and traipse to Wildflower to recover. It was a necessary release, but it meant we'd have even less sleep. Sometimes, when he hurt one of us too much, we couldn't even go out because we couldn't walk or were too exhausted, which made it all even harder to bear. On days home from school, I would lie in bed all day, feeling numb and shut down. For us, the box room was like a prison. I almost preferred the shed to the box room because Mr Stabard was coming to hurt us so often upstairs at night now. Mrs Stabard would let us lie in bed if we were off 'sick', but she wouldn't look after us. Some days I would feel paralysed when I woke up, and I'd roll over and face the wall, not bothering to get up. There would be no food, books, treats, drinks, amusements, or extra blankets. And certainly, no hugs, cuddles or comfort. Of course, our foster mother wouldn't call the doctor, and we wouldn't have friends to visit. Instead, they would totally ignore us. If we were hungry, we'd have to tiptoe downstairs to steal food and often lived on Winalot and water. We'd stuff a sock full of it when we did the washing and then hide it under the wonky floorboard in our room for the next 'Winalot party' in the woods. However, it was often the only food we had on our days in bed. Mrs Stabard must have known full well that we were 'sick' because of her husband's horrendous night visits, but she did nothing about it. She was a very shut-off person, like a zombie a lot of the time, very emotionless unless her grandchildren were around. I couldn't understand why she was so nice to them and then so horrible to us. I began to feel the Stabards just kept us there in the poxy box room to meet his sexual needs and to do the housework for her. We really were their slaves.

I also knew they claimed all sorts of things for us as foster children, which we never benefited from. I saw Mrs Stabard filling in forms on the kitchen table for money from Social Services. I could see they claimed for trips away, holidays, household items, clothes, shoes, special equipment - you name it. When there were ten of us in the room at one time, they must have been getting an allowance for each child for food, heating, and clothing. That was a lot of money – running into thousands of pounds a year. Yet we all had a starvation diet, no real clothes or bedding, toys and certainly no treats. Where was all the money going? Who was getting the benefit of it? Mr Stabard worked full-time until he retired when I was about eleven, so what did they do with the money? They didn't live a luxurious lifestyle, and I never saw them go on holiday themselves. However, later Mrs Stabard would go and stay for weekends with her married children. They only ran one car (we never went in it) and lived in a council house. They never threw a party or had friends around for a meal. So what did they do with all the cash? And why didn't Social Services check up to see if it was being spent on us properly? Perhaps they were saving it for their pension, or he spent it on drink – he always had loads in the house.

As I got older and understood more, I began to feel even more trapped and outraged than I had before. These questions were emerging in my brain, and I had no one to ask or turn to. I was never alone with the Social Services visitors, the doctor or the dentist. Now that I'd left primary school, I didn't know Mr Harrow anymore, and my new teachers treated me like an idiot, so I couldn't talk to them. The people I knew at church I'd never spoken to and the ones who 'cast out the devil' with us weren't people I'd ever want to trust. I didn't know any grown-ups I could actually talk to, and I so desperately wanted to ask someone, 'Is this normal?' or 'Can they do this?' or even just, 'Is this right?'

It made me absolutely livid to think about the whole situation, and I was most furious with Mrs Stabard. She had been a nanny before she married and brought up children herself; how would she have liked it if someone had treated her daughters or son this way? The answer was that she didn't see us in the same category as her own children, just like the masters in Roots didn't see the slaves as people. We weren't human, so we didn't count. This thought also made me fly into a rage. All I ever wanted was one hug, one tender moment; for her to say, just once, that she cared about me. The tragedy was I would have done anything for her. I wanted her to love me, so I did everything she wanted in the hope of getting one loving smile or embrace. Yet every time I thought I'd earned her love, she would turn away and leave me to her husband's horrible clutches. That made me scream inside with such pain and rage that I thought I would melt down.

Even worse (and I loathed to admit this to myself), as much as I feared Mr Stabard and hated how he hurt me, I wanted him to love me too. I didn't want to feel all this pain and confusion. After all these years of doing these things to us, I thought he must love us somewhere deep down. I felt very attached to him – I'm ashamed and confused to say – even though he hurt me all the time. Sometimes he would be a bit gentler, such as at Christmas, which was confusing. But then he'd be brutal, and he'd hit us. He was sometimes even more violent to the other two girls, which I thought was almost a twisted sign that he loved me more. Surely, he must, after all this time? If either of them cried after he'd raped them, he'd smack them around even more ruthlessly, as he hated tears or any sign of weakness. I would be pleading with him to stop, wanting him to turn around, say sorry, and give us all hugs and tenderness. But, of course, he never did. He'd just go away and leave us all in tatters.

Unfortunately, I was now getting so angry and bitter that I began to distance myself, even from my sisters. At times I got mad at them and even picked up a knife and threatened with it one day when I felt my temper was going to overflow. I didn't always want to be the protector for the two other girls – I wanted them to protect me for a change. After one night, when he raped all of us, one after the other, and we'd had to watch helplessly, I went crazy at the other two girls. I was utterly sick of looking after everyone else – what about me? Why didn't we all fight back? They tried to do that in Roots, although I knew they seldom won. They both just looked at me like they were frightened of me as well. I think I was beginning to scare myself. It was like I had a demon inside me – maybe the very demon the Stabards had told me all these years was actually in me. If they thought I was evil, then I would be evil. I didn't care anymore; something was going to give.

It wasn't just me who was starting to rebel. There were times when Hope challenged Mr Stabard, and I was scared for her and us. One day, he told us to pick up a cup of coffee he had dropped on the floor and clear up the mess. Usually, we would scurry to do it, but this time, for some reason, Hope was riled. She stood in the kitchen, hands on her hips and just glared. Mr Stabard was confused. He was also a bit drunk, and he stormed over.

'Clear that up.'

'No.'

I couldn't believe what I was hearing.

'I said, clear it up.'

'Why should I? You dropped it'.

Mr Stabard's eyes bulged with fury, and I could see he was about to lash out at her. I tried to will her to stop, but it was clear she was going to stand her ground. In two strides, Mr Stabard came over and slapped her face – whack.

'I will not have disobedience in my house. Clear it up when I tell you.'

He was red and sweaty, and by this point, she knew he had defeated her, but she took her time clearing up, so I joined in, terrified of what had just happened. Something had gotten into Hope, and I had noticed her becoming increasingly mouthier around that time. It worried me as I felt it put us all at risk. However, I was becoming more explosive too, and sometimes it was my turn to suddenly flip. Occasionally Hope and I sniped at each other, but mainly we were fighting Mr Stabard.

Another day I trashed everything I could get my hands on. I remember going berserk and smashing up all the grandchildren's toys. Over the years, we had always focused on them because we had absolutely nothing, and the grandkids had everything. I was in the kitchen with the other two girls on this occasion. I was preparing supper as usual when one of the grandchildren called me 'wog' over and over. He had gone to the toy cupboard, got some toys, and taunted me with them. That was it: I just lost my temper. I dropped my vegetable peeler in the sink, stormed into the hall, straight into the toy cupboard, and started stamping on the toys. I ripped up board games with my bare hands, pulling toys apart. I got a doll, put my fingers in her eyes, and ripped her hair out. I got their teddies and soft toys and pulled off their legs and arms. I had enormous strength in my rage and kept trashing and ripping until I had broken every last toy.

Afterwards, I was absolutely shaking with fury. It was like an uncontrollable stream of energy; I even sent myself to the shed to cool down. I sat in the shed, supper half-prepared and waited to hear the grandchildren's pained reactions. I heard a shriek and crying, and I admit, it was satisfying. It felt like I'd finally got my own back as they'd now know a little about what it felt like to be bullied. I had never considered myself a nasty person, but now I sometimes worried I was becoming one of them because I enjoyed hearing these spoiled children's pain. As I sat there, enraged, I thought about how we weren't living a life that kids lived; we were living an adult's life, doing all the cooking, washing, cleaning and being Mr Stabard's sex slaves. Ripping things up and hurting the grandkids' toys were really the only weapons I had. Why shouldn't I get my own back?

After I'd smashed up the toys big time, Mr Stabard just replaced them, and I was so livid that I smashed them up again. It was war. I started losing my temper all the time now. Anything could set me off. I didn't care anymore. It was like the genie was finally out of the bottle, and I couldn't put it back. The more I lost my temper and trashed things, swore and shouted at the Stabards, the more my foster father would taunt me that I was 'crazy', which made me lose my temper even more. On reflection, I was nearly twelve, and my hormones must have been all over the place. I was behaving like a normal adolescent but in very abnormal circumstances. The backstreet abortion had really been the last straw, the final trigger and I felt I could take no more...and yet the abuse continued relentlessly, just as before.

On one occasion, I felt so angry when being taunted that I put my fist through a kitchen window. The Stabards were very surprised by this, but they weren't concerned as to whether I had hurt myself or whether they'd pushed me too far. Mr Stabard just said, 'Oh look, she's gone crazy again,' and I was humiliated even further, which made me feel even angrier. It was a bit like I imagine cockfighting or dog-fighting to be like – you starve, abuse and chain up an animal and then let it loose on another unsuspecting opponent. I'd been starved, abused and chained for so long that the Stabards could easily goad me into flipping my lid – to my foster father's sadistic amusement. I would no longer do what the Stabards wanted, and they began to get scared of me. I was seriously out of control and began to challenge them back. I liked that feeling – that I could wield some power over them. I wanted to scare them as they had scared me. I wanted to hurt them like they had hurt me all my life.

Smashing a window was very satisfying, just like smashing up toys. It gave me a release, made me feel better, and for a fraction of a second, I felt I had got my own back. But, as always, the Stabards had 'right' on their side, and one night, after I lost my temper and started trashing things, they called an ambulance. When the paramedics arrived, I could see Mr Stabard talking to them outside in the front garden, pointing towards me back in the house. I was terrified and ran out to the garden to hide in 'Our Home'. Somehow, they got there before me. Suddenly, two white men came towards me in green uniforms, and I was petrified. I started kicking out and tried to bite them. I'd been pushed to the limit and was fighting for my life. If they called me 'crazy' all the time, I'd show them how crazy I could be. I was thrashing and trying to get away when one of them came towards me with a syringe, and then suddenly, everything went dark.

I was angry at the lies to cover up the wrongdoing in the heavy burden they all put on me to pretend everything was okay. I couldn't pretend anymore. I liked being crazy as they didn't expect me to be able to speak out later in life. They thought 'stupid dumb jennie' would be so damaged, so slow, so crazy that they would be free from ever being found out.

12

SECTIONED BEFORE I REVEAL
THE TRUTH

'Jennie's behaviour has been very disturbed, and the staff have been unable to cope. We had to place her on the geriatric ward due to the lack of beds available. Age 11.'

(Doctor's NHS notes 1985)

When I came round, I thought I had gone to hell. It was the opposite of when I took the pills and ended up in heaven. I was in a long, white-walled ward with probably about forty beds. It was an adult ward, and I was the only child. I couldn't believe what I saw around me, and I had no idea where I was for a while. People were wandering around in their robes, half-naked, crying, screaming or shouting. It was absolutely terrifying. There were a lot of old people who looked like skeletons. There was a man with his privates hanging out of old stripy pyjamas, talking to himself all the time. There were old ladies propped up in chairs, supposedly watching TV in a common room, but they were asleep and drooling or talking to themselves. There were zombies everywhere – walking up and down the ward or sitting in high-backed chairs, rocking backwards and forwards. These people were totally out of their minds. It was hell on earth.

Nobody spoke to me. Nobody explained anything. I was petrified. Eventually, a nurse told me I had been 'sectioned'. I didn't know what that meant. She explained that I couldn't go home because the hospital had me under their control. It was like I had gone from one prison to another - just like that. Sectioned? I had never heard the word before. I was eleven going on twelve, and the doctors had now imprisoned me in this echoey, cold madhouse. I found out I was in a psychiatric hospital (which has since been closed down) built over a hundred years ago. It felt like it. It also smelt like it - the whole place stank of wee, poo, vomit and sweat. People were lying in bed groaning, crying out in pain. I'd never, ever seen anything like it in my life. I saw people in white coats and nurses in uniform holding people down on beds and injecting them while the patient screamed and shouted swear words at the top of their voices. I saw three or four nurses wrestling a patient to the floor, dragging them along the floor, and finally tying them up to a bed. I was terrified to death.

It was clear that the Stabards had sent me here to punish me even further. Yes, I broke the toys and put my hand through a window, but was I really mad? I thought the Stabard's house was bad enough, but this was a hundred times worse. Were they teaching me yet another lesson about how evil I was? I had to be bad to be locked away here. People were out of their minds, and many patients had been here for years and years. Old people with sticking-out white hair and no teeth came over and stared at me, drooling. I felt like an animal in the zoo, and they were taking a look at me. Men came up, put their faces right up to mine, and grinned madly at me with stinky breath and black teeth, making me shriek with fear. I was not safe here; I was going to be hurt here, too, was all I could think.

When I went out to the bathroom, it was utterly disgusting. There was wee all over the floor, poo on the seat and brown finger marks on the walls – it was more disgusting than anything I'd ever seen. The bath was old and had black rings around the inside, and someone had gone to the toilet in it. I felt sick just going in there. How could I be here? How was I going to get out again? Would I be here for the rest of my life? Maybe the Stabards had made a deal with the doctors never to let me out again? At that point, even going back to the horrors of the shed and the box room felt preferable to being here.

I was in the mental hospital only a short time after the abortion, so I felt I was somehow being punished even further – for being angry about being hurt and abused. None of it made any sense. However, nobody came to talk to me. Nobody asked me anything. Nurses would wander around, talking loudly to patients like they were the kids at my ESN school – as if they were simple or stupid. The nurses just seemed interested in dishing out pills to everyone and keeping things to a very rigid routine. And that's where this place reminded me of the Stabard's house. It was very rigid, full of rules. You had to do what they wanted you to, or they punished you somehow.

The food was also totally nauseating. It was just a grey slop. There were lumps of cold potato, with hairs sticking out and green and black 'eyes', which made me feel sick. Then there was the watery, grey mince which was inedible, even for me, who had eaten Winalot sandwiches and dog poo casserole. There was tasteless, overcooked cabbage, rubbery meat and solidified gravy. I couldn't bring myself to swallow most of it, and I had a really hardened stomach since I'd been starving most of my life. The other thing that reminded me of life at the Stabards was when they gave me tablets. The nurse came along and snapped at me:

'Take this.'

She stood stern-faced over me while I had to swallow a load of little pills, numbing my mind. The tablets numbed my thoughts, my feelings – even my taste. They made me feel like someone had removed all of my emotions. Now I was like one of the zombies on the ward. I lay rigid in bed and stared at the ceiling, watching the hours go by slowly while people shouted, screamed, cried, swore and wet the floor all around me. My tongue felt like a swollen slug and stuck to the roof of my mouth, and I was always terribly thirsty. I couldn't get anyone's attention, and nobody spoke to me. The nurses weren't friendly like in the other hospital. There weren't any other children on the ward, and I felt very peculiar being the only one. There were quite a few other black people there, though, which I found rather strange. Why were there so many locked up in here? Usually, you don't see so many black people in one place.

One day a doctor came, dressed in a smart, dark suit, surrounded by many nurses and other doctors in white coats. He looked like a very posh man, and he stood way down at the end of my bed and stared at me for ages. One young doctor had a clipboard and was scribbling down something all the time the head doctor was there. The posh man just looked at the clipboard at the end of my bed and talked to the nurses and the doctors, ignoring me. I couldn't hear what they were saying, and I just lay there, inert, in my hospital gown (which, embarrassingly, didn't do up at the back) while they talked to each other over my head. Then the main doctor shouted at me from the end of the bed with his booming voice.

'So, Jennie, how are we today?'

I didn't know what to say. How was I? In this hellhole? What did he think I thought about this stinky, nasty place? I was scared I'd be very rude to him if I said anything at all. I didn't know how much I should say about the Stabards and what had been going on at home or whether he meant how I was this minute. The drugs I was on made my mind fuzzy, and I felt very confused. So, I didn't say anything to him. I just lay there, pulled the sheet over my face, and hoped he'd go away. I could hear them talking, so I peeked out again and saw the doctor with the clipboard writing something else down.

'You know, it won't get you anywhere being this angry,' boomed the big chief doctor to me.

He looked like a fierce headmaster who looked down his nose at me, and I didn't like him one bit. What did he mean - it wouldn't get me anywhere? Did he think I was choosing to feel furious? He'd be angry if he'd been through what I had. But I said nothing. I felt very intimidated by this man and didn't know what to say to him. All I could see was a lot of grown-ups staring at me with fierce faces, like angry masks. Nobody looked like they cared one jot about me – as usual.

'You know your foster parents care about you, don't you, Jennie?' said the doctor in front of everybody. 'I think you're being a bit ungrateful.'

Ungrateful! I would have gotten up and thrown something at the doctor if I hadn't felt like I was made of lead. I turned on my side, away from his glare, and closed my eyes. I felt very tired and didn't want to look at him and the whole staring gang anymore. I missed Faith and Hope and wished they were there with me. They'd understand. Even a glance or a twitch of a cheek would mean something between us. We could read each other like books. I knew every little mannerism of both of them, and they knew mine. With that man at the end of the bed, we would have exchanged a look and then giggled quietly. We would have understood that we all thought he was a complete idiot who understood nothing about the whole sordid situation. Then when we were in the woods, we would have acted out the entire scene again and fallen apart, laughing helplessly at how ridiculously pompous he was.

The next morning the breakfast trolley, pushed around by two nurses, didn't stop at my bed. I was starving, and breakfast was the only half-decent meal of the day – I could have some cereal and a glass of milk at least. I asked the nurse if she could give me some food, but she said no because I was going to surgery later. Surgery! I had just had 'surgery' at that big Victorian house, which was terrifying. The last thing I wanted was any more. Just as I was starting to get very upset, another nurse came over and injected me. After that, I calmed down very quickly; I felt like someone had fed me a giant marshmallow. I couldn't speak or move or do anything.

Later, two men in white coats rolled me onto a stretcher and wheeled me down to surgery. I felt very lonely but far away from my feelings, like watching the men push me along the corridor. Once I got there, they lifted me onto a bed – what must have been an operating table – and I saw loads of medical equipment. Someone in a green gown and mask peered over me and looked at me coldly. They picked up my wrist and looked at their watch, something medical people always seemed to do. I just stared at the blue eyes over the mask, and I couldn't tell if it was a man or a woman, which seemed very strange.

Then they were holding up a syringe. No one said, 'Jennie, we are going to do x or y to you,' they just did it, and I just lay there paralysed, unable to stop it from happening to me. I felt helpless, and I couldn't speak at all. I was totally in their hands. Then I felt the needle go in – a sharp prick – and I fought to keep awake. I didn't want to go to sleep; maybe they would kill me; how did I know? I thought I was in a torture centre of some sort. Despite my struggles, all went black, yet again. When I came around, my head hurt a lot. I felt like someone had punched it on both sides. I couldn't remember anything either. I didn't know my name, where I was, or how long I'd been there. My head was thumping and thudding. It felt like a ball that someone had sucked all the air out of, slowly filling up again with air. I felt so peculiar. I slept and slept and wasn't interested in anything. The next time I saw a nurse and was awake enough to speak, I asked what the operation was.

'ECT,' was all she said.

I didn't understand.

'What's ECT?' I asked.

'An operation on your head,' is all she said.

ECT. Electro-Convulsive Therapy. It entailed thousands of volts pushed through my brain to give me a kind of fit; I found out much later. I was eleven; they had sectioned me and given ECT. I was 'crazy Jennie' who didn't need anything explained to her. I was a mad, black girl who was ungrateful, difficult and bad-tempered (as the Stabards told me over and over) and who ought to count her blessings (as the nurses and doctors told me over and over). People had taught me all my life that others could come and do what they liked to me. They were free to abuse my body, and now my brain could be too. A few days later, I woke up to find Mrs Stabard standing at the bottom of the bed. She had her navy coat on and her usual shut-down expression. She was holding something; when I looked, it was a packet of crisps and a tube of sweets. I couldn't believe it. She had never given me anything like that before. What was she up to? She came and stood by the side of the bed and looked awkward. No kisses. No hello. No chit-chats. I was furious, and I didn't want to talk to her. So, I blanked her. How could she put me in this mad place? It was her fault I was in this hellhole. She put the sweets and crisps on the side table, and I brushed them onto the floor. I didn't want them. It was too little, too late, and I was angry. How dare she pretend in front of the nurses and doctors that she usually gave me sweets and crisps? It was all a show, just like the last time after I took the pills. In the hospital, she pretended she cared, but when we got home, she didn't care. How dare she act as if she treats me well when she actually lays us out for her husband to rape at night! I put my eyes down and refused to look at her. I did that a lot, and I knew she wouldn't like it. I wanted to shut her out, to teach her that she had hurt me.

'Jennie,' said Mrs Stabard flatly. 'How are you?'

How am I? I couldn't bear to hear her voice, pretending she cared about me. Suddenly, I felt this enormous surge of rage in me, and I reached out and picked up the table on wheels that went over the bed, and I threw it at her. Mrs Stabard stepped sharply sideways, shocked, as the table whizzed past and skidded across the ward, slamming into another bed on the other side. A couple of people screamed, but someone else cheered, and for a moment, I felt triumphant until I saw the men thundering down the ward towards me. Mrs Stabard had retreated and was standing passively watching, saying nothing at all, as four hefty male staff held me down while one injected me. Everything disappeared down a black tunnel yet again.

I awoke in a small cell-like room with a jacket that locked my limbs from moving.

13

TARNISHED CHILDREN

*'Jennie is the only one who has presented any
difficulties with her foster parents.'*

(GP's report)

I was in the hospital for several months after that,
although I really have no idea how many. Being trapped
in hell, it all felt like it went on for weeks and weeks. I had
no idea whether it was day or night, winter or summer,
weekday or weekend, as the days all rolled into one great
big blob of nothingness. The boring routine was the same
every day. I just hid in bed under the sheets or lolled in a
chair in a flimsy hospital dressing gown and watched all
these people wandering about, half-dressed, moaning,
throwing fits and shouting obscenities. I was eleven years
old and locked up, against my will, with all these deeply
disturbed adults. After the ECT, the nurses gave me loads
of pills, making me feel woozy as if I were looking at life

through a thick pane of glass. I felt very remote from my feelings as if someone had switched off my emotions.

In all those weeks, nobody really came and talked to me. The nurses would drift by, chatting to each other, eating our leftovers (more to the point food we had again - leftovers were the bit they didn't initially want) and shouting instructions to the patients – they always spoke to us like we were really thick. They would mainly give us pills, while the male nurses were always ready to wrestle somebody to the ground or tie them to a bed. The doctors would waft around every other day, and the big chief doctor would come round once a week and boom at me from the end of my bed. I learnt to ignore him – I was too intimidated by him to know what to say. I just wanted to keep everybody out. I didn't want to look anyone in the eyes anymore. I had stared into Mr Stabard's horrible cold blue grey eyes, bearing down on me at night, enough for a whole lifetime. His cold stare haunted me. At least here, I was safe from him, for the moment. But this crazy prison, where they locked me in with all these mad people, was just a different kind of hell on earth. I didn't know what I was doing there or why I wasn't in a children's ward. I definitely felt being stuck with all these crazy adults wasn't anything new; in fact, these adults were just different crazy adults to those who lured me into taking my child's body. Maybe this was this part of my punishment? Perhaps everyone here believed I was evil, which was part of my 'purification'? Maybe the Stabards had convinced the big doctor that I was so bad that I had to have my head squashed in by electric volts and my emotions flattened by millions of pills, and then I'd be 'pure'? I still longed to be cured – to no longer be a naughty girl that had to be locked away.

Being in the hospital was like a game, in a way. Nobody ever sat down next to me, took my hand and asked me what was wrong. Instead, I spent my life double-guessing what they wanted me to say, and then I'd try to give them what they wanted. In the Stabard's house, I always had to watch what I said. Any question or command always had a 'right' answer; if I got it 'wrong', they would punish me. The horrors of the airing cupboard and the shed stayed with me and taught me to be very careful. So, I'd learned not to take any question at face value and to work out what the grown-ups wanted and give it to them. I wanted to please people, even in this madhouse.

One day, a nurse came along and stood by my bed. She took my wrist, timed my pulse with her watch, and put a thermometer under my tongue. As she was doing all this, which was part of the daily routine, she suddenly said:

'Do you hear voices?'

I didn't know what she meant. Voices? There were voices all around me shouting all the time. I didn't look up at her. I'd learned that talking to people only led to them hurting me, and I didn't want to let people get too close anymore. I said nothing but tried to work out what she meant and what answer she wanted. Why was she asking me a question with a thermometer in my mouth? She wasn't making it that easy to talk, was she?

Jennie,' she asked again, more intently this time. 'Are you hearing voices...you know, in your head?'

In my head? I didn't know what she meant exactly. I did think about Mr Stabard and all the horrible things he called me and the nasty things he did to me. I 'heard' that all the time – I had nightmares about it and constant images of his face in my head if that's what she meant. I was also thinking about Faith and Hope – I missed them and worried about them all the time and loved remembering the things we said to each other and the games we played in the woods. So, I certainly 'heard' them in my mind while sitting in this awful place hour after hour and wished they were with me. I'd always had a strong imagination, probably because I'd had so little real stimulation from books and toys, so I relied on my mind to keep me amused either for hours in the shed or now in this brutal ward. So, in a way, I did 'hear voices'. I shrugged. I didn't know what she wanted me to say.

'So, you do? You do hear voices?'

She seemed pleased with my shrugging, so I shrugged again. Then I nodded.

'Sort of.'

'Aha!' she said.

She seemed very pleased now. I felt glad about her reaction, so I looked sideways at her. She was smiling. I liked to please people; I was always looking for the love, care and attention I'd never got. This nurse, whom I had become quite fond of during the weeks, patted my hand and said:

'Okay - okay, we'll do something about it for you, Jennie.'

'Well, that was a result,' I thought. Somebody's going to do something about me at last. Whatever that something was. I had no idea what this conversation, if you could call it that, was all about or where it would lead. But something clearly had happened, even though I wasn't sure what it was exactly.

Meanwhile, I had to concentrate on getting through the days. It was all I could do to avoid stepping in the poo and wee in the bathroom and keep my head down when accosted by patients wandering the corridors. The food was disgusting, but I got it down the best I could and mainly spent my time sleeping. That was the only good thing about being there: I slept and slept and slept. I felt tired all the time, as the medication made me feel like a robot, and I just snoozed my days through the weeks ticking by as I moved towards my twelfth birthday.

The whole time I was in the hospital, nobody visited much. Mrs Stabard came occasionally, but I always felt indignant with her shows of kindness, so it was never a good visit. I never saw Faith or Hope, and I really missed them. I would lie on my bed trying to remember the beauty of Wildflower Woods, our private paradise on earth. I sometimes took myself on a mental holiday, imagining climbing out the window, shinning down the trellis and padding down the garden barefoot. I would eventually be up on the hill, wind in my face, stars and moon above, feeling free. I would breathe in deeply, just envisaging the indigo space of the starry sky with its friendly moon face. I would smile as I remembered our times running through the dead leaves in our trench area (an old Second World War shelter I later discovered) or skidding down the chalk runs on our wet bin bag liners. I hugged these memories to myself, and then I'd come to open my eyes and see I was still in this nightmare – nothing had changed.

Eventually, they let me out. As I was about to leave, the big chief doctor came round and told me I had a 'diagnosis' – whatever that was – and they would give me some medicine to make me feel better. Diagnosis? Was that the same as 'sectioned?' As for medicine, I was sick of it. It just made me feel like the living dead. In his booming tone, he told me that I would have to have an injection at the doctor's surgery once a month but that my nice foster mother would take me there. He glared at me from the end of the bed.

'Now, Jennie, I'm expecting you to be a good girl and take your medicine and behave better at home,' he commanded in front of everybody.

I managed to peek up at his face through my lashes. I was embarrassed, but I nodded. He was definitely like a strict schoolmaster. I knew they liked me to nod here.

'Good girl.'

And then he wafted away, surrounded by the doctors and nurses, like a giant gander with a loyal gaggle of geese. Afterwards, the nurse came with a little silver tray and a syringe. She pulled the flowery curtains around my bed and asked me to roll on my side. I felt a sharp sting in my bottom – it really hurt.

'What's this for?' I managed to ask.

'Schizophrenia,' is all she answered.

'Skitty, what?'

But she was gone, and I had no one else to ask.

I knew I heard voices, many at times, but they felt like me but weren't me. I called them my me's. I'd reassemble my pain and carried parts of my trauma like a deep dark suitcase until I could carry them myself.

I would zone out when life became difficult and completely blackout, sometimes for just a split second and others a bit longer. I would find my life playing right before me, yet I couldn't get to it as I was in a trance, but a trigger made me see it. Sometimes I would wake up in a strange place without remembering how I got there. I thought I was going mad. I thought they were right about me; mad, bad Jennie. It all made sense in 2022 when I was diagnosed with DID dissociative disorder. Nobody told me before then, but the explanation released me from a life sentence. I no longer had to be ashamed of who I was anymore. It was normal due to what my life experiences were. But sadly, to this very day, many still don't understand it, especially those who work in the mental health field.

That's so difficult because you know you have to pretend again to be a good well-controlled person so that they can tick the boxes, so I don't get sent to the hospital again.

The Stabards came and took me home. On return, life continued just as before. Nothing changed. I don't know why I thought it would be different, but I did. I had been totally terrified by my trip to the hospital, and the drugs also made me much more docile, so at first, I actually felt relieved to go home. I just returned to the old routine for the first few weeks. Almost immediately, Mr Stabard started coming into us in the box room at night again. I discovered Faith had gone into hospital as her condition had worsened, so we'd actually both been in different hospitals simultaneously. But Hope and I were back in the shed, back doing the chores and back to being 'hurt' by him.

I was also back at school. The teachers said nothing about my being away, and I missed nothing. I was back in the classroom with kids with many disabilities and many other black children. Most of the kids there had had some bad beginnings in life. Many of them had difficulty speaking or reading, so we did a lot of colouring. We were back to bricks and blocks and then more blocks and bricks for a change. The teachers gave us cards that we had to put into sequences according to colours and objects, which were incredibly boring and repetitive. I noticed the teachers just spoke to each other often and sort of ignored us as if we weren't really worth bothering about.

We did gymnastics, but the gym was small, and all we were allowed to throw was a small softball at each other because they thought we couldn't handle doing anything else. Since there was no running, swimming, or anything hard or stretching, I missed my athletics badly. I tried hard to calm down at school because I didn't want to return to the nasty hospital again. But I was very bored all the time. Occasionally, I'd sneak a Daily Mirror into school to check I could still read. I was surprised I could, and I would say to myself, 'I can't be that stupid after all, can I?' because I could still make out stories. After a while, I did make friends with one girl, Abigail Greer, who saved me from total isolation. She was an older black girl who had told me about my monthly bleed being a 'period', which I wouldn't have known otherwise. She was beautiful, and I would have done anything for her. She became very influential on me. I guess she could sense that I was very desperate and vulnerable and needed someone to talk to.

Of course, I never told her what was happening at the Stabards – I don't think I had the words to explain any of it, and I didn't know whether it was 'normal' or not – but I became very attached to Abigail and did all sorts of things for her. I would run and fetch for her like a pet dog, as I wanted her to like me. I was even becoming a slave to other children. Meanwhile, back at the Stabards, I wanted them to understand that I was not going back to being the silent doormat that they could always do what they wanted to. Whereas I tried to behave at school, I began to find it harder to keep my cool at home. I did try when I first came home from the hospital, but when Mr Stabard came in at night and started the rape business all over again, I found it hard not to be angry. I found his behaviour at night even more disturbing now. After putting the light bulb in, he would take my nightie off, make me stand in the middle of the room, and look me up and down. It was like he was assessing me. He seemed very interested in my breasts now, which sickened me. He played with them all the time and even sucked on them like a big baby, which embarrassed me terribly and made me want to throw up. I didn't know where to look or what to do when he did it; it seemed so very personal.

He still often brought the Sellotape as he hated me looking back at him. My venom would show through my eyes. Drunk, shameless and feeling in complete control of us, he would still hurt me in front of Hope and Faith when she was there. Whilst I was in the hospital, the other two children, Raj and Prathi, had returned to their own mother. I assumed that Mr Stabard's night visits had continued, just as always, while I'd been away – he wouldn't have wanted to deprive himself. Hope hadn't been to the woods without me, though, as she felt it wasn't the same when I wasn't there, and she was scared to go there alone.

The Stabards were still watching Roots and kept up the weekly ritual of seeing it with their adult daughters, Carla and alice. They even brought the grandchildren round to watch with them all, so we'd have the whole family baying at us afterwards, like blood-thirsty hyenas, trying to intimidate and humiliate us. I absolutely hated these weekly sessions of being openly tormented, but the Stabards seemed to think they had a right to inflict it on us. We didn't spend as much time in the shed now, but after the horrendous Roots routine, they sent us to our dingy box room with nothing to do. Now I was officially crazy – or so everyone said – I felt I had a licence to do crazy things. I hated how the medication made me feel, all woozy and woolly in the head, and I often fed my pills to the dog. The dog was a dopey old thing and just slept all day once I'd fed her my tablets. I hated feeling so drugged up all the time, so I felt justified. I didn't want to hurt the old thing, but I didn't want to take all the pills myself.

Mrs Stabard also used my 'crazy' label as an excuse to get even more money. I noticed her filling in loads of forms all the time to social services , claiming I had broken things and saying she had to replace them. This was a lie, but they got themselves money for new lamps, sheets, blankets and all sorts because she claimed I was always trashing the place. I wasn't – at least not then – but it made me feel I might as well have done. One of the few positive things about me going to the child guidance clinic was that the services referred me to a very nice doctor for individual sessions. I remember Mrs Stabard taking me there one morning instead of going to school. We walked up a hill to the centre of town, and then, to my amazement, I went in to see the doctor on my own. I was very scared of going in, but she was a lovely woman who sat at a low table with me and put me at ease.

She got me to draw a picture of 'my family'. I drew the house and put Mrs Stabard and my two 'sisters' in the picture, but I wouldn't put Mr Stabard anywhere. The doctor seemed quite concerned about why I wouldn't draw him, but she was warm and encouraging. I also drew the shed in the back garden and called it 'Our Home'. The kind woman doctor kept asking me why I wouldn't put Mr Stabard in the picture, and I didn't know what to say. I hated him and didn't want him anywhere near me, so leaving him out of the drawing seemed the best thing to do. I also made Mrs Stabard very small in the picture, smaller than me, and the doctor asked if she was another foster child. I said, no, it was Mrs Stabard. She kept asking why she was so small; again, I couldn't answer. I just felt she was small because, somehow, she did nothing for us, but I couldn't explain that. I did all the work at home, so it seemed natural to make me bigger – or maybe I felt responsible for looking after the house and my sisters and being the focus of Mr Stabard's perverted attention.

I really liked talking to the doctor, and I found doing the drawing very interesting, so I was pleased when she said, "we'll do this again next week.'

It was the very first time someone had listened to me and asked probing questions, so I really looked forward to going again. However, the next week, I found that Mrs

Stabard had written in and said we couldn't make the session. When I asked her if we were going, she shook her head. She didn't answer when I asked why. I felt terribly disappointed like I was going to cry buckets, but I held the tears back. Later I felt anger, which added to the burning resentment growing inside me.

If the sessions had continued, I think, in time, I might have been able to describe what was happening at 97 Forestlane Way – which is precisely why the Stabards deliberately ensured that my visits stopped. They were terrified I might spill the beans. I was very sad not to see her again as she was the first person I felt had taken any real interest in me. This single act by the Stabards condemned me to at least another twelve years of mistreatment and abuse.

However, one day, soon after, something weird happened at school. The new headmaster, Mr Pringle, entered my unruly classroom, got down to my level, and asked me to come immediately with him. I thought, 'Oh no, I'm in trouble again,' because I'd been losing my temper a lot lately. We walked down the corridor to his big office. When we got there, he opened the door - imagine my surprise when I saw a room full of people, including a police officer in uniform. I shrank back against the door frame, shaking and trying to hide.

Mr Pringle said gently, 'It's alright, Jennie, just come on in', so I followed him gingerly, absolutely terrified, into the room.

14

FREEDOM OR DANGER

'Jennie is lucky to have the Stabards as she is an unattractive and inarticulate child with many black moods.'

(Social worker's report 1978)

I wanted the floor to open up, let me fall in and hide from all the adult eyes. I was absolutely terrified as Mr Pringle went and sat down in the big chair behind his desk. I stood to one side, trembling and feeling sick, trying to hide, and I couldn't look at anyone in the room. I put my two fingers in my mouth for comfort. My heart was racing. The policeman sitting there in his smart black uniform was scaring me. What had happened? What had someone said? Was someone ill? Had someone died? It raced through my mind that Faith somehow gave the game away while I was in the hospital. Or maybe it was something completely different. Maybe Mr Stabard died in a car crash – I had wished it so many times, but now I didn't want it to be true. I had no idea what to do or what to expect. I was so used to being excluded from everything in the world I was clueless about what to do when the world actually sat up and took an interest in me.

'Jennie, don't worry,' Mr Pringle said in a kind, gentle voice.

He could see I was shaking violently. I wanted to cry, but I bit my lip, as usual.

'These people here just want to ask you a few questions.'

My knees wobbled uncontrollably, so Mr Pringle stood up, got a chair and put it behind me. He then put his hand on my shoulder, and I plopped down onto it. It was a relief to sit. Then a man spoke from across the room. I hadn't really noticed him before. He was dark-haired, middle-aged, and smartly dressed, and he explained he worked for Social Services. The policeman was there because it was a criminal enquiry. My heart nearly leapt out of my mouth at the word' criminal'. Was I going to prison, finally? Mr Stabard had always threatened it. I looked sharply at Mr Pringle, who whispered:

'It's okay, Jennie. It's okay. It's about Raj and Prathi.'

I blink. Raj and Prathi? What does he know about them? Of course, they had gone home while I'd been in the hospital. They lived with us for nearly four years, and I felt sad at their return, as I'd gotten fond of them, even though we'd all had to share our cramped space. I'd felt quite jealous of them taking up the beds in our box room, although sorry for Raj, who had been 'hurt' a hell of a lot by Mr Stabard. I suddenly have flashes of Mr Stabard forcing Raj to put his head down onto Mr Stabard's horrible stinking thing. I'm nearly sick on the carpet at the thought.

Mr Pringle explains that Raj and Prathi went home to their family and told them some not-very-nice things were happening at 97 Forestlane Way. My heart is pumping so loud; I wonder if they can hear it. I keep my face straight. The children haven't slept since they got home and are very distressed and confused by what has happened to them. I feel my eyes widen with fear as I listen. Oh my God, it was finally all going to come out. I feel a whole mixture of emotions rushing through me, although my head is still like porridge due to the pills I'm taking. Someone had finally come to rescue me, to save us! I wonder where Faith is and why she isn't here as we are still at the same school.

I think I might now be released – like the slaves in Roots when they finally got freed, and I might go and live somewhere where people treat me nicely. And then it pops into my mind, quick as a flash, what Mr Stabard had always said – what he had told me for twelve years over and over and over like a broken record – that if I speak up and they take me away, he'll have to kill himself. I will be responsible for his death. As much as I hated him, I didn't want him to kill himself. I don't want that responsibility.

Given that I'm 'crazy', will anyone believe me, anyway? What if I say something, and the Stabards both deny it? Surely the authorities will believe them rather than me, a mere schoolgirl – and a dumb, naughty ESN schoolgirl at that. Anyway, I often have temper tantrums, which they may think would justify my mistreatment. All this is racing through my mind as the man in the corner (who I don't like the look of) starts explaining something.

'I'm Mr Venetti,' he pipes up. 'I need to know if you've seen Mr Stabard do anything he shouldn't. . . to Raj and Prathi.'

I sit riveted on the chair. I look down at my hands and pick imaginary fluff off my dress. I always do this when I feel anxious; I pick, pick, pick while I think about what to do. I bite my lip and shuffle on the chair. I can't look up; it's too scary.

'Jennie,' Mr Pringle's voice still sounds gentle, unlike the man from Social Services, who looks mean. 'Mr Venetti needs to know the truth, you know. You won't be in any trouble. Just tell us the truth. Tell us what you know.'

I look at Mr Pringle. He's quite a young man, with reddish hair and pink skin. He's got nice shining blue eyes and a warm smile. I think he's someone who actually likes children, even ESN ones. But what can I say? Where would I start?

'Do you think your foster parents have ever done anything to harm Raj or Prathi?' asks Mr Venetti again, sounding a bit impatient.

I don't like him one bit. I think of Raj's head pressed on Mr Stabard's thing, crying afterwards, and being sick. Eventually, I nod. I can't look up, but I nod. My fingers are picking away at my skirt. The policeman is scribbling something down in his notebook. I feel very put on the spot. I suddenly think I'll be locked up myself if I give anything more away and look up at the policeman in fear. Why are people always looking at me and writing things down?

'Raj and Prathi have said some pretty serious things, Jennie,' Mr Venetti says again, looking quite fierce. 'Do you think they are really telling the truth?'

I nod slowly again. I bite my lip.

'What do you think they have said?'

I can't look up. Finally, I mumble that I think Mr Stabard hurt them at night. He liked to touch and do things to them – and make them do things to him. And he would lock them in a shed in the garden and a cupboard, saying they're bad. There's a shocked silence in the room. Mr Venetti clears his throat.

'And do you honestly think these things are true?'

He's glaring at me. I feel he's angry. Pick, pick, pick at my dress with my fingers. Pick, pick, pick. I have to keep my emotions under control, but I'm shaking anyway. Even the pills aren't numbing me enough not to feel scared and tearful. I nod.

'You realise how serious this is, don't you, Jennie?'

I see a glint in Mr Venetti's eye, and I just want to run out of the room. I put my two fingers in my mouth again to stop myself from crying and pick at my dress rapidly with my other hand. I start rocking.

'Jennie, Jennie,' says Mr Pringle gently, 'don't worry, we just need to know.' He pauses. 'Is it happening to you, too?'

I can't think, I can't breathe, I can't open my mouth. Pick, pick, pick, pick. What shall I say? If I say 'yes', all hell will be let loose. If they don't believe me, I'll be sent back and be 'sectioned' again and have more ECT in that vile hospital. What if Mr Stabard hears and kills himself? Or kills Faith and Hope as I don't care about him killing me - he might even doing me a favour if he did.

Oh my God, I don't know what to say. Anyway, wasn't I crazy now? I'd been labelled a 'skitty thingy', so who'll believe a mad girl? Oh God, what should I say?

'Jennie?'

I can't look up. My eyes are blurred, and my mouth's dry. I don't know what to do. I want to cry, run away, and leave this room with all these grown-ups. Why won't they leave me alone?

'Jennie, can you answer, please? We need to know.'

Mr Venetti sounds very sharp. I look up at Mr Pringle through my lashes. Then shake my head.

'No?'

'No.'

I look down. Pick, pick, pick.

'So you're saying that Mr Stabard has been hurting Raj and Prathi, but he hasn't hurt you or your sisters, or anyone else?'

I shake my head. Inside my head, I'm screaming, 'Go on, tell him, go on, tell him – say it.' But I'm too scared. I'm too terrified to do it. If the truth be told, I love Mrs Stabard and desperately want her to love me back. Even though she's cold to me and does horrible things, like laying us out for him at night, I still forgive her. She'll never forgive me if I say something. What if I leave home; where would I go then? I've always held out that it would all be alright one day and my foster mother would eventually love me. If I shop her husband, she'll never talk to me again, that's for sure. And as for him, I hate him, but I also want his attention. Strange as it may seem, I was actually very attached to him, although I loathed what he did to me. Somehow, I was used to it, and it almost seemed like a warped kind of relationship. At least it was a relationship – without him or them, I'd have nothing.

I was full of such twisted emotions that I couldn't make sense of it all. I didn't want Mr Stabard to kill himself, and he had drummed it into me that he would do that, so I felt completely responsible at that moment for keeping him alive. Wouldn't I be truly evil if he died? And Mrs Stabard would hate me forever if I was the cause of him going away or dying. I was also afraid that I might get locked up again and, this time, in a real prison.

How did I know whether these people in this room were being straight with me? I had learned not to believe what adults told me, and I was really scared of people in authority.

'Are you absolutely sure he's never touched you in ways you don't like?' pipes up the policeman finally.

I look down.

"No, sir, he touches them, not us,' I hear my voice mumble.

'You are absolutely sure?'

I nod. Mr Pringle turns to Mr Venetti and the policeman, and they speak quietly for a moment. I don't listen. My heart's racing. I'm thinking, 'Oh God, why did you say that? Why don't you tell them? Go on, tell them! Go on - this is your chance!' I look up at them through my lashes, wanting them to ask me again, but they are talking seriously to each other. All the time, my mind's racing, and I'm panicking inside. I don't know what to say or how to return to what I've just said.

Part of me feels at least I've helped Raj and Prathi. But part of me feels horribly loyal to the Stabards, like the authorities won't send me away from them now. I was scared I'd end up in an even worse situation, like in the hellish hospital. I couldn't tell them, as absurd as that might seem. I had a chance to escape, and I couldn't take it. How mad was that? The minute the word 'no' was out of my mouth, I wanted to shout 'yes' but couldn't. I was too scared. Something stopped me; some invisible thread or cord bound me to them. After all, I had been with them all my life, since I was three months old, and how was I to know that the whole world wasn't like it was at the Stabards?

The meeting was suddenly over, and Mr Pringle took me back to class. Mr Pringle said nothing to me except a quick 'Well done.' I think he was disappointed in me or something. I sat the rest of the afternoon, unable to think straight, just building blocks, one block on top of another, like a zombie. Then I'd knock them down angrily, as I kept thinking I missed my moment when I could have left. I should've taken it, but I didn't. I regretted not taking it almost immediately. I'd been so scared by the situation with all the adults and the seriousness of the meeting. Maybe if one person had asked me face-to-face, like the nice lady doctor who'd got me to draw, or just Mr Pringle or the policeman – I might have said something. I didn't like the look of Mr Venetti, he'd made me feel scared, and I felt I couldn't tell the truth to him at all. I didn't know why. The rest of the afternoon, I felt atrocious. Like always, I caught the minibus when it was going home time. At first, I didn't speak to Hope, and then I told her what had happened. Her eyes opened wide.

'Me too,' was all she said.

We discovered that she had also been interviewed that afternoon by the same people and had said exactly the same thing. Hope had said it was Raj and Prathi, not us, who were being 'hurt' by Mr Stabard. We couldn't believe it. When put on the spot, she had felt she couldn't give the game away, either. And now she regretted it as I did. We sat in total amazement as we drew up to the road near Forestlane Way. We had both had a near escape, but now we were returning to our hellhole as usual. Wasn't that a sign that I was truly mad? I could have gotten away that very day, but I didn't. So, doesn't that mean that I deserved all I got? What a fool.

When Mrs Stabard opened the door, we knew we were in trouble immediately. She gave us her stern look and then pointed down the hall, meaning we should go straight in. When we got to the lounge door, I could hear voices. Mrs Stabard pushed us past the door, and we entered the kitchen. We were just going out to the shed, very frightened, when the lounge door opened and suddenly, there was Mr Venetti, shaking hands with Mr Stabard. Mr Venetti? They seemed very friendly towards one another, like old pals. Mrs Stabard saw me looking, and she shooed me out to the shed with Faith and Hope, and we were quickly locked in. Half an hour later, the door was flung open by an absolutely livid Mr Stabard. He grabbed me by the hair, started pulling me across the floor, and beat the shit out of me. He pummelled me, slapped my face, and kicked me before starting on Hope. He gave us the worst beating I can ever remember having. He was blowing steam out of his ears.

'But', I kept saying while he was hitting me, 'I didn't tell, I didn't.'

'You made up stories, porky pies— you're evil, you know that?'

He lay into me again, slapping, punching and kicking me into submission. He told us the police would charge him for the other two, and if he went to prison, he'd kill himself, and then it would be our fault – did we understand? But I felt outraged, as I hadn't given the game away about us. Didn't he understand that at all? I couldn't say anything because he didn't give me a chance as he was so intent on slapping us into the far end of next week. I discovered a lot later that Mr Venetti had worked with the Stabards when they volunteered as workers in the children's home that eventually shut down after abuse allegations about some of the workers there. The home had sacked Mr Venetti in disgrace. It was a local children's home, but somehow Mr Venetti had got himself back into working with children again – God knows how. It meant that he had gone straight to Mr Stabard, warned him about what was coming, and told him what we had said in our separate interviews. We had had our near escape – with the policeman and Mr Pringle there – and we had blown it due to a warped loyalty. Meanwhile, Mr Venetti had protected Mr Stabard instead of us. Perhaps unsurprisingly, Raj and Prathi's case against Mr Stabard was eventually dropped six months later due to insufficient evidence.

15

INDIGNANT CHILD

'Mrs Stabard is to be congratulated on all the effort she makes for this very difficult, moody girl.'

(Social Services' report)

I had missed my chance to escape, and now I was trapped yet again. I would never be free now. I was furious with myself for not getting out when I could and furious with Hope for not speaking out, either. I knew I couldn't really blame her for doing the same thing as me, but I wasn't feeling very rational about it all. I was still furious with the Stabards for everything they demanded from me and did to us. I was constantly resentful, a boiling cauldron of rage simmering away, threatening to blow at any minute. At first, after the whole psychiatric hospital episode, I tried hard to behave better. The pills 'numbed' me down, and school was mind-numbing, too. I tried my best to keep calm. But the old regime continued, and Mr Stabard still came in at night, even though he was under investigation about Raj and Prathi. I guess the fact that we hadn't given the game away made him feel very secure with us: he had silenced us well and truly, as far as the authorities were concerned, so he still felt safe doing what he liked with us.

Once the police dropped the case, he was obviously smug – he somehow believed he'd never been in the wrong in the first place and was a model foster parent. So, my life continued on its usual treadmill from twelve years to about fourteen or fifteen. I would try to be calm and then have a volcanic blow-up after several weeks or months of trying to be 'good'. I would trash things badly, and the Stabards would either deal with it by locking me in the airing cupboard for days or in the shed or – if I got too violent and I smashed up the toys or pulled a knife on someone – they would call an ambulance, which would cart me off to the madhouse for a few days or weeks. The psychiatrist usually put me on new or bigger doses of the old pills, and they began injecting me with stronger antidepressants and other things, like antipsychotic drugs.

Around this time, the doctors decided I was 'paranoid', which meant I thought someone or something bad was out to get me all the time. It was genuinely true: someone bad was out to get me – and I lived with him. In a way, I felt like the authorities were also out to get me because apart from the one woman doctor who had tried to understand my story, nobody had ever asked me a single question about why I was so angry. The ambulance to the hospital and increased drug regime felt like another 'out-to-get-me' experience. So, I felt increasingly more paranoid, especially since I was always sent back home to the 'saintly' Stabards and reminded by everyone that the problem was all mine. It was all in my head, clearly, and they were not to blame. I had a crazy mind, so I should be grateful for all I had at home. To my mind, that was truly crazy.

Mr Stabard had retired by this time. He was now in his mid-sixties and had become utterly obsessed with my body, particularly my breasts. He would hang around the house all day when I was home and up in the box room (we weren't always in the shed all day now we were bigger), and he would come in unannounced and just ogle my body. He would typically stand at the doorway and stare at me for a very long time. He was creepy in the extreme. It made me feel very self-conscious and awkward. I'd usually sit on the bed, making me feel less vulnerable than lying down. He'd shuffle in for a crafty peek, like the dirty old man that he really was.

...'Take it off', he barks.

I ignore him, knowing what he wants but willing him to go away. He takes a few more steps into the room towards me. I can smell his boozy breath in the air.

'Take it off - your top. Take it off; show me.'

He stands a few feet away, his eyes glazed. I look at the ground or my knees, wanting him to disappear, feeling my cheeks flush with embarrassment. In the end, I take my top off to get rid of him. He goes very quiet momentarily, and I can hear his breathing getting heavier. He fumbles in his pocket as if he's looking for something. I fight the desire to stand up and punch him or scream in his face – instead, I start picking at my skirt with my fingers, trying to control my temper. I just want to shout, 'Go away, you filthy old man,' or 'Leave me alone!' but I don't dare, as he'd punch and slap me into submission.

'Take your bra off.'

I take it off reluctantly, shivering. By then, I've given up fighting him off and want it over with. I sit there, naked to the waist, in a freezing cold room, staring at the floor, and he stands there, inches away, licking his lips and drooling over my young girl's body. It feels disgusting. Like I'm a piece of meat displayed in a butcher's shop window. Eventually, having had his fill, he goes away, only to return later that night to start his sleazy ritual all over again. After putting the light bulb in, he starts the usual business, telling me to take my top off so he can see me. I feel so disgusted with myself and ashamed of the other two watching. I have to cut myself off from my body and my feelings just to deal with it . . .

Mr Stabard usually seemed to favour me more than the others, perhaps because I was more physically developed than them then. The only relief for me was that it saved the other two from too much abuse, especially as Faith was very poorly now and didn't look like she would survive much longer. Since going to ESN school and starting her periods, Hope had become more rebellious than me, often challenging our foster father, which made him angry. Then he would punish us all by withdrawing food or locking us in the shed all weekend. I was in a difficult position and often volunteered to do what he wanted to save the other two from being hurt and us from a more horrible punishment later. I hated him for putting me in this position and loathed him as he satisfied himself on my young flesh. But hating him did me no good and simply fuelled my mounting anger. Even though I was always angry and increasingly rebellious by the minute, I still didn't dare to do things I'd been trained not to do. For instance, I would never have dared to go into the lounge, sit on the sofa, and put my feet up. I still feared the Stabards enormously, especially as they were continuing to bring home the church people to exorcise us every few months. They still drummed it into the three of us that the devil possessed us, and we had to be purified. I think they truly believed this, and it was sincerely part of their warped worldview that black skin meant evil. The Stabards had brainwashed us so entirely that we weren't worthy of sitting on the sofa and turning on the TV for ourselves; we would not have done it. It was unthinkable.

We took the odd risk as we got older and became more rebellious. I remember once or twice going into the beautiful bedroom next door to ours during the daytime and sitting on the beds. It felt incredibly naughty like we were committing a major crime. Now we were in our early teens; we wanted to look in the heart-shaped mirror above the dressing table and imagine ourselves living in this bedroom like proper teenage girls. We'd all sneak in, hoping the coast was clear and they wouldn't hear us, and we'd pretend it was our room, and we'd lie on a bed each, with our hands under our heads for a few minutes, imagining we could sleep there. It felt fantastic. The soft duvets and springy mattresses, the carpet under our hardened feet, the flowery curtains and the pictures on the walls all made us feel like princesses – for a few precious minutes, anyway. Then, terrified of being caught in the act, we would rush back to our box room, close the door and giggle at our wild adventure to the wonderland of the room next door. It was a small but important victory in the war against the tyranny of the Stabards.

We were genuinely defiant in other ways, too. Sometimes we stole things. We were still going to the woods to save our sanity, but now we took food and even alcohol along. We would get into the larder, pour some gin or vodka into a plastic juice bottle, and take it. This was particularly helpful in winter when it was cold. It was great if one of us was hurting badly after Mr Stabard's so-called 'purification' treatment. We would have little parties and feel naughty but excited about our escapades. We stole whatever we could get our hands on - bits of pork pie, slices of ham, cake and good old Winalot. We were growing girls and hungry all the time. We still had to eat the rubbishy leftovers from dog bowls and were occasionally chained to the door to watch the Stabards eating if they were in the mood. Either way, we were constantly empty-bellied. We got better at slipping food into our mouths while preparing dinner. In our desperate bid to survive, we felt we had to be as stealthy and clever as possible. We also learned from Roots how the slaves survived by learning to be manipulative and stealthy, hiding things, pinching things and using their wits to scavenge. You'll do whatever you need to get through it all when you're desperate.

Something happened during this time that caused me a great deal of grief and created even more anger. The Stabards' grown-up children still visited regularly, and all were married themselves with children, so the Stabards now had eight grandchildren. Bernard was in his thirties and was a big strapping muscle man. His son, Kevin, was one of the children who had always hated us. He always used to shout 'wog' at us and taunt us when we'd been watching Roots. He'd been a ringleader in throwing food at us at the children's parties and always enjoyed making us feel small. I don't know why he hated us so much; maybe he resented us being there for taking up his grandparents' time and attention. I don't think he ever forgave me for trashing his toy train set, which I had done one Christmas when I went berserk. Bernard never stopped him – I don't think he had ever forgiven us for upsetting his son, either. Also, as Mr Stabard's son, he had absorbed his father's hatred of black people all his life, as had his two sisters. Hope and I were in the kitchen one afternoon when Bernard dropped something off for his parents. We shouldn't have been there, we should have been in the shed or our room, but we'd tiptoed downstairs and were scavenging for something to eat. For some reason, the Stabards were out somewhere – maybe doing some shopping for an hour. I was about fourteen at the time, which made Hope about twelve. Faith was in the hospital, as usual. We never liked Bernard and were genuinely afraid of him as he was very burly and had his father's aggressive attitude, especially towards us as black girls.

. . . Hope and I are in the larder, just off the kitchen, rummaging quietly when he suddenly appears.

'What are you doing here?'

Bernard stands in the middle of the kitchen, hands on hips, looking very demanding. He knows we shouldn't be there, especially in the larder, because we must always wait for the Stabards to feed us. We were not allowed to help ourselves to food. We look at the floor and freeze, hands behind our backs.

'I said, niggers, what are you up to?'

He always uses terrible words to attack us. We're used to it, even though it hurts and makes me fume.

'Cookin' supper,' says Hope unconvincingly.

There's no sign of steaming pots and pans. Hope always speaks for us first these days; she's now braver than me. Bernard strides across the room, grabs her by the shoulder and spins her around. In her hand are a crust of bread and a chunk of cheese. He turns me around, and I'm holding some apple pie.

'You greedy, thievin' little wogs.'

I feel a surge of fury but bite my lip, too scared to move. Bernard grabs the food from our hands and throws it in the waste bin in front of us. He's smirking, looking very pleased with himself.

'Caught you red-handed, haven't I?'

We both stood riveted to the spot. I hate this man almost as much as I hate his father – he has the same menacing, cold stare. I want to slap him. Instead, I stare at him fiercely, trying to communicate my hatred with my eyes, but Hope is more courageous and confrontational. She's mouthy today.

'We can eat if we want to,' she says boldly.

Oh, God. I clenched my jaw at her defiance.

'You what?'

'We live here'.

Bernard puts his face right up to Hope's, snarling angrily now.

'What did you say, you little black bitch?'

I'm terrified now and get hold of her t-shirt and try pulling her back towards me, hoping to slide around the room and escape to the hall. I sense he will get very nasty; we just need to get out of there. Bernard has his nose right up to Hope's. She's looking down at the ground, trembling.

'I said, what did you fucking say, wog?' he spits at her.

'We can eat if we want', she repeats in a tiny voice.

'Oh, you can, can you? We'll see about that'.

Hope darts a look of pure fear at Bernard.

'Don't tell', she pleads, suddenly terrified.

'Oh, don't tell', he mimics nastily.

Then he puts his face right up to hers, even closer.

'How you gonna stop me, nigger?'

Hope's incensed at him for using the 'n-word' yet again. It always reminds us of the dreaded Roots. So, she raises her eyes and locks her gaze on him defiantly. They stand, face-to-face, bound together in a staring match. I will her to look down, to stop and move away. We might be able to end it there and then, but he has other ideas.

'You owe me, bitch', he hisses at her through clenched teeth.

He really hates us with his father's venom – it must be in the blood. Without any warning, Bernard suddenly grabs and throws her flat on her back on the tiled kitchen floor, which is, as usual, covered in dog pee and animal droppings. Hope shrieks and is winded. Bernard is suddenly on top of her, holding her down with his thighs straddling her, his knees pinning her to the floor, and his hands pinning her arms above her head. I stand with my hands over my face, terrified, holding my breath. When I peek through my fingers, he has pulled up her skirt, got his thing out, and is in her. On the hard, unwashed kitchen floor - right there and then, Hope lays, with her legs open, looking sideways with no emotion on her face and just lets him do what he wants. Years of training with Mr Stabard have taught her not to resist but to go limp and blank it all out. Bernard moves in and out of her very fast, grunting and groaning, like a dog on heat, and then it's over. It's very quick. He springs back off her, and I can see her legs spread uncomfortably, looking shocked. Bernard goes over and gets some kitchen roll paper. He zips himself up, and hands Hope some paper to wipe herself. She doesn't move, so he bends over and wipes her. I'm amazed. It's such a bizarrely tender gesture, given that he's just raped her on the kitchen floor, in broad daylight – in front of me. She sits up and pulls her skirt down over her knees, a crushed look on her face. Suddenly Bernard bends over her and pulls her up to her feet by her arm. He half-hugs her – which is very odd, too – almost to say sorry for a moment. Then, without a word, he rushes out of the house.

She stands there looking at the floor, totally numb and blank. She's no longer standing up for herself; she was put in her place and tamed by yet another 'master'. Horrified by what's happened to her, I go over, put my arm around her shoulders and steer her out of the kitchen. We go upstairs to the box room together in total silence, all ideas about food completely forgotten by now. Hope crawls onto the top bunk (which is a treat as it's our favourite place, the safest place to sleep as 'he' can't climb up to it) and turns to the wall. I sit on the hated bottom bunk and wonder if I could kill Bernard with a knife the next time I see him. I imagine stabbing him in the chest with great pleasure. Maybe I could torture him or even cut his privates off? What right has he to come in and do that to my little sister? How dare he punish her for taking food which belongs to us anyway? Don't the Stabards claim money to feed us, then keep us starving most of the time? I hear Hope sobbing softly into her pillow, which she doesn't often do these days. She used to cry more when she was little. I stand up and put my arm around her, but she shrugs me off. She's too upset for comfort.

'We'll go to Wildflower tonight,' I whisper. 'I promise.'

She doesn't answer, just sniffs and keeps her back to me, hunched around in a foetal position. I stroke her bony back gently, feeling terribly guilty that I didn't do anything to stop the bastard. How dare he! We were nothing to him. Just animals. Actually, beneath animals. Eventually, Hope lets me comfort her gently, at least for a while. As I stroke her hair, I keep telling myself that I could have hit or pulled him off. I feel so angry with myself all over again as if it's my fault that I let him rape her. I should have done something to stop him, although what could I have done? I feel helpless, powerless and sickened to the core. What if he tells the Stabards we'd been out of bounds getting food – then there'll be even more hell to pay tomorrow. We certainly can't tell them what he's done – or anyone else, for that matter. With his wife's blessing, Mr Stabard does it all the time himself anyway, so what will they care?

After this horrendous incident, Hope became even more rebellious and unruly at home. It was a major turning point in her life with the Stabards. Until then, I had been the one who gave them the most trouble. I always seemed to carry all the anger for the other foster kids. But this incident on the kitchen floor, the bald-faced crudeness of the attack, somehow tipped Hope over the edge. She began to talk back to the Stabards, which meant she got beaten more. She also started stealing things, and we joined in. It was only little things, like a few pence or some extra food, but it was another way of getting our own back. One thing we did quite often was to nick one of Mrs Stabard's Sunday brooches and hide it for a week or two under our wonky floorboard. It just gave us a hollow sort of pleasure to confuse her about where she had put something – she was now in her sixties and getting more forgetful about things. It also meant going into her bedroom, which was a dare, making us feel more powerful.

We also did something very naughty to Mr Stabard one Sunday. He had now lost most of his hair, although it had been white for as long as I could remember. He bought a toupee (no doubt with our childcare money) and very proudly wore this to church on Sunday. One day Hope found an ant's nest at the bottom of the garden when we were cleaning out the aviary. She showed me, and almost without a word, we hatched a plan. The ant's nest found its way under Mr Stabard's toupee, and loads of ants settled in the false hair. The following Sunday, he wore it to church. We watched in church as he scratched his head, neck, and ears during the service. We nearly wetted ourselves as we saw him wriggling and scratching as the ants climbed down his neck. Halfway through, he took the toupee off, and we saw him turning it around in his hands and looking inside it, clearly puzzled. Then he half-jumped, half-shouted out, and we saw the wig fly over the pew and land in the aisle. We nearly had a fit and just managed to keep our composure when he shot a fierce look over his shoulder at us. Luckily, we were mistresses of the straight face by then, and we kept our eyes down, faces blank, although we could feel his eyes boring into us. He was fuming all the way home, and we knew he was longing to lash out at us, but we shot in the house and out to the shed and leant against the door the minute we got back. He must have had too much to drink after church since he fell asleep in the lounge, snoring loudly and never came out to give us a walloping.

We felt victorious: 'Operation Ants in the Pants' or rather, in the wig, had worked! These minor victories meant an enormous amount as they were like little islands in a sea of almost unremitting misery. We seldom won, so winning a tiny battle in the war that was life with the Stabards raised our confidence. Until then, nearly all of our ire focused on Mr Stabard. He was the target of our daily fury, and it was against him we fought the hardest. I still wanted Mrs Stabard's love, but I would never earn it, particularly as she was so remote and cold all the time, to us at least.

One day the social services woman came for a routine visit, and I heard Mrs Stabard telling her that I was Mr Stabard's 'favourite' and that we had a 'special relationship'. She made out that Mr Stabard was very nice and gave me special treatment. I felt livid about this. Later that day, when the social worker had gone, I threw all the washing and ironing on the floor and refused to clear it up. She was standing in the kitchen, pointing to the stuff on the floor, and I refused to pick it up and sort it. It was a major stand-off. She then said if I continued to be bad like this, she would call an ambulance, and they would take me away. Knowing I hated that hospital, she used this as the ultimate threat. I rudely answered that if she did that, I would tell the hospital everything that was happening, and then she'd be sorry. They'd both be in trouble and imprisoned forever until they rotted and died. I walked out of the room, triumphant. That would show them.

That night I was due for a bath, a rare treat. If I was lucky, I had baths about once every couple of months. Since the days of the chocolate treatment, I had felt scared of them. I always kept my clothes on in the water for added protection. I was washing my feet when I suddenly felt someone behind me, and something went over my head. I was pulled under backwards and tried to gulp some air as I went down. I felt the water close over my head, and I freaked out. Someone was dunking me under. My hands went up to my head, and I worked out I was under a sheet or something heavy with water and that a pair of strong arms were holding me down. I fought wildly to sit up, entangled in the wet sheet and kicked my legs, holding my breath and feeling like I might burst, before being pulled backwards and dunked under again. I was lashing out with my arms and legs, still holding my breath but needing more air and desperately trying to get the sheet off my head. Then someone shouted something from downstairs in the house – it sounded like Mr Stabard wanting something – and I realised with total shock that it was Mrs Stabard doing this to me. It wasn't him. It was her! I was horrified and amazed. With an almighty push, I finally got myself upright and pulled off the sheet. As I desperately gulped in the air, I saw her back disappearing out the door, sleeves up, arms dripping wet. I just couldn't believe Mrs Stabard had done this to me. She'd actually tried to drown me! I never knew she was that strong – or that angry with me. I couldn't believe she hated me enough to try and kill me; I was devastated. I loved her and wanted her to love me back. I sat under the dripping sheet, absolutely desolate and shivering with fear for some time afterwards. I listened to the Stabards' voices downstairs and wondered if I would ever get out of their 'care' alive.

16

FIRST CONTROL I HAD OVER ME

'Jennie is of low average intelligence and appears emotionally immature but copes fairly well with her foster home.'

(Social worker's notes 1977)

After Mrs Stabard attacked me in the bath, I started running away. She'd never done anything so openly violent to me, and I felt totally betrayed. I had sort of gotten used to his mistreatment - but from her? I always held out that she would eventually love me one day. Now I realised that she hated me just as much as he did. Now I had nothing to lose, nothing to hold me back. I'd lost respect for her, which hurt a lot. I was nearly fifteen, and one day, after we'd had a massive argument, I just slammed out of the house and went where my feet took me. I felt very unsafe, so I took off and walked and walked and walked. I roamed the streets, digging my fingers into my face, scratching and pinching my skin and trying to hurt myself. I also slapped and punched myself as I felt so agitated and trapped.

People stared at me on the street; some would shout 'crazy' and spat at me, but I didn't care. After all, I was 'crazy Jennie', wasn't I? I began to hurt myself whenever I felt I'd explode and needed a release. I'd get a vegetable peeler or a knife, and I'd slice into my flesh. Usually, I had a go at my arms. For a second, cutting gave me a different release from when they did it. It was a real feeling of relaxation when the blood came. Then it would really hurt in a sharp, deep, nervy pain. I'd also take one of Mr Stabard's razor blades from the bathroom cupboard and slice myself with that - feeling a fantastic release of all the pent-up anger – it was a strange sensation. If they hated my black flesh, then I did, too. I needed to dig into something and hurt myself to release the tension.

I didn't like the pain, but I used to be fascinated by watching the blood bubbling up and beginning to pour; I was almost mesmerised by it. As the wizard did to me, I also burned myself on the legs with Mr Stabard's cigars. I was in control during my self-harm, not them. Sometimes the burns would go septic. Hurting myself became a habit – an addiction. I think I was absolutely desperate and simply didn't know what else to do. If Mrs Stabard saw my cuts afterwards (to which I often stuck a bit of toilet paper to stem the flow), she would say nothing. She'd just look briefly and turn away, uninterested.

Faith was also getting desperate at this time and was never around. She was almost permanently in the hospital, and I don't think I really saw her again after I was fourteen or fifteen. I missed her a lot as she was a gentle soul who loved the woods and somehow created a bridge between Hope and me when we weren't getting on. Meanwhile, Hope and I was arguing a lot. I don't know if it was our age or whether we were both so fed up with our lives that we didn't know who else to take things out on, but we constantly argued. We were caged up together, and sometimes, I felt totally infuriated with her. It wasn't her fault. She was more provocative than I was, and after the rape, she began to go off the rails. I was worried she would get us into even more trouble, so I tried to quieten her down for all our sakes. I still carried the weight of being an older sister, and now Mr Stabard only had the two of us to satisfy him; he used us more frequently, which we hated.

The neighbours complained because we would argue and shout in the box room or the cramped shed. We wanted to give the Stabards a hard time. We needed to let off steam, and we would swear at the top of our voices – it was our kind of protest, and I don't think we cared at all if anyone heard. Going to school was still frustrating, and I was always bored out of my brain. One day Mr Pringle called me into his office, and I thought, 'Oh my God, I'm in trouble again.' The memory of that meeting with the policeman and the horrible Mr Venetti was still raw – the day I'd failed to take the chance to escape. That was something else I cut myself about. However, I was amazed when Mr Pringle said he had decided I could try to do an exam at the local school if I wanted to. I was shocked; what did he mean? He explained that he thought I was good enough to sit for a CSE (Certificate in Education) in English at the local comprehensive. Instead of staring at the floor, as usual, I looked up and saw he was smiling at me. I couldn't believe that somebody was saying that I was capable of doing something positive at last.

'I think you can do it, Jennie,' he said. 'I've noticed you wanting to read things and being bored in class.'

I couldn't help a huge grin spreading across my face. Me - go to a proper school and read books, like the other 'normal' kids? I felt excited but scared at the same time. Mr Pringle could see that I was nervous.

'Don't worry, they know you're coming, and they'll settle you in,' he said. 'We'll take you there and back.'

I couldn't believe that someone was actually thinking about me and offering me something good for a change. It felt absolutely amazing to feel someone was on my side for once. True to his word, I went to the school and studied alongside the other ordinary children in an annexe in the playground. A teacher took me there a couple of times a week. Mr Pringle kept saying, 'you're not stupid, Jennie, you're really not,' but I found it hard to accept. All my life, I'd had it drummed into me that I was stupid, bad, crazy – you name it. I loved the reading – I drank in the books – but I must admit I was quite an unruly student initially. After so long messing about with building blocks, I found the whole experience of going to a proper school quite daunting. It took me a long time to get the hang of it. After all, going from primary school to the ESN school, there had been no real discipline or order. We didn't really have to apply ourselves.

Also, being on the pills constantly, my brain was fuzzy, and I found it hard to concentrate at first. But I soon began to grasp the routine – even enjoy it – and I was pleased to finally be doing something constructive. As I began to settle down, I even learned to write essays. I felt immense pride in what I was doing, although I never told the Stabards about it. I tried hard to behave better at school, especially showing Mr Pringle, I was worth his trust. So, I made a big effort to be calmer at both schools I was attending. I liked the annexe and the lessons and enjoyed the feeling that I was learning. I liked knowing things, and I felt less tired and achy in the head now that I was finally using my brain. I felt like I was exercising my mind, like a muscle, and I really liked it. I began to have a feeling of satisfaction in myself. The teacher at the comprehensive put me in for my CSE but tried to persuade me to go for my GCSE as well. I was terrified.

Mr Henderson, the English teacher, kept saying, 'Jennie, you can do it, you know.'

But I was scared. It felt like a step too far, too fast.

He kept encouraging me, but I kept saying, 'No, I can't.'

I said I needed more time, but I think I was scared to try and fail. I didn't take the opportunity when they handed it to me and regretted it afterwards. Still, I had absolutely no support at home, and I guess it felt too stressful to deal with on top of the Stabard's regime. However, I gained a lot from the fact that two teachers actually thought I was worth investing in. It made a big difference to my self-esteem: they didn't think I was totally worthless. Back at the ESN school, my friend Abigail Greer began to get me to do things for her which were against the rules. I think I was desperate for a friend at any price and had made myself useful to her. She was older than me and was using me to bring in alcohol from Mr Stabard's huge supply, which I would sneak out in a juice bottle, just like I did when we went up to Wildflower Woods. I would also pretend I could buy her things from the clothes catalogues she brought to school. I'd never seen anything like these things, but I would promise to get her stuff to buy her friendship. I couldn't actually buy them, and she'd get disappointed in me when I didn't come up with the goods (literally), saying I'd let her down badly. I'd feel terrible and go home and hack at myself with a razor blade, feeling more useless than ever.

Abigail also wanted to introduce me to boys. When we went into town or walked home together, a part of the way, she would stop and chat with boys and then start kissing them. I would stand behind her, watching, terrified. I didn't like all that, and it freaked me out. After all the years of Mr Stabard abusing me, I wasn't in the least bit interested in boys. Sex meant something horrible to deal with, nasty, humiliating and painful. Emotionally, I was as naïve as a child. Also, no adult had ever given me any proper information about my body, how it worked, how babies were made, or about sexual hygiene, even though my periods started when I was nine, and I'd had an abortion at eleven years old. I had been sexually abused since infancy and yet knew nothing about the birds and the bees, courtship, love or any of that stuff. So, when Abigail was standing there snogging the boys, I wanted to get as far away as possible. It confused me, and I didn't want to be involved in any of it. As far as I was concerned, it just led to one thing – trouble. Even though the men who abused me were men, I still felt this was dangerous and feared for my safety in school.

Meanwhile, all my frustrations came out at home. I didn't respect Mrs Stabard anymore – not after the bath episode – and I let her know. My temper was uncontrollable, and any stress about the exam I was taking or the trouble I was getting into with Abigail would come out with me trashing furniture, throwing things and shouting. I couldn't think straight and would lose my temper over the slightest things. I think the drugs I was on also made me more aggressive. I took loads of pills daily, and the more I took, the angrier I seemed to get. But I was numb at the same time, feeling heavy and dull and yet furious like an underground fire burning deep down, and I couldn't put it out. I was still going to the mental hospital for check-ups and sometimes because I'd freaked out. The Stabards called in the paramedics to teach me yet another lesson.

Around this time, there was a lot of discussion about what would happen to me next, which made me very insecure. Hope was going off the rails now – she was out with boys a lot and had started drinking regularly. I could see things would get very difficult, and the Stabards said they couldn't look after her much longer because of how she behaved. But they also discussed my future. They would never talk to me but talk about me when I was in the room like I wasn't there. It was like, 'What shall we do with Jennie when she's sixteen?' Not, 'What would you like to do, Jennie, when you're sixteen?'

Apparently, at sixteen, their official job of fostering me would come to an end, and I was free to go. I remember one of the social workers coming to the house, and there was a meeting in the lounge about me. I didn't get consulted or invited in, but I listened at the door and heard them discussing my future. They never asked what I wanted. The Stabards never said, 'We'll support you going to college,' or asked, 'Is there a course you'd like to do?' Nothing like that. The attitude was: 'Dumb Jennie can't think for herself. She's crazy anyway, and there'd be no point in talking to her, so we'll make decisions for her over her head.' I was an awkward teenager, and nobody knew what to do with me - least of all me. I was coming up to finishing school, and I managed to get through sitting my exams, which I enjoyed, even though I was nervous. And then, two things happened, which triggered a lot of further upset.

First of all, I had a huge bust-up with Abigail. I had tried to win her friendship by giving her things and pretending to buy her clothes, but she finally got fed up with me and dropped me. I was devastated. The only friend I had ever made had dumped me, and I was back to being just lonely old 'crazy Jennie'. Secondly and even more devastatingly, Hope disappeared. She left after a massive row with Mr Stabard that started over the washing-up. After the kitchen floor attack, she had really changed. She was bitter and angry all the time, even at me. Although she was only fourteen going on fifteen, she was much older than her years and furious, like me, about everything. When she finally blew her stack, refusing to do what Mr Stabard wanted, he hit her so hard that she decided to cut free. She told me she couldn't take any more, but we'd said that so many times. I had never thought that she would do that. We had been through so much together, and I believed we would be together the rest of our lives – or at least keep in touch. Of course, we often fell out – we argued and squabbled, just like sisters do. I often felt jealous of her because I thought she was prettier, thinner and more confident. But I loved her. She was my sister, my family, my world.

One day after school, she wasn't on the minibus. She just didn't come home or any night after that. After a couple of days, Mr and Mrs Stabard called the authorities, and there were meetings. They spoke to the school. I think, more than anything, Mr Stabard was terrified that she would tell on him. He certainly cared about himself more than her welfare. As far as I know, she didn't blab. She just disappeared, just like that. I don't think the police were ever involved – I think the Stabards were relieved she'd gone. I was absolutely devastated she was gone, and I cried myself to sleep every night. Our little room was suddenly very empty. I also felt much more vulnerable to attack from Mr Stabard, as I was left to fend him off alone. I felt a mixture of anger and pain of loss for Faith and fear that he could really have me when he wanted me now.

Looking back, I think she blew a fuse and just got on a regular bus and went to another town – probably with boys she'd met and snogged after school. I think she'd had enough and was so angry that she was even prepared to leave me. Her getting into alcohol and drugs scared me as I felt she was going down a dark path, and I couldn't save her. I heard years later that she had got heavily into drink, hard drugs, and prostitution and had finally become homeless. I have no idea whether she is dead or alive, as I never saw or heard from her again. With Hope gone, my world fell apart. I felt utterly terrified being alone in the house with the Stabards, as Faith was now almost permanently hospitalised. Mrs Stabard would coldly say she wouldn't return either – or good riddance. I mourned daily. It was like I'd lost part of myself. It all got so much harder after she'd gone.

Over the following months (probably to replace their lost income), the Stabards did have a few babies for short-term fostering for a while – and I would have to look after them in cots in my bedroom, of course. The Stabards were now well into their sixties and not really up to it anymore. I was an utter handful and strangely didn't actually want to leave them. With school ending, Hope and Abigail no longer around, and Faith away, I felt extremely insecure. I hated the Stabards, but I didn't know anything else. I wanted to escape but didn't know where to go. I was now living alone in a terrible triangle with the Stabards. I slashed at myself, pinched my face, and punched myself desperately. One night I cut myself very deeply in my groin with a razor and bled so much that they eventually called an ambulance, and I had to have stitches. At least I had a couple of days respite, with nice food and a comfy bed. However, it just confirmed to everyone how crazy I was. Back home and desperate, I stayed awake at night, trying to figure out what I would do. Where was I going to go? Who would have me? What would happen? I was very afraid of the big wide world out there and terrified of the crazy world in here. I had no idea what on earth I was going to do next.

17

BID FOR FREEDOM

*'Mrs Stabard patiently cares for this difficult
teenager well, despite being challenged daily...'*

(Social worker's report)

The loss of Faith, the disappearance of Hope and even
Abigail left me unhinged. I hadn't expected my sisters
to disappear as they did – so quickly and finally. Although
Faith had been sick for so many years, and I could see she
was deteriorating, I didn't expect her to just disappear
in a puff of smoke. The Stabards never included me in
what was happening with her; I never visited her in the
hospital, and they didn't give us any information when
she was away. Of course, I loved and cared for her, but
I couldn't say my goodbyes or ask any questions, as the
Stabards wouldn't answer them. I have no idea how
things ended for her – she just went off the map. To this

day, I feel sick that I never saw her again. Was she alone at the end? Did she know I cared? I hope she did.

All this was coupled with the prospect of leaving school and with losing my one and only friend, Abigail. Leaving school was no big deal on the one hand, in that it had given me so very little in terms of skills and learning. In many ways, it undermined my confidence rather than built it. But I did feel pleased that the teacher had chosen me to study and take an exam right at the end, and that did make me feel I wasn't entirely stupid. But I'd missed so many vital years of basic education by wasting time playing with building blocks and colouring in. How would I ever catch up? So, I didn't feel confident when I was leaving school.

My friendship with Abigail also seemed to set a pattern for what would happen in the future. The Stabards had taught me to be a slave, and I would take up a slavish position in my relationships from then on. I would always try to please people, to my detriment, and then finally explode with anger once I felt pushed too far. I didn't know what a healthy friendship was. I had such low self-esteem that I thought the only way someone would be friends with me would be if I tried to earn it – to please them, even if it meant putting myself at risk. I had learned to try and sacrifice myself for my sisters. That pattern continued well into adulthood.

What's more, the Stabards were contemplating getting rid of me now. They could throw me out at sixteen. The irony of this situation was that now I had the chance at freedom; I didn't want to leave because I was frightened of the world. The mental hospital had made me terrified about what might lie outside. If it were all like that, I would rather stay at the Stabard's, unbearable as it might be. It was a case of 'better the devil I knew'. At the same time, I still deeply regretted not having the courage to leave when Raj and Prathi made their accusations. I had failed to stop the Stabards. When their case failed – much to Mr Stabard's smug satisfaction – I felt my cause was lost. If they couldn't prove a case against them and had a birth mother and family fighting for them, then what chance did I have to convince anybody of the reality of life at 97 Forestlane Way?

It's hard to describe, but I felt totally stuck with the Stabards. It was like I couldn't leave, and I couldn't stay. The alternatives seemed less appealing. I hated them, but I feared the unknown. They did not help me in any way to find a good way to move forward. Neither did Social Services nor the mental hospital staff when I came in contact with them. I felt stuck between a rock and a hard place, meaning I stayed with what I knew for the time being, even though it was bad for me. In the end, the Stabards agreed to keep me on (I guess for more money), and we continued living our weird dysfunctional lives in a terrible triangle. Mr Stabard still visited me at night two or three times a week. He forced himself on me, Sellotaping my eyes shut and Mrs Stabard still pretending she didn't know what was going on. They still shoved me in the shed, the airing cupboard and the box room, occasionally for punishment, but I fought them more each day. I felt less powerful being on my own without Faith and Hope, as although we hadn't talked to each other about what was going on, we had always understood each other without words. Our visits to Wildflower Woods were the most magical, miraculous times and saved our sanity. Now that it was just me with this strange couple who could do what they wanted with me, I felt I didn't even have the woods to escape to – it wasn't the same experience without the other two. Without the release of being in the woods at night, my temper got worse as I became more trapped and fearful. When I left school at sixteen, I would be up in the box room all day sometimes, wondering what the hell to do with myself, feeling utterly lonely and desolate. Then Mr Stabard would appear in the doorway. He would never knock. He had no idea I might want privacy as a teenage girl or need my space. He would still ogle me, feeling himself through his trouser pocket and demanding to see or feel my breasts. I was just there, on-demand, for him to play with – his property and sexual plaything.

One day, I'd had enough of all this, and I had a terrible temper tantrum, trashed the kitchen and stormed out of the house to walk the streets like I often did. I was fighting the urge to slash myself and instead was pinching and hitting myself. Then I suddenly spotted a big poster for the YTS – the Youth Training Scheme, a government-funded training opportunity for teenagers. All at once I thought it might be an opportunity for me, so I decided to try and pursue it for myself. I felt lucky I could read at least; otherwise, I would have missed it. I went home determined things would now change. I went to the Job Centre two weeks later without mentioning it to the Stabards, who would have laughed and discouraged me. After taking my ticket, I sat for ages in what looked like a hospital waiting room. When they called my number, I spoke to a man through a window, and he filled out forms. He asked me what I would like to do, and I shrugged. I had no idea. He offered me a job of stuffing envelopes which sounded really boring, or catering, which sounded like yet more hard kitchen work.

I ended up applying to work in a hospital. They offered me a placement working in an old people's ward in a big local hospital. By that time, I felt like a hospital was like another home. You got meals and a bed, and in the normal hospitals I'd been to so far, the staff could be nice and friendly, and the environment was clean and bright. The idea was welcoming, especially when they offered me a room with food and board, all paid. I thought it sounded a bit like heaven. At least I'd get away from Mr Stabard and could sleep at night without being pounced on. However, I didn't tell them about my medication or history.

I thought the drugs I was on made me braver than if I hadn't been taking them. I was so numb I was more

cavalier than I would have been if I'd fully felt my fear.
So I said 'yes' without thinking about what it meant. I
had never lived anywhere alone or been away from the
Stabards except when I was in a hospital. I had no idea
what it meant to be free. I was like a slave who was finally
given their freedom but had no idea how to use it – how
to manage money, buy my food and clothes, or build
relationships at work. These things are very complicated
if you don't know about them. I threw myself into the
unknown without knowing what I was getting into. I
guess I was very mixed up at the time – still fuming about
everything that had happened and was still happening
– and I was so lonely without the other two girls that I
needed to move somehow. Being doped up to the eyeballs,
I couldn't think clearly about what I was doing. A big
feeling of 'I'll show you', aimed mostly at the Stabards,
but maybe also at my sisters for leaving me in the lurch,
drove me. A few weeks later, the care home sent me a letter
which told me I had an appointment to meet the manager.
Mrs Stabard opened the letter and read it, then handed it
to me, looking annoyed.

'What's this?'

I looked at the letter and shrugged. I was excited and
frightened but didn't want to show my feelings to Mrs
Stabard. I knew she'd try to stop me.

'You won't last,' she said, turning away.

I felt like a pricked balloon deflating.

'Yes, I will. I'm going to do it'.

'You won't last five minutes.'

I felt stung. She just wanted to keep me locked up. I'd show her – I'd show them – that I could do something. I thought of the comfort of the nice hospitals, cleanliness, and freedom. I had to leave; I couldn't stand it anymore.

'I'm going.'

Mrs Stabard turned and walked out of the kitchen, and I felt petrified, but I also felt determined and thought: 'I'll do it for Faith, I'll do it for Hope – I've just got to try.'

I had a proper uniform, brown and white checks and a paper hat. I was an auxiliary, and I felt quite proud of myself. I had a real job - a proper role in life. I think inside my head, I had imagined the hospital would be nice and orderly, and I'd have my meals cooked for me and would be able to get a good night's sleep when I needed one. However, reality hit once the ward sister handed me a long list of chores, a mop and a bucket and looked sternly at me. I thought, 'Here we go again. I came here to escape, but I am doing the same thing as at home.' Then I ended up working in the grotty geriatric wards. I had no idea how to work with people, and I'd already spent my life cleaning up, cooking and working hard. However, I couldn't believe it when a nurse told me to wash some of the old people. This meant removing their old clothes and pyjamas – some had soiled their beds – and cleaning their private parts. After years of abuse, I couldn't bear to touch them 'down there', not even the women. The men lay there, waiting for me to wash their bits, and I felt such hatred for them and I couldn't go near them. I knew it wasn't their fault that they were old and helpless, but the stench, combined with my bad memories, often meant I wanted to be sick. The sister came up to me during the first week and said:

'Mr Brown says you haven't washed him.'

Without thinking, I replied, 'How can he know I haven't washed him? He's blind!'

Only once I'd said it did I realise how stupid it was – I can even laugh at it now. The sister stared at me like I was a total idiot. I hated Mr Brown for telling on me because I felt I was now in my own little world in the hospital and could play at being an auxiliary. Truthfully, I just wanted to be in my little clean room, asleep in a nice cosy bed and fed hot meals. I needed some nurturing, some respite from it all. Unfortunately, the sister didn't have the time or inclination to train me, and I have to say, I don't think I had the right attitude. I had no idea what working in the outside world entailed.

I really just wanted to go to work for a bit of a rest from the horrible home the Stabards had forced me to work in all my life. While working at the hospital, I found a guy called Johnny wandering outside one day and brought him in. He stank of booze (worse than Mr Stabard!), but I bought him some sandwiches and a drink from the automat and even let him sleep on my floor. I felt very sorry for him as he had nowhere to stay. It was all very innocent: Johnny didn't touch me, just crashed and snored. I got into trouble when a staff member discovered what I'd done. I had no idea what you did at work or how normal people behaved, and I just thought the poor bloke was in need and that I should help him. I got the sack, and six weeks later, I returned to the Stabards with my tail between my legs. I just felt stupid all over again. Stupid, crazy Jennie had messed it all up. I'd tried to escape and had fallen at the first hurdle. Boy, were they smug! When I told my foster parents I'd lost my job, I got a load of 'I told you so's'. Worse than that, the day I got home, Mr Stabard was waiting for me.

Mrs Stabard was out somewhere or other. When I came back in the door, after six weeks of trying to do the job, he didn't say hello, but he just grabbed me by the hair, dragged me up the stairs backwards and beat me so hard that he broke the little finger on my right hand. He swore at me, kicked me in the stomach and thumped me until he had beaten me to a pulp. My finger was in agony, hanging limply at an odd angle. He also raped me on the landing floor – right there and then on the spot – then threw me in the airing cupboard for two days. What really terrified me was him saying that I'd have to start at stage one all over again to be purified. What a welcome home.

18

WILDERNESS YEARS

... 'hopefully, Jennie will be able to live with her foster family until she is discharged from care... her security is being threatened by the efforts made by Social Services to revitalise the links with her family of origin...

The Stabards are, I feel, deliberately sabotaging any connection with the girl's birth family.'

(Social worker's report 1980)

I was back in the fold. I was back to the horrendous, punitive regime - at stage one of my purification programme, which meant the Stabards locking me in the shed, shoving me in the airing cupboard and enduring degrading drunken night visits from Mr Stabard at least twice a week, sometimes more. They ridiculed my foray into the world; they laughed at me for being so gullible.

My foster parents didn't offer me guidance; they just poked fun, riled me, and punished me for getting wound up.

Meanwhile, my sister's absence left me heartbroken, as I missed them so badly. I was left to deal with the madness of my hidden hell alone. I was desperate for friendship but had no idea how to make friends or how to talk to people, exchange information, or build friendships based on mutual respect, care, trust and even love. I had only attached myself to Abigail in a slave-like worshipping way or to waifs and strays – like Johnny in the hospital, to whom I gave a floor for a few nights. I wasn't the faintest bit interested in 'boyfriends' either, in the way that Abigail or Hope had been. I wasn't keen on kissing boys, flirting or doing any 'normal' teenage stuff. Perhaps I felt that anything to do with sex would lead to more unnecessary pain and trouble. Dabbling with boyfriends would open not just a can of worms but a whole barrel-load. After all, how could I explain my physical experiences with Mr Stabard, which had been going on for as long as I could remember? What boy would understand that? I had never had any innocent pecks on the cheeks, casual flirtations, or first kisses. And I felt I never would. Indeed, Mr Stabard had never kissed me or shown me any tenderness or love. The kind of perverted act he subjected me to was the opposite of loving, tender sex.

I was wary of getting entangled with anybody in any way that would lead to something that intimate. How would I ever trust anyone? Any physical touch would make me feel explosive rage. I think the feelings involved would have been too enormous to deal with. I already felt out of my depth, so I avoided them – telling myself I was fat and unattractive anyway. I had been called ugly for so long that my self-esteem was at rock bottom, and I never expected any boy my age to find me attractive. Boys, sex and attraction, were a minefield, and I had no idea how to cross it. Thus, for the next two to three years, from leaving school at sixteen until almost nineteen, I was in a kind of wilderness at the Stabards. I did try to make one male friend after Hope left; I met Mohammed at the ESN school and had quite liked him. He had a very difficult background, with a lone, alcoholic mother who brought home violent boyfriends who beat him up and abused him. I felt I had something in common with him. Perhaps I felt sorry for him too. He was another waif and stray I could help. I think it made me feel more powerful to help someone else. I wasn't interested in him sexually, although I think he was quite interested in me. It was rather like we were two lost souls trying to find our way in a tough, hostile world.

I bumped into Mohammed in town one day, and we chatted for some time. We struck up a sort of friendship, and naively, I thought it would secure me a Valentine's card from him, just for me, or something like that, from someone who thought I was worthy and strong. I wanted the status of a boy in my life without all the physical and emotional complications. It sounds silly, but I thought if I were nice to him, he would be my Valentine, and then I would be a normal teenage girl and an attractive one to boot. Sadly, my innocent little plan didn't work out. One night Mohammed arrived at my front door in a real state, and the Stabards actually took him in. After a big bust-up with his mum and her nasty, violent boyfriend, he was homeless and came to the Stabards for refuge. I didn't know what to do with him, but the Stabards contacted Social Services. I think they arranged (I guess they got money, as usual) to look after him for a while. They placed Mohammed in the box room with me – where else? We slept in separate bunks, like brother and sister, but sadly Mr Stabard soon sucked him into the madness of his regime. One night I woke up and found Mr Stabard 'hurting' Mohammed in the same way he had hurt Raj. Mr Stabard was drunk as usual and had Mohammed kneeling, head at crotch height, pushing his mouth onto his foul thing. It was disgusting. Even though Mohammed was sixteen, he was overpowered by Mr Stabard and forced to undergo his own so-called purification treatment. I was horrified. I hadn't really wanted him to come and stay in the first place, and now he was being pulled into the Stabard's sick world. So, I did something really silly after that – or perhaps just very desperate. A few days later, I took twenty pounds out of Mr Stabard's wallet and then made out Mohammed had stolen it – which outraged Mr Stabard and confused Mohammed. He was duly shipped back to his abusive mother. It was the only thing I could think of doing to get him out of there. Trying to protect someone else at my own expense was typical of me – that's what I'd always done. It was more painful for me to live with someone else being 'hurt' by Mr Stabard than to deal with it myself. It was similar to when I used to say to Mr Stabard, 'Take me, take me instead of them,' to save Faith and Hope from his torture. I guess it made me feel better about myself to shoulder the responsibility.

My logic was that my friend's drunk mother and violent boyfriend couldn't be as bad as Mr Stabard. I felt hugely guilty for not warning Mohammed about what he might be getting into at my house. I never spoke about what was going on at home. He had no idea what he was doing when he knocked on the front door and asked the nice Christian people for help. I felt a responsibility to get him out of there, even if it meant framing him for something he didn't do. Needless to say, I never got my Valentine's card; and that was the end of that sorry relationship. Mohammed said nothing about what had happened to him either, as far as I know. Anyway, who would have believed him? He was just another unwanted, damaged kid who nobody liked much, had nowhere to belong – just like me – and had found himself falling into the nasty clutches of Mr Stabard.

Meanwhile, the Stabards continued to discuss what to do with me (over my head) as I was getting 'troublesome' to them. They made it absolutely clear to me that they didn't want to adopt me and actually couldn't 'afford' to do it – a joke, considering that all their foster children had brought them riches far outweighing their expenditure on them. I had wondered, at one point, if they would adopt me. I didn't like them but didn't know where else to go. I was very anxious to belong somewhere, even if that somewhere was vile. Deeply rejected, my temper tantrums continued to escalate wildly. Maybe the Stabards feared I would go on trashing the place and, as they got older, I would start to fight back against them? Perhaps I was too much for them to deal with long-term? Whatever it was, it was clear that saying they couldn't afford me was just a feeble excuse – and despite everything, it really hurt. My foster parents' rejection of me made me even more insecure and angry.

Why didn't they want to adopt me? What was wrong with me? If they had had me all those years as a house slave and sex slave, why wasn't I good enough to adopt? Their rejection led me to think more about where I had come from in the first place. Now that I was a teenager, I began to wonder about my birth mother and my own 'roots'. I longed to know more about my family of origin but was absolutely terrified to ask about them. Who would I ask? How would I go about finding out more about them? I couldn't ask the Stabards, who would never have told me the truth anyway and would have just said something insulting about them. I eventually had a chance to ask about my birth mother when a social worker visited the house for a regular check-up. I wrote them a little note in secret and asked for help to find her.

I think the social worker made some enquiries on my behalf, and I was told on a later visit, in a fairly off-hand way, that the trail to my mother had run cold. She was somewhere in London, but no one knew where exactly. However, she'd had more kids after, a couple of boys. So, I had two half-brothers? Wow. They couldn't tell me anything more than that. It was a real shock to think my mother was still alive, still walking the streets, breathing, eating, and living a couple of hours away from me. Did she ever think of me? Did she ever wonder about that little baby she seemed to give up so easily? It made me even more upset to think about being so totally rejected by my own mother. If she hadn't given me up, I wouldn't have ended up at the Stabards and endured sixteen years of hell. I was furious at her for giving me up and enraged at the Stabards – it was all so unfair and confusing. Why was my life like this?

I would go on a rampage when I felt very aggrieved, and things got too much. As usual, I would smash things up, and the Stabards dialled 999 to get me back into the psychiatric hospital. I would be at home, taking it all on the chin, until it got too much and then I would explode and be turfed out of the house and off to the hospital. There I would be drugged up or given ECT and left to stew in a mixed adult ward full of very distressed people until I had calmed down. Nobody would talk to me in the ward – my drugs would just be altered or increased, and I'd lie in bed like a zombie, watching the clock until it was time to leave. Then I'd return to the house, shed, and Stabard's abusive regime. I'd be docile until the anger built up into an unbearable rage and boiled over again. Round and round and in and out, I'd go. I began to feel like I was living in a world of revolving doors. No wonder I was confused and anxious all the time.

Meanwhile, I tried a few more jobs caring for older people in my calmer periods. I went back to the Job Centre every so often, sat in the soulless waiting room, took a ticket, and talked to a bored counter clerk, who usually frowned at my file. Inevitably, they sent me to one old people's home after another. I didn't want to work with older adults, but they kept sending me to those places, probably because it was what I did the first time around on the YTS scheme. Each time I came up against the same problem. The staff would ask me to do some personal hygiene tasks, and I just couldn't. I think the years of being pounced on by Mr Stabard had put me off getting too close to older people for life. Plus, the lack of privacy I had experienced made me very loath to touch someone else 'down there'. Each time I would return to the Stabards to face a beating, humiliation and further purification.

Then, after one of his particularly violent and humiliating 'I'll-teach-you-a-lesson-you-ungrateful-black bitch' sessions (conducted on the landing floor after being pulled upstairs by my hair by an irate Mr Stabard on my return from yet another failed job), something happened. It was something that would escalate my problems with the Stabards in a way I couldn't imagine as I starved and sobbed quietly in the airing cupboard for two days after the brutal rape. It was something that would change my life forever and would, in the short term at least, send me down into further depths of pain, confusion and despair – the likes of which I had never experienced before.

19

BABY BLUES

'It'll be very sad to see the cycle of deprivation repeat itself once again. Jennie is of low IQ, retarded behaviour, lacks any social skills, and she is now a mother.' - Family centre 1988

(NHS psychiatric notes: Dr Brown)

Mrs Stabard had the weirdest habit. If she wanted to know whether I had a period, she would come to the box room and pull my knickers down to look inside them. She'd done this for as long as I could remember, so I was used to this indignity. She wouldn't say a word and just pointed to me to yank my trousers down or dress up, pull down my knickers and peer into them. Or she'd say, 'show me,' and I knew what she meant. She would give me a sanitary towel, just like that, without a word if there were any blood. I was used to her doing this strange degrading ritual and thought nothing of it. I didn't really pay much attention when she started doing it quite a lot. She continually monitored me, watching me with her dead eyes and following me around the house. Now I was on my own with the Stabards; I became very aware of how much she was interested in the condition of my knickers. She seemed desperate to know if there was any blood; when there wasn't, she seemed very grumpy about it. I had no idea why – not at first, anyway.

One day – I must have been eighteen at this time – Mrs Stabard came into the box room early in the morning again and pointed for me to follow her. We went to the toilet together, and she made me wee on a white stick with a little plastic window on one side. She stood behind the toilet door as I did it and said:

'Don't look; pass it to me.'

I had no idea what it was for, but she took the stick away and didn't speak to me again that day. I was used to her quirky ways and didn't think much of it. They never included me in any discussion, so I forgot about the bizarre incident. However, a few days later, the three of us – we made the oddest triangle between us – went to the doctor's surgery together. Mrs Stabard told me beforehand to say I'd found out that I was 'pregnant' – although I wasn't entirely sure what 'pregnant' meant exactly – and that I had to say that a boy I knew had done something bad to me. Because of that, I was to say that I didn't want him involved in the whole business.

When I got to the doctor's surgery, I was very apprehensive. Once we went in to see him, Mrs Stabard talked for me, saying a boy had raped me – I jumped when I heard the word – and that the boy was no good, but that I would keep the baby and the Stabards would look after it. When I heard her say 'the baby,' I totally freaked. What baby? What had any of this got to do with having a baby?

Meanwhile, the doctor asked me to lie on his couch behind some curtains, and he felt my belly. I didn't understand at all what was going on. He asked me to do a urine test, which I was very used to, as I always had urine infections. He tested the urine with another stick and wrote some things down, and my head was buzzing with fear and confusion. All the while, Mrs Stabard talked to him about me over my head, as usual, like it was the most natural thing in the world. There was a total assumption that I would keep 'the baby', and there was no suggestion that it would be got rid of, like in previous times. I was so shocked and remembered getting off the couch, feeling my legs trembling like jelly under me. What on earth was happening to me? What did it all mean? Would they take me to the horrible woman in the big house again? My whole existence was one big question: why, what, who and how?

After that, I felt sick in the mornings. It was nausea similar to when Mr Stabard 'hurt' me, as I often felt ill afterwards, like when they took me to that woman's place.

I felt very woozy, odd and hungry all the time. I noticed my body was changing too. My breasts got bigger – which fascinated him no end – and I got larger all over. I didn't want to get bigger as I already felt I had a weight problem and didn't want to put on any more pounds. They never sent me to a class to understand what was happening to me, so I was full of fear and ignorance.

I must have found out I was pregnant just before Christmas in 1987, as I turned nineteen, and by the New Year, I felt something moving inside me. It was like I was just a body, carrying Mr Stabard's and possibly others' babies (that I would never be able to find out), like it had nothing to do with me. I freaked out more. I had no idea what was happening, and I thought the devil had grown in my belly because I had been so bad. I linked what Mr Stabard had done to me (because I was evil) and the growing lump (which must be evil too). It sounds crazy, but I was terrified of what was growing there and wanted it all gone. I was so scared that I ran away one day. I ran and ran, and then, when I was out of breath, I walked the streets of my market town with its leafy lanes for a very long time, feeling desolate and alone. When I returned in the evening, Mr Stabard was waiting for me. As always, he had drunk a lot. He grabbed me the minute I came through the door and started slapping and hitting me around the head. He didn't kick or punch me in the stomach like usual, but he slapped and hit me on the arms, legs and back.

The next day, when I saw the midwife at the clinic, she asked what my bruises were and how I'd got them, as I had loads by then. I looked like a black and blue punch bag.

Before I could breathe or think what to say, I heard Mrs Stabard pipe up, 'Oh, that's Jennie's ex-boyfriend. He turned up, and she let him in, so he hurt her again.'

The midwife nodded, tutted, and wrote it all down, and I just sat there thinking, 'This is crazy.' I wondered who was crazier, me, the Stabards, or the midwife – why did everyone believe my foster parents when they always lied? The midwife spoke to Mrs Stabard about putting me in a 'safe house' whatever that was, but Mrs Stabard assured her that it wouldn't be necessary as they were there for me. I was sitting there thinking, 'Yes, please. Please take me to a safe house – anywhere away from these dangerous people.' I still didn't know what was moving around inside me. I had no idea a baby moved as it grew, so I sincerely thought I had a devil inside whenever I felt a kick. I had been so brainwashed over the years to think the worst thing possible about myself, so how could I have something inside of me that was actually good? People kept saying I was pregnant, but I didn't understand what that word meant.

At night, I would lie awake, willing the devil inside of me to stop moving; I thought if it were still, I would be less evil. I would watch my stomach moving, like a possessed thing and think something grotesque would burst out of it any minute – a bit like in the film Alien, which I saw a lot later. I thought whatever was inside would break out of me and rip me apart, but I had no idea exactly what it was. It was evil and terrible; that's all I knew. The Stabards had their grand plan, and I was part of it – but definitely not in on it. I heard little bits and pieces of conversation if I listened at the lounge door, and I could tell that Mrs Stabard was quite excited. It was like I was carrying a baby for her – like I was a body for her husband to use to have a baby with – so I, as a person, counted for nothing. I was like an envelope carrying a package for her.

Meanwhile, her husband carried on coming into my room to look at me all the time. He was very fascinated by my breasts, which were now very large, and my belly, and he didn't leave me alone. He kept pestering me at night and wanting to do what he always did, and I didn't want him to, but I couldn't stop him. I felt so ashamed, with the devil inside me, like I'd broken all the rules. I kept very quiet about what was happening to me and hid away in their house. I didn't tell anyone that I was pregnant, not that there was anyone really to tell. I felt very lonely at this time and really missed having Faith to talk to. I wished she had been there – not that we spoke about things in depth, but because we would have gone out to the woods and laughed, or a look would have passed between us, and I would have known that she understood how I felt about the whole thing. I was on medication throughout the pregnancy and still felt very angry. But the worst thing was being completely unprepared for what was going on. I didn't read any books about pregnancy or go to any classes. Nobody told me what to expect or how to handle it all. I had no idea what happened to get the baby out – I was terrified of the whole experience. In all its largeness and unpredictability, I hated my body: I hated not understanding what was going on inside of me. I also hated it being part of him.

I ended up going to the hospital because I had what they called 'pre-eclampsia'. I didn't know what that was, but I didn't feel well. I felt dizzy and strange as if the devil had taken over my whole body and had got a grip on me from the inside out. Then the pain started. It was August 1988, and it was hot, and I was terribly uncomfortable. Mrs Stabard was there the whole time. I didn't ask her to be there; she just was there, like a big blob on a chair, watching me coldly. She wasn't interested in me at all. She just seemed very fixated on what would come out of my body. The pain was agonising, like nothing I'd experienced before, and I was petrified. It went on and on and on, and eventually, the doctor ripped the baby out of what felt like my bottom, and he said I had to have stitches. I didn't know where the stitches were or what they did; I just knew that everything hurt too much and that I was exhausted. I fell asleep immediately afterwards, and when I came round, Mrs Stabard was holding the baby and cooing over it. I couldn't get my head around it. After all that, there was now a baby in the world torn from my body, but somehow it wasn't mine. Mrs Stabard took charge of the situation from the start and tried to control everything.

She accused me of not 'bonding' with the baby from the word go. Bonding? I didn't know what bonding meant! No mother had ever loved me or held me in her arms. I'd never been nurtured and shown care and attention, so how was I supposed to know what to pass on to a newborn? I felt completely at sea and didn't trust the two people who were supposedly looking after me and my baby. All I knew was I felt tearful and exhausted. What on earth had happened to me? How would I be responsible for another human being when I had so little control over my own life? When I got my hands on the baby, I looked down at the perfect little being, which filled me with terror. It was completely dependent on me to look after it. How was I going to do that? I had no idea. I had no money, training, job, security, or proper family behind me. The Stabards didn't want to adopt me. No one had told me what would happen once the baby came out. How was I supposed to look after it?

There was an assumption I'd just know what to do, but I had absolutely no idea. I felt nothing but fear and resentment, holding that little bundle in my arms. How dare this little being come into the world and make me responsible for her? I'd have to protect her all my life. I'd always had to put others first and look after everyone else's needs. And now I had a baby to look after twenty-four hours a day on top of everything else. Would I never be free? For years I'd protected my sisters as much as possible, and now, I had to start again with this one. It all felt too much to bear. Somehow, someone decided the baby would be bottle-fed right from the start. I had milk in my breasts from day one, and as they ballooned bigger and bigger, they hurt like hell. Nobody asked me if I wanted to breastfeed my baby. I didn't know how to or what was involved, but when the nurse came in, she would hand Mrs Stabard a bottle, not me, and she would pick up the baby and feed her.

It felt like Mrs Stabard had told the nurses she would have the baby, and I didn't want her. But that had never been discussed – not with me, anyway. I did feel very confused about the baby, as I didn't understand what I was getting into when I was pregnant, so once she was there, I was overwhelmed. However, she was mine, not Mrs Stabard's and I felt very mixed up about who was doing what. The more Mrs Stabard fussed over her, fed her and cooed at her, the less connected I felt with my daughter. I didn't feel she was mine to pick up, cuddle, or feed. Nobody said, 'Jennie, you hold the baby this way or feed her that way.' I just sat there, watching Mrs Stabard do everything, feeling like I had nothing to do with the situation. I just felt exhausted and very out of it.

It was as if Mrs Stabard did everything she could to keep us apart. She didn't want me to bond with the baby, whom I called Anna Bella, after one of the dolls I wished I'd been able to play with as a child. However, there were moments when I peered at Anna Bella, especially when she was asleep, when I was overwhelmed by the beauty of her little face and eyelashes. I couldn't believe this gorgeous little thing had been tucked away inside me all that time rather than the devil. But my overriding emotion at that time was one of utter helplessness. I was full of mixed feelings and unable to think straight. I think I had a hefty dose of 'baby blues' and felt very detached from Anna Bella. I couldn't tell anyone how I felt because I feared the Stabards would snatch her away if I did, or the doctor would put me back in a mental hospital.

My foster mother played silly games with social services and me, pretending somehow that the baby was hers but expecting me to do most of the care behind the scenes. Once we returned to the house, Mrs Stabard would not let me take Anna Bella for walks in the pram. Instead, she would take her out and push her like her mother. Mrs Stabard wanted the nice bits – the cuddles and the feeds – but she didn't want to change her nappy or have her wake her up at night. I had to do that in my usual servant role. Then when we went to register the baby's name, Mrs Stabard came with me and insisted Anna Bella's surname was Stabard-Brookes and not just my surname, Brookes. I didn't want this to happen, but Mrs Stabard took over filling in the form. It made me even more confused - whose baby was she? When I'd asked them to adopt me, they had said no. But now I had a child; they wanted to put their name on it like it was theirs. Clearly, they didn't want me, but they did want the baby.

Gradually I began to twig that Mrs Stabard saw the baby as hers since it was her husband's – albeit with me. She couldn't talk about it openly or acknowledge it to anyone. It was a twisted situation, but that was the truth. She saw me as a surrogate mother for 'their' baby as if I was just a vehicle to provide them with another one of their own children. I didn't count as a person in my own right. I must be honest and say I didn't know what to think about the baby. They hadn't prepared me for her in the least, and now here she was, needing my attention constantly, so very vulnerable and crying, sleeping, pooping and feeding around the clock. Was this now the end of my youth? Was I ready to be a mother? Did I have what it took? Or would Mrs Stabard take her over from me and be her real mum? Would I be relieved if she did, or would I resist? When Anna Bella cried during the day, Mrs Stabard would be there before I had time to cross the room, picking her up and making me feel inadequate.

Although I had looked after kids all my life when Mrs Stabard dumped them on me, I was not ready for the responsibility of motherhood myself. I was too young, too inexperienced. I needed help to be a good mother, but I didn't want help from the Stabards, who I thought were terrible parents. After all, look how they'd treated my sisters and me! While I'd been in the hospital having the baby, they had taken the bunk bed down, so there was just one bed in my room now, with a Moses basket for Anna Bella. Once we were back home, Mr Stabard started coming into me at night, just like before, as if nothing had changed. Even though I had been through childbirth, had stitches and had a new baby to look after, he would still come in drunk and expect to do his usual stuff with her in the room. I felt sickened by him. My breasts were still hard with milk for the baby, and he would suck them, drinking her milk. I hated him for that. He didn't care that I was sore and exhausted; he just took what he wanted and rolled out of the room. And then the baby would start crying, and I'd get no sleep.

But then, one thing really started worrying me, making me extremely anxious. Mr Stabard started getting very interested in the baby. He wanted to be there when I changed her nappy and would stand there, staring at her for a long time, with his cold blue eyes, and I'd feel very strange. I didn't trust him at all, and I felt he was getting far too keen on her. I didn't know how to keep her safe from him. I didn't want him touching her, yet he would stand over the basket, swaying slightly, licking his lips and drinking in her naked little body. It made me shudder to think what he was working up to. He kept saying, 'Let me hold the baby,' or 'Leave her with me,' but I wouldn't.

Then one evening, I went to the toilet, and when I returned to the box room, I found him holding Anna Bella and trying to take her nappy off for no reason. I grabbed her, which made her cry with shock and lashed out at him.

I felt like a tigress protecting her cub. How dare he touch her! He was revolting, and I didn't want him anywhere near her. I told him to get out and shouted at him, and he slapped my face hard, cutting it with his signet ring. The next day I went to the doctor myself with Anna Bella, showed him the cut on my face and said my boyfriend had come round and had beaten me up – I don't know why I was still protecting the Stabards. I guess I felt too scared of them. The doctor referred me straight away to a local women's refuge, and that very night we moved in. Anna Bella was just three months old. It was a dark, bitter November night. I felt lonely and terrified, taking my little bundle in her navy carrycot to a secret address. As I settled into our new room, I felt like the most unprepared and inexperienced mother of a young baby that had ever been on earth – and I'm sure it showed.

20

TRAINED NARRATIVE

'Mum has rejected her child – says she reminds her of the girl's father who had promised to marry her after the birth but now refuses to do so . . . we are aware of her childhood experiences of abuse. We don't feel it is necessary for Jennie to deal with this.'

(Women's refuge worker's notes)

Despite my best efforts, I wasn't a 'natural' mother. I had no idea what I was doing. I felt awkward and scared, cack-handed and naïve. I resented the baby, especially as I saw him whenever I looked at her. *His* face. She was the spitting image of Mr Stabard, and I hated that she was the result of one of his horrible night attacks. How could I feel anything else? Even so, I felt protective of her. She was just a little baby, after all. There were moments when I looked at her, and my heart would melt, and I would see her little fingers and toes and just want to put my arm around her. It was all very confusing.

However, the refuge was warm, clean and friendly. I was in a room with bunk beds, and for a moment, it filled me with fear that it would be the same regime as at home. Here I was watched all the time, just like at home, but in a different way. At least at the refuge, I could go and sit in the lounge or go to the kitchen (they were out of bounds at the Stabards), but there always seemed to be someone there with a clipboard making notes about what I was doing. I had made a story up which I was sticking to. Mrs Stabard had started it all off with the tale she'd told at the doctors originally about the violent boyfriend who raped me. Not knowing what else to do, I continued the myth of the boyfriend, knowing all the time that the person we were both talking about was the man who was supposed to be my foster father and Mrs Stabard's husband. That seemed very weird, but the doctor, the hospital staff and the refuge people had 'bought' the story, so I continued to sell it.

The truth was that I felt so confused I didn't know which way was up. I had not set out to be a mother at eighteen, but now I was; I had to deal with it. I certainly had never wanted a baby with my foster father, but he had raped me so many times I'd lost count – probably thousands of times. And as I had been having periods for nine years, it was unsurprising that something eventually happened. But now, the outcome of the abuse would be with me for the rest of my life. How on earth was I going to deal with that? The baby tied me to him forever, precisely why Mrs Stabard was trying to get in the way and take over. She wanted to prove I was a stupid, crazy girl who hadn't bonded with her child. Well, in a way, she was right because I hadn't really bonded yet, and I was feeling powerless about how to look after this little thing that was now solely in my hands. I couldn't even look after myself properly, let alone a new baby.

Because Mrs Stabard had done so much for Anna Bella, I wasn't skilled at things once I got to the refuge. They soon noticed. For instance, when I made a cup of coffee, I carried the baby under my arm like a rugby ball while I poured hot water into my mug. They were horrified and sat me down and told me I was doing it all wrong. I was upset; I'd put her under my arm to protect her. But they had to teach me how to hold the baby, cradle her in my arms properly, and then put her down and make my tea. I felt very defensive and embarrassed, worried that people were always having a go at me and making out I was stupid or else making notes about my every move. However, they obviously had a point, and I had to learn the hard way how to do things the right way. I also hadn't been making Anna Bella's bottles up – Mrs Stabard had been doing that. She made me feel like I couldn't begin to get it right, so I left it to her. When I made up Anna Bella's feeds at the refuge, I don't think I did it correctly, so she started to lose weight. The refuge got worried, and social services put the baby on a 'failure to thrive' list, which meant she was in danger. Again, I felt terrible. I was trying to do my best for the poor little thing, but I was probably inept at making her feeds and forgot what to do most of the time. I was still on about thirty daily tablets of antidepressants and antipsychotic drugs, which made me very numb and forgetful. I think they also made it hard for me to be emotionally aware as it felt like I was trapped in a sort of rubber suit all the time, removed from the world.

I'm not sure whether Anna Bella's failure to thrive was due to my not paying her enough attention and being unable to respond to her needs or whether, with so little experience in maternal care, I couldn't make her feel really loved and secure. I just didn't 'read' my daughter's needs and demands very well. I think I also still had the 'baby blues' during the three or four months I was in the refuge, which nobody really picked up on because people already thought of me as 'depressed'. My depression was anger at my situation. If I wasn't a model mother, sometimes it was because I couldn't bear all the responsibility. I'd been looking after children for most of my life, and now I had to look after one that the pregnancy had thrust upon me.

To make matters worse, she didn't feel like mine some days, as she was the product of something so painful. So, in those early days, it was hard not to reject her – at least at first. Yet, despite all this jumble of terribly mixed-up and painful feelings, a new emotion emerged gradually.

I found myself feeling very tender towards my daughter. I began to look at her and saw a sweet little face and gorgeous fingers and toes. I began to want to hold her close, rock and protect her. These feelings came and went alongside the other emotions of annoyance, frustration, and resentment. I didn't want any harm to come to her – not a jot – but I didn't know if I wanted to have her with me for the rest of my life. At the same time, Mrs Stabard started putting pressure on me to come home. She wanted us both back, she said, when in fact, she just wanted the baby back and me to do the work. She would call and beg me down the phone:

'Please come home; we need to see the baby.'

I was bewildered as to what to do. Part of me was pleased to be wanted, even though I knew it was just for the baby, and I felt stupidly tempted. However, I did learn some things from the refuge. Although it was very tough to be responsible for the baby all the time and hold my own amongst total strangers, I did learn more about the world. I watched other mothers with their babies and learned from them. There were many mixed-race and black women with terrible life stories, so I didn't feel entirely alone in that respect. I didn't talk about my history, as I didn't have the words yet. I didn't even know where to start, and I didn't think anyone would believe me anyway. I also didn't trust anyone enough to tell them the truth. It was such a messy tale. Where would I begin if I tried to tell where my baby had really come from? If I finally spoke out, would I be blamed and shamed? I carried the shame for us all, somehow.

Meanwhile, Mr Stabard was sending me messages, through Mrs Stabard, that if I didn't bring Anna Bella home soon, he would cause me considerable trouble. He knew how to pull my strings, even at a distance and after four months, we returned to the Stabards' house. Again, I could have broken free at this point, disappeared from the refuge to somewhere else, far away, and never gone back - but I couldn't imagine doing it then. It's hard to explain what a hold the Stabards had over my mind. The brainwashing I had received for years left me feeling completely in their power. When Mr Stabard threatened me, I felt like I had to comply with what he wanted without question. I imagined he could come and get me from the refuge or steal away the baby I was beginning to bond with, so I felt it was better to go there myself. What a huge mistake I made.

Social services had placed her on a Child Protection Register because she still wasn't putting on much weight, although she was improving slowly. But when I returned, Mr Stabard was more interested in Anna Bella than ever. At first, he was no longer so bothered about me, which was a relief, but he showed a very unhealthy interest in his daughter. He started leering at her in her cot and hanging about, telling me to take her nappy off. He wanted to see her naked all the time. I just wanted to protect her and was frightened I would lose her. I was afraid he would do something to her, and how he kept drooling over her kept stirring up terrible memories in me. It felt like everything was coming to the boil. Mr Stabard's constant pawing at the baby made me so angry that I thought I would burst. I had to keep the lid on my temper; otherwise, I would lose Anna Bella, so I began to feel suicidal like I just wanted to smash myself into pieces. I struggled against these feelings as I knew I couldn't do anything to myself and keep the baby. However, a month after I returned to the Stabards, I took an overdose – only a small one, but enough to get me back into the hospital. It was a desperate cry for help, the only one I knew how to make. They recommended I see a psychiatrist, and I got sucked back into the mental health system. I badly wanted to keep out of it, for Anna Bella's sake, but after the overdose, they took her into care for a few weeks while I recovered. I think they thought the Stabards were too old to look after a baby as they were in their late sixties now, and I was unbelievably relieved.

However, once I returned home with them after a few weeks away and reunited with Anna Bella, Mr Stabard started hanging around again. It made me both sick and furious - how dare he? One afternoon in the spring of 1989, he came up to the box room and hung over the cot, looking down at Anna Bella. I was waiting for the health visitor to come for a check up.

The baby was gaining weight, and he kept asking, 'Are you going to change her nappy?'

I knew he wanted to see her naked body and look at her 'down there' - I feared I knew exactly what he had in mind. I didn't trust him, having seen him with so many children over the years. I remembered the chocolate business starting as far back as I could remember. I had flashbacks of those early days in the shed or the bath when the water turned red, and he would shove the chocolate into me and push it in and out brutally until I was ripped and bleeding. I remembered the creepy bouncing games on his lap and the hard object underneath. I could feel all those times he put his fingers in me and hurt me hard. My life played right in front of me as flashbacks flooded in. I looked at my baby, and I saw red. I launched myself at him. I thumped him and kicked him, and scratched his face. I screamed at him to leave her alone.

'I'm gonna tell everybody what you've been doing to me here. I know what you want to do to her, and I won't let you. Y' hear?'

It was like a major panic attack, as though I had looked over a cliff and seen how far down it was and realised I didn't want to fall. I knew what he would do to her because that's what he did with young children and now perhaps even his own.

I picked her up and held her protectively, repeatedly shouting at him, 'You're not having her!'

I didn't want him anywhere near her. I felt sick, I needed him to get away immediately, so I pushed and kicked him out of the room and barricaded myself in. I could be very violent when unleashed. I was hysterical. I pushed all the furniture I could against the door. I had to protect the baby against him – against him doing to her what he had done to me all my life. I knew I hadn't been the mother I was supposed to be. I wasn't really good enough for Anna Bella. Still, the one thing I knew I had to do was protect her from all the horror of the pain, degradation and humiliation I'd been through in my childhood. I didn't want Stabard to brainwash her into thinking she was evil or had to be 'purified'. I saw the beauty in her. I couldn't bear the idea of her going through all the terror of the constant raping I had been through. It was a nightmare, and I was trying to protect her from becoming another of Mr Stabard's helpless victims.

The next thing I knew, there was banging on the door, and a man's loud voice was shouting:

'Open up, Police.'

I was absolutely terrified. I went over to the window, where I saw the light flashing in the road; there was a police car and an ambulance outside, and paramedics and police were talking to the Stabards. Mr Stabard was talking and pointing up to the box room, shaking his head, and I could imagine all the lies he was telling. He was pointing to his face. I imagined him showing his scratches and saying I was 'crazy' and that I had launched myself at him in an 'unprovoked attack'. My place, as always, was in the wrong. Where else? I was mad and bad. Again, I heard a knock at the door.

'Jennie, open up.'

This time, it was a softer voice of a woman, but not Mrs Stabard. I waited.

'Jennie, you need to let me in. Is the baby okay?'

I looked down at Anna Bella. I held her tight in my arms, and she looked a little scared, or was I imagining it? I thought, 'What shall I do? What's the best?' The voice came again.

'Jennie, listen, we can talk about it … just open the door.'

I couldn't think properly with everyone speaking at me at once, those outside the door and those inside me. My me's were frightened, and some said to me, let them in. Others said they got it; if I didn't, others said don't, we can hide or run to the woods.

The woman eventually persuaded me to open the door. I didn't want to hurt the baby. Reluctantly, I pulled the furniture away from the door with one hand, bit by bit, holding Anna Bella carefully to me in the crook of my other arm. I didn't want to let her go. He might get his filthy mitts on her if I left her for so much as a second. I cautiously opened the door just a crack, and there was a policewoman and a female paramedic. As the door opened, someone pulled it open wide as the policewoman was talking to me. Although I couldn't really understand what she was saying, a paramedic stepped forward and took the baby out of my arms. Meanwhile, another got behind me, and I felt the inevitable sting in my behind. The next thing I knew, nothingness.

21

THE TRUTH WILL OUT

'I can confirm Jennie has a diagnosis of paranoid schizophrenia disorder which renders her unfit to care for the child.'

(Social worker's notes)

When I came around at the hospital, I was very confused. At first, I couldn't work out where I was or what had happened. My first thought was for the baby – where was she? A panic gripped my heart, and I looked around me at my single bed and the psychiatric patients wandering around and pulling their hair, or lying in their beds, moaning and groaning. I couldn't imagine what had happened to her. What had they done with her? My baby! Where is my baby? I tried to get out of bed, but my legs were like rubber, my head hurt, and I felt very woozy and sick. I fell back on the pillows, distraught. What on earth had happened to me? And then I remembered the dreadful scene with the paramedics and the police – but Anna Bella had been with me then...and the paramedic had taken her away. So where was she?

Eventually, a nurse wafted by, and I tried to grab her attention but failed. Then another came and took my pulse and temperature. I demanded to know where my baby was, but the nurse just said she was safe and resting. Confused, I lay back momentarily, staring at the ceiling, but then I was gripped by panic. Was she back with the Stabards? If she was, how could she be safe? I called out for the nurse and tried to get her to tell me where my baby was – and I realised she must be back with them.

...I know exactly what he will be doing. He will be creeping in ...pulling down the blanket and taking off her nappy... and...I just want to scream, shout, and cry to get someone to understand what we are dealing with here.

With a cool expression, the nurse stands over me and makes me take my tablets. There are about thirty pills, and I swallow them, shaking all the while. At this very moment, he might be touching her, hurting her, and I'm stuck in this bed, unable to protect her.

My job, as her mother, is to protect her. I have to look after her; I don't want the same things to happen to her that have happened to me all my life and to every other black child that has got within inches of Mr Stabard. But how can I get someone to understand? When the nurse is gone, I make a plan. No one realises that I am always making plans. I have to double-think everyone always; my me's plan a lot to find the best ways to survive. If I think they want something from me, I give it to them - then they will take me seriously. So I believe, for instance, when the nurse comes up and says, 'Do you hear voices, dear?' I say, 'Yeah, I do. I hear voices.' I think she means, in my head, when no one's talking. But the thing is, I don't hear voices, like the way she says. I just say I do, and then the nurse looks pleased. She goes away and comes back with an injection or more pills, and I sort of feel I am playing the 'pleasing people' game each time just for peace.

As I lie in the hospital, fretting for my baby, I make a plan. I have to get them to understand how desperate I am. I don't want to return to the Stabards, but I also don't want to stay in this mental hospital. I want my baby back and must show them how upset and hurt I am. When nobody is looking, I explain.

You see, you have left my baby with a man who has raped me since I was a baby. That's why I'm here...with you all telling me I'm a mad woman who hears voices. It's not only me who Stabard abused, but countless kids like me. There are my two sisters – one has probably died now, and the other, she's gone off the rails and onto drink, drugs, and boys. Anyway, there's been loads of other kids who could tell you about my foster father. He likes having sex with kids, you see. And I'm worried he's going to start on my daughter.

By the way, did you realise my daughter is his, too? No, it's not the product of me and some boy I picked up, as it says in my notes. No, it's actually the product of a rape by my wonderful foster father.

All this is going through my head. These are the 'voices'. The truth. How can I say it? Who will listen to me? My me's, and I know the truth. Who will believe me? I take an overdose – as I have done several times and will go on to do many more times – because I want someone to listen. But, I am sorry to say, it has the opposite effect. Instead, you increase my drugs. And I'm given ECT, which eliminates my mind, my memory. And so I am back to square one. Another square one; another purification of sorts...

I spent much time determining if he had done something to the baby. My memory disappeared sometimes, and I couldn't recall what I had done - I would forget days. Sometimes I would look at her and feel detached. I would tell the nurse that I sometimes smacked my baby because I lost my memory, like when Mr Stabard hurt me. I thought I must have turned into him as why couldn't I remember. It didn't matter how much I tried to remember - my daughter would be asleep in her cot; but how did I get her there? I was a remote control that many people pressed different buttons that muddled me. My head always hurt as it was in a constant tangle working out the games these people played and what was happening to my baby and me. It was so heavy to carry, and knowing nobody would want to listen to me, I had no choice but to carry it, or my me's carried some for me.

Her little face would remind me of his, and I wouldn't want to look at her. Then I would think, 'That's not fair. She's my baby – it's not her fault they made me have her.' Then I would remember to pick her up and cuddle her. That's what mummies are supposed to do, aren't they? I would stroke her hair, ensure I had washed her, and feed her a bottle. I would enjoy that as we sang and read stories together, and so would she. Sometimes I would look at her and wonder how I would cope with motherhood. How was I going to protect her? And then, against my will, I was sent back to the Stabards with loads of pills and instructions to be grateful that I had a home with good foster parents and had to learn to control my temper. I was just someone who heard voices and had a bad temper - the bad girl. The new medication made me feel paralysed, frozen, and unable to move my face or body. Taking it meant walking around, feeling like a zombie.

Back at the Stabards, I was fearful and tense. Mrs Stabard kept trying to take over the baby again. I would have just gotten used to looking after her independently and feeling more comfortable about the whole thing. Then she'd swipe the baby away and feed or take her out in the pram without telling me. And then I'd come into the box room and find her husband hovering over the cot, lifting the blanket and peering at Anna Bella with that leering, drooling look I knew only too well. He would sneer at me and give me a look that said, 'I'll get her; you just wait, black bitch,' then I'd want to kill him. I'd rush in, shove him out of the way, and grab her out of the cot, and she would cry, startled awake by my fear. I'd hold her close, feeling desperate, not knowing how to get through all this and get her away from these people.

One night I greatly feared what he might do to her and me. I was lying awake in the box room, and she was in her cot. I must have nodded off and came to with him swaying over the cot. I jumped out of bed and shouted at him to get away. I was terrified. He tried to grab me then, and I fought him off. It was terrible, a real tussle in the middle of the night, with the baby screaming in the background. She must have been about six months then. I dressed, grabbed her, and took a load of pills before leaving the house. It was all I could think of to do in my warped, fearful way of thinking. Then we went out into the night. I pushed her in her buggy, and I've never felt more desperate as I walked along in the early morning hours. I wanted to fall and sleep forever but kept pushing the buggy until she calmed down. I walked into the centre of town – it must have been about three in the morning – and a police car drew up alongside us. They asked me what I was doing, and I said I was taking the baby for a walk...but that I'd taken some tablets.

They put us both in the car and took us back to the local general hospital. I had my stomach pumped yet again, and we were back in a mother-and-baby unit. The social worker was sitting there when I came around, with the curtains closed around the bed. In a kind voice, she asked me why I was taking my baby for a walk at night, having downed a load of tablets. Didn't I know how dangerous it was, putting us both at risk? While she was talking, she put her hand over mine. I looked at her face – it was kind, she looked nice – and I finally found the words:

'He hurts me.'

She looked at me and didn't say anything at first. She squeezed my hand.

'What do you mean?'

'I've got to protect her from him.'

She looked worried then and leant forward towards me.

'Does he do something he shouldn't?'

I nodded. Hot tears started scalding down my cheeks. I couldn't stop them. I nodded and sobbed. I'd held it back for so long, but now I couldn't keep it in anymore.

'I don't want something to happen to Anna Bella.'

The social worker wrote something down.

'Can you take her into care?'

She looked up at me, surprised.

'Why Jennie?'

I couldn't explain that I didn't feel confident enough to look after her myself or be able to protect her from him, and at the same time, I knew I didn't want her to be at the Stabards. I was in such a state I didn't know what was possible and what wasn't. I felt relieved that the truth was finally out but scared about what would happen as a consequence. I remembered the horrible Mr Venetti and the beating after the Raj and Prathi meeting. If Mr Stabard knew I'd told on him, he'd kill me.

As it was, nobody did anything. Amazingly, although this social worker told me she believed me, she did nothing. I didn't know if I was relieved or not. Sometimes I wanted him punished; other times, I was relieved nothing had worsened. I felt alone in the world and scared about what would happen if it all came out in the open. I was confused that the police didn't arrest him and no one asked me to do anything. Like before, the hospital and social services kept sending me back to the Stabards.

It was 1989 when I finally spoke up about the Stabards, and it was written down on my record – as I have read it since – but nothing was set in motion to change anything. Mr Stabard wasn't arrested or questioned. Both of the Stabards were given an award shortly afterwards by the local authority for thirty years of service as a foster father. They were in the local papers, receiving his award, smiling at the camera. The church praised him, and he was cheered by the British Legion. People patted him on the back, toasted him with wine and beer and said what a great job the Stabards had done for all those poor, disadvantaged, black and disabled children that nobody else wanted.

Meanwhile, I bounced in and out of the mental hospital, swallowing pills and desperately trying to keep my daughter out of his clutches. I had begun telling the truth about Mr Stabard. Still, no one believed me, so they made me feel. No one did anything, which made me think, 'What was the point of saying anything when social services will still send us back to live with them?' A pattern emerged during the first year of Anna Bella's life. I would return to the Stabards, and he would sniff around the baby, so I would do something desperate, like an overdose. Then the Stabards would call the police, a doctor would section me, and Anna Bella would be left behind with them. Of course, this would make me even more desperate and likely to do something self-destructive. Sometimes Anna Bella would be taken into another foster home for a while, which would make me feel relieved, but I would miss her so much that I would ask for her back. It was a terrible trap. Everybody seemed to think I was 'crazy' and a threat to the Stabards, the baby and myself. I think I was behaving crazily, too, as I didn't know what else to do. Every time I tried to get some attention – the only way I knew how – the Stabards would call the police, and I'd end up back inside the hospital. Everyone would look at me and say I was an unfit mother, paranoid and 'schizo'. These words echoed what the Stabards had told me all my life about being evil. I felt everyone thought I was the problem, and no one understood why I had the difficulties I did. I had no power, no voice, and nobody was listening to me. I would see the psychiatrist, usually a man in a suit or a white coat, who would come around and ask me things. He would never say, 'Tell me what it's like at home?' Instead, it was all about whether I heard voices or not. I wanted to scream at him, 'You don't understand what's happened to me,' but where would I start?

After a few months, the council finally offered me a flat in the town, and I moved in with Anna Bella. At first, it was great. We were in our own little place, and I began learning to look after my daughter properly. I started to feel very fond of her and loved holding her, watching her smile, and responding to things. I wasn't always a good mother, though. I was sometimes forgetful as the drugs slowed my responses, or I missed days. Sometimes I put her on the bed, and she rolled off, and once I put her in a bath for a few seconds when it was too hot. I didn't mean to, but I did make mistakes. If the social worker saw or heard about it, there would be a flurry of people coming around and observing me, asking me questions and telling me off. They always wrote on their clipboards.

I had to go to a day centre, so they could watch me and make sure I learned to do things properly. All that was fine, as I knew I needed to learn how to be a good mother, and I wanted to be one. But no one had told me that they had given Mr Stabard a key to our flat since, somehow, they believed that he still had some connection with me despite my telling of his abuse. One night, I woke up to find him standing in our bedroom, leaning over the bed where I was sleeping with Anna Bella next to me. I screamed out. The baby woke up and started screaming too. He'd let himself in while we were asleep, he tried to grasp the baby and grab at my breasts, and I had to kick and punch him off. He eventually left, swearing at me and saying he'd kill me. I was shaking like a leaf and no longer felt safe in the flat. In the end, I took some tablets to calm myself down, put Anna Bella in the pushchair and started walking around the town – again in the early morning hours. I just wanted the tablets to numb me, to blank out the panic and the fear.

I went to a park I knew and sat on the bench. It was pitch black, and I could see the calming stars and moon. Somehow it reminded me of Wildflower Woods, of being in the soft embrace of nature. I felt safer and more serene when trees and grass surrounded me. It was cold, but I didn't care. I could breathe out here. Our little haven of a flat was no longer safe, as Mr Stabard had access to it. He could let himself in and do things to us anytime – and I could do absolutely nothing about it. He could rape and kill us, and no one would even know. As I sat on the bench, hearing the wind whispering in the trees above and watching Anna Bella sleep, all snuggled up in her buggy, it came to me, in a flash, that I would never be free of the Stabards. I realised I could never escape this man who had ruined my life. The only thing I could do was save my daughter's life. Somehow, I had to keep her free of him. It didn't matter what happened to me now - but it did matter what happened to her. I had to keep him off her, even if I used desperate measures. When a policeman eventually found us, I was nearly unconscious, but she was fast asleep. He took us to the local hospital. I told them I had felt like hitting the baby, and so they took her into care. It was the only way I could protect her – tell them the lies that they could understand. No one was doing anything to help when I told them the truth – so lying was my only real option. In a mad world, I had to do mad things for us to survive.

22

SUCKED INTO THE SYSTEM

'Jennie now clearly likes her daughter and is physically close to her. Anna Bella likes to snuggle into Jennie when she is tired or upset and will always look to check that Jennie is close by. She recognises her voice and footsteps and will giggle and coo freely at Jennie. There is good eye contact, Jennie will smile and talk and responds to her demands, comes prepared with nappies and clothes and takes pride in her achievements and appearance.'

(Social worker's report)

I was my own worst enemy. My strategy for getting people to take me seriously was acting out against my best interests. I often felt so frustrated, so pent-up with fury and powerlessness that I felt I had to do desperate things to get people to take me at my word. I didn't feel like I had ever been listened to properly. Instead, people had labelled me *'crazy'*, which was how people saw me: that and all those other nasty words: ugly, fat, stupid, wog. Now I had begun to admit to one social worker a little bit about what was happening at home; I frequently started having horrific nightmares and flashbacks. It was like opening Pandora's Box – everything began to fly out. I kept seeing Mr Stabard's face all the time; that horrible, overbearing, staring face coming at me in the dark. It was like he was a Bogey Man, and he half-scared me to death. I couldn't bear to have the light off at night. I was like a child myself.

However, after a year of yo-yo-ing in and out of the hospital, back to the Stabards, out to a flat, back to a hospital, and then to new accommodation or a women's refuge, I had begun to bond with my daughter. I'd made terrible mistakes in the first few months and battled many emotions. Becoming a mother was a steep learning curve, but I was much more comfortable in my new role when Anna Bella was nearing her first birthday. I still had many obstacles to overcome. I had no job, no money and was very dependent on others. I had very few skills besides the obvious ones of cooking and cleaning, as I used to do for the Stabards. My education was limited, and I had no idea what I could do. I'd also had so little exposure to normal life that I found it difficult to imagine how I would make my way in the world, earning a living, running a flat, making friends, having a social life or (God forbid) a sex life. I depended on doctors, hospitals and social workers and lived on handouts. I had no idea what it would be like to be truly independent and able to make choices for myself and my lovely daughter.

During this first year of Anna Bella's life, I would become depressed and suicidal every time I returned to the Stabards or had any contact with them. Then, when I was alone, I would be anxious that he might find us and break in as he had done to my safe haven flat. Or days would go by and I wouldn't see anyone other than the baby, and I would begin to feel claustrophobic. I wasn't coping well, but I also didn't trust anyone and was very isolated. I missed my sisters very much at this time and wished they had been there to share the baby with me. We would have had fun going out to the woods together. I would have loved to have had some of our riotous birthday celebrations and dances under the moon with Anna Bella and her two 'aunties'. They were the only two people in the whole world who, I felt, understood me in any way at all. Only they had been through the Stabard life – if you could call it that – and only they would know what a hellish existence it had been. They understood what had made me like I was – no one else did.

I was unprepared for life, and when I panicked, I would want Social Services to take the baby and put her with a proper family. Then I would worry – what if they were just like the Stabards? Could I trust that any foster parents treat children well? After all, the council had just awarded the Stabards a huge prize despite all the pain they had subjected their foster children to. Then I would fear the social workers would trick me and send Anna Bella back to the Stabards, despite me asking them not to. It was a terrifying time. I must have seemed mad to those in authority as I often changed my mind. I just didn't know what was right, what I should do, or which way to turn. I wanted a kind parent or nice understanding person to tell me, 'Jennie, do this, then it will all be fine,' just like the good fairy in the Cinderella story, I needed someone to guide me, to help us. Only I didn't know if I could trust anyone; or even if anyone in the world was actually trustworthy. The other thing, which didn't do me any favours, was that I had become quite addicted to the hospital. Not to the horrible mental hospital – which I never liked - but to the ordinary local hospital, where they had nice clean sheets, cooked your food and took the worry off my shoulders. It was like I was looking for a good family to look after me.

I developed a terrible habit of overdosing to get into the hospital for a respite from the Stabards (when we ended up back there) or from struggling on my own in a soulless flat. I'm not proud of owning up to this part, but I also got hooked on the idea of taking tablets, particularly as they numbed out all feelings for a while. It was a relief to take them, perhaps like an alcoholic feels relief when they get drunk and disappear into oblivion. When I took an overdose, it was a desperate cry for help. I seldom took enough for it to be potentially fatal, although I did once or twice when I really meant it. Mostly I was saying to the authorities, 'Help, I can't cope. I need someone to listen to me.' It was the only way I could think of to get attention for our plight.

Of course, taking pills backfired – badly. A council social worker decided to campaign to relieve me of my role as Anna Bella's mother. To be fair to this woman, Margaret Vallelly, she was doing what she thought was best. She was new to my case, and when she saw my notes and met me, she obviously thought she had to protect the child first and foremost - from me. I must have seemed completely out of control, and she didn't like me at all. I didn't like her either. She always looked at me like I was something the dog brought in, and she didn't think I was a capable mother. My prescribed drugs bombed me out so much that I must have seemed a bit slow and zombie-like.

However, I did love my daughter, and by the time she was a year old, I was beginning to get real enjoyment out of being with her. Every day she was doing new things, and I felt proud. She had finally put on enough weight and was sitting up, crawling, and now trying to stand up. I was amazed to see how she was becoming a real little character, and she also looked very lovely, with deep brown chocolate eyes and a sweet little face. She had dark curls and was becoming a toddler in front of my eyes, a real little girl with her own personality. I felt I had gotten past the shock of the beginning of her life and that we were now moving forward together.

By the time Anna Bella was nearing three years of age, two major things were happening. First, Margaret Vallelly decided to end the situation for good by insisting that Anna Bella be adopted. Secondly, I was assigned a new psychiatrist, a woman from outside the area, in a new post, who had a completely different view of my case. These two things happening simultaneously would set things on a collision course, as the social worker would want to take Anna Bella away from me while the psychiatrist felt she should stay with me. All the time, I was being sucked further into the system, and people who still knew nothing about the truth of the situation was deciding on the future for my daughter and myself. Worse, in the social worker's case, she was not interested in what had happened to me. After all, there were already notes on file about my accusations of abuse, which had sat there for years without anyone doing anything about them. Margaret Vallelly was only interested in the child. In her view, I was a bad, mad mother, and my daughter would be much happier with a steady, happy home elsewhere. She may never have said this to me directly, but everything she did, from the moment she started the job in 1991, was focused on taking my daughter away from me.

In the interval, something extraordinary was happening with the new psychiatrist, Jacqueline Brown. When I first met her, she struck me with the fact that she was very different from all the others. She was a woman in her late twenties (most of the others had been men in their fifties or older), and she was quite stern and brisk in her manner. Dr Brown was straight-talking and straight-dealing, and she didn't beat around the bush. She told me, in no uncertain terms, that I had to stop messing about with overdoses. It was like she sussed me out immediately, which was quite unnerving. I think she could see that something was making me take the pills as a cry for help – although I wasn't telling her (or anyone else) why I was doing it all the time. She was very direct and told me I had to shape up. I had to play ball with her if I wanted to keep my daughter. At first, I was furious. Here was another person telling me what to do. How dare she! I felt – wrongly, as it turned out – that she didn't understand what was going on with me. In actual fact, Dr Brown turned out to be my biggest ally and my greatest saviour. She looked through my case notes afresh and began noticing things no one else had noticed. She saw something obvious that everyone else had studiously ignored. Dr Brown noticed that I had spoken about abuse years earlier to a social worker – and yet I was being sent back to the same foster father who I said had abused me. Why was that? Why indeed? Dr Brown began to ask difficult questions and gave me some advice to help my case.

She explained that if I wanted to keep my daughter and not let her be adopted, I would have to prove that I could look after her well. To do that, I would have to stop taking overdoses, and I would have to get off my medication. Dr Brown said she thought the drugs weren't helping me

- she even thought they were making me worse. Too right! All they did was make my mind feel like porridge which someone had left out to go soggy in the rain. Why on earth was she the first person – the only person – to question my treatment? However, the path was not clear, and it was going to be long and winding. It was not like I could do what she wanted overnight. My reaction and overreaction cycle was hardwired, and it would take me a very long time to trust her enough to take her sound advice. This is where I was my own worst enemy.

Meanwhile, I received a letter telling me that the council was now vigorously pursuing a 'freeing order' to leave the path clear for them to have my daughter adopted. It was almost as if at the very moment when I was beginning to straighten up, with someone fighting on my side, the council was pressing ahead to snatch my daughter away. I couldn't believe it, and it sent me into a tailspin. I decided I wanted to fight with Dr Brown's help, but what I didn't realise, or calculate well enough, was how much power the authorities would have when they set their minds on doing something like taking a child away from its mother– especially if they deemed her both bad and mad. I also didn't realise how difficult it would be to clean up my act. Each shock wave about imminent adoption would panic me, making me want to overdose as a desperate protest. I felt like I was being sucked further into the system with every day that passed.

23

SAD FAREWELLS

'Jennie has a history of depressive illness and deliberate self-harm...at least partly as a result of adverse experiences in her foster home.

Both mother and daughter are bonding very well - Jennie's daughter looks for her when she is out of sight, and they sit together for hours, playing with art and reading.'

(Psychiatric report by Dr Brown)

Instead, I rushed it, and in doing so, I pushed them all away. I'd scared them off, making me feel even more distraught. At the time, I knew the authorities were closing in on Anna Bella and me. Living alone, I hadn't coped very well and had been in and out of the hospital like a yo-yo. I had gotten into a downward spiral, and although Dr

Brown kept warning me, I had to resist acting that way. I didn't seem to be able to do what I needed to do. It was a bit like cutting myself – which I was still doing. When the urge to hurt me was upon me, resisting was challenging because it gave me such a feeling of release. I managed all the masses of confused feelings roaring around inside of me by cutting myself, running away, or opening a bottle of pills. I needed some release, so these had to do as I had no other outlet. A couple of times, I'd said, 'I'm going to kill myself', which sounds incredibly self-indulgent, given that I had a child in tow. But I can't convey how desperate and alone I felt all the time, like the walls of the world were closing in on me, and I couldn't cope. Of course, I was very aware of my daughter's situation, but I also felt the enormous pressure of meeting her needs every minute of every day. I had no partner to talk to or family to back me up; everything always came down to me. I still missed my sisters terribly, and the Stabards rejected me, so I was back to where I started, or so it seemed.

By 1992, when Anna Bella was four and I was twenty-four, the council had followed Margaret Vallelly's lead and was pushing hard for a 'separation order' – in other words, they were trying hard to separate me from my daughter. Most days, Anna Bella and I tried to get to the day centre to give the day structure. I was also determined to learn more life skills, like handling money and filling in forms. At the same time, I was terrified I might lose my daughter, and then I'd have nothing left to live for. My mental health record was being used against me constantly, even though Dr Brown and my social worker, Gus, were trying to support me. Gus continued to try to put me in touch with my black roots, but I was wary.

I knew that doctors had labelled me 'paranoid' many years ago. Yet, the people from Social Services increased my paranoia all the time. I knew Margaret Vallelly was trying to get Anna Bella away from me – whenever I met her, she was openly hostile and constantly scrutinised me. Someone with a clipboard always seemed to be scribbling down what I was doing right or, more likely, what I was doing wrong. I remember Anna Bella falling over and grazing her knee, and I bent over, hugged her to me, and looked at her knee. The social worker in the day centre told me I was smothering her and she should learn to toughen up. She said, 'It's only a little graze, don't pick her up.' It was all very odd because when Anna Bella had fallen over and cried another time, they told me to pick her up and not ignore her! I couldn't get it right, and I knew they were always writing down stuff about me and my parenting skills (or lack thereof) and discussing me behind my back. I might be paranoid, but I had something to be paranoid about. They were still talking about me, not to me, and they did want to take my daughter away. So I wasn't that crazy – I was right.

Even though Dr Brown would tell them that I was now well-bonded with Anna Bella and my mothering skills were coming on, Social Services were determined to see me as a mad, bad mother. It was like a war, and I had to keep fighting, but sometimes I would get so tired that I would begin to flag. Mainly I was on my own in the fight, then someone like Gus, my social worker, would come on board and fight alongside me for a while, but then get tired and give up or be moved on, and I would be on my own again. Another example of how they tried to make out I was not functioning was the mind games they would play on me to test me out – which I know sounds a bit paranoid, but I think it is true. For instance, if I were to meet with a social worker at ten in the morning, I would get there at ten, but they would call my mobile at nine-thirty, saying that I was late. If I mentioned I thought the meeting was at ten like we agreed, they always looked at me like, 'Well, she's mad; what does she know? She would get the time wrong.' I felt they were trying to trip me up and trick me, and it would all go down on my record.

If I spoke up for myself and argued with them, I was being 'difficult' or 'stroppy', 'uncooperative' and even 'aggressive'. Social Services were against me every inch of the way. They always said I had a 'low IQ' and 'poor mothering skills. Even though they knew I was petrified to go home to the Stabards, as I was scared for Anna Bella's safety there, they always supported the Stabards against me. After all, they had appointed the Stabards as foster parents in the first place, so they had to defend them, even though I had made the abuse accusation. So Social Services saw the Stabards as the only possibility. I wanted to do anything in my power to stop Mr Stabard from doing to my daughter what he had done to me, so I protested as much as I could. Social Services said they'd continue to pursue legal adoption regardless as the only solution.

Eventually, the authorities sent me back to live with the Stabards, to my absolute horror. I hated it back there and was miserable being stuck in the dingy box room with Anna Bella again. At least we weren't shoved in the shed together. Around this time, Mr Stabard had to go away for a while, and I was amazed at how different things were. Mrs Stabard remained as remote as ever from me but very friendly and sweet with Anna Bella. We rubbed along together without much friction. I became more stable with him far away and enjoyed motherhood much more. I particularly relaxed because I knew he wouldn't appear at my bedside in the middle of the night, and I didn't have to watch over Anna Bella twenty-four hours a day. I could actually get some sleep, and my daughter could rest easily. It was noted, even reluctantly, by Social Services that the stability of my situation had improved. My mothering skills were better than ever. Out of my window, I prayed to the stars and moon at night that he would never return. If things had continued like that, it might have been okay. But it wasn't meant to be, and after a few months, Mr Stabard returned home, and my heart sank as I heard his hated voice again in the hallway. There was eventually a major crisis when Anna Bella was about four and a half. The authorities had never noticed that Mr Stabard had a drinking problem, and if they saw, they turned a blind eye. He was drunk again every night and regularly rolling into my room. I hardly slept, as I had to be vigilant all the time. He made it crystal clear to me that he wasn't interested in me anymore and that it was time for Anna Bella to take my place. I had already noticed a disturbing change in her behaviour. I feared that something had already happened to her, somehow, as she began to scream when I used to change her nappy. I had no idea why she would let out this high-pitched shriek. There were a couple of times Mrs Stabard had taken her out for a walk in the buggy, and I wondered if that had given him a chance to get his hands on her, in some way, when I was out of sight. I always tried to protect her, but he was very sneaky. He had never put Anna Bella in the shed or bathed her – I had been very careful to keep her close to me – but there were odd times when he must have had access to her when Mrs Stabard had charge of her without me around. I was terrified that something had already happened, especially when the screaming started like that.

She was now around the same age as I was when he started hurting me. I dreaded what he got up to when I wasn't there (such as when the doctor had me shut up in the mental hospital). All I knew was he was utterly untrustworthy and unscrupulous and had no respect for anything or anyone – even his own flesh and blood. He just wanted to have what he wanted and when he wanted it, especially when drunk. He even drank first thing in the morning these days, so he was drunk much of the time. The man was a beast, and it made me so furious we were stuck there with him that I could hardly breathe when he was near us. One night he staggered into our room as usual, at about two in the morning, while Anna Bella was fast asleep in the little child's bed, they had gotten for her. She looked like a beautiful fallen angel, with long, dark curls spread out on her pillow. I must have dropped off because I suddenly woke and found him swaying over her, pulling down her blanket. He was staring intently at her, with his drooling, leering look, and I leapt out of bed and rushed over to him. I tried to pick her up, but he aggressively pushed me out of the way. I knew he wanted her all to himself to satisfy his sick urges. I wouldn't allow him to hurt my daughter the way he'd hurt me, so I grabbed some clothes and started to put them on, thinking we had to get out of there, fast.

He remained focused on Anna Bella, who was awake now and looked scared. I was rushing round the room, trying to find her clothes, my bag and stuffing things in desperately, trying to get out of there. Mr Stabard, intent on having Anna Bella, stooped over the bed and started pulling her pyjamas down. I leapt on his back, pulled him off, and tussled. I was fierce and full of fury, and as I pushed past him, I threw him against the wall, grabbed Anna Bella and my things, and rushed us out of the room. He was slow on his feet, as he was quite old now and very drunk, and I made it down the stairs before he got to us. I carried on putting on my coat as I lifted Anna Bella into her buggy, covered her up and rushed out of the house.

A telephone box was round the corner; I found some coins and phoned the emergency services. I told them I was hitting my daughter and that I might harm her. I said I couldn't cope with her and I might even kill her. I didn't know what else to do. I think it was the first thing that came to my mind. I was so scared of Mr Stabard. I knew that the authorities always believed him over me, and the only thing I could do was sacrifice myself for her safety. I knew that if the police arrived and I said he was trying to hurt her, they would recognise the address and my name and remember all those times the Stabards had called the police to take me away to the mental hospital. They'd had me sectioned from that house, and I was labelled schizophrenic, psychotic, depressed and paranoid. Why would the police believe me now over them? In my twisted, panicky logic, it was the only thing I could think of to get Anna Bella away from Mr Stabard – which sadly meant getting her away from me, too.

Suddenly, I saw the police car and ambulance arriving, their lights flashing. It must have been about three in the morning by then. They took my little girl away, having checked her over for cuts and bruises, and I felt relieved she was going with the police to somewhere safe. I saw her little face disappear into a car, and I felt terrified I might lose her, but I had to protect her. Seeing her go was such a wrench, but I was more scared for her safety than anything else I could think of. I certainly didn't care about myself. I believed, in my heart, that the authorities would never take a baby away from its mother, especially if that mother showed signs of progress. So I thought that she would be with me soon after that.

However, that night I went home, after the police had taken my daughter away, Mr Stabard came into my room – it must have now been about four in the morning – and he raped me with such violence, hatred and brutality, it is a wonder that I am still alive. He had drunk even more after the police had dealt with me, out on the street, and when I came back, he slapped and punched me, knocking a tooth out. I was bleeding from the mouth, and he was utterly furious with me. He couldn't have my child, so he took his anger out on me. He kicked me in the face and punched and slapped me all over my body. After he raped me, I was a bleeding, blubbering wreck, but I felt, at least for tonight, I had saved my daughter from the grasp of this perverted and sick man.

After this, I took a major overdose and ended up again in the hospital. I was at my wits' end, but at least I knew my daughter was away from the Stabards. I was terrified that despite everything I'd done to protect her, he might have already found a way to hurt her, and I was terrified of how it might affect her. What I didn't understand at that time was how far things were proceeding with social services and how successful the hostile Margaret Vallelly had been in turning the circumstances against me. Even though Dr Brown was writing positive things about me, social services put Anna Bella out to a foster family – not the Stabards, thank God – and I felt reassured for a little while that I had done the right thing. But then I found out, to my horror that the authorities had sent Anna Bella to another faraway city. I was distraught. I thought she would be with a temporary foster family (a loving and kind one), and I would see her soon. Social services told me I could visit her, yet every time we set a date; it would somehow be cancelled, rearranged and then cancelled again.

I thought it would be for a few days, a week, or weeks, but six months passed, and I had not seen my daughter. All that time, I was in a mental hospital. I took repeated overdoses as an act of desperation, trying to bring attention to my terrible situation. Unfortunately, the doctor increased my drugs, although Dr Brown had been trying to get them down to a lower level. As they told me, they sectioned me for my 'own safety', and I had more ECT. I just wanted to see my daughter and missed her terribly. Anna Bella was usually with me every day, and we had our little games and songs we played. I missed her sweet smile, little voice, and enjoyment of everyday things. I loved her smell and having warm hugs with her. Now she was gone, and I couldn't find out how to get her back. I felt utterly desperate, and the authorities told me I should get a solicitor, which I did. However, I didn't know how to deal with any legal things. The social workers who tried to be on my side, like Gus, helped me do this, but we were up against the might of the system. Meanwhile, Dr Brown would keep telling me that if I wanted to get my daughter back, I'd have to stop trying to hurt myself. I would try, but then the feelings would take me over. I would feel distraught, lonely, and completely despairing, and I'd trot out of the hospital and get myself some pills, and then wham, I was back at stage one, yet again. Eventually, the doctor discharged me, and I was re-housed in a flat in my town; but I couldn't settle down there. I missed my daughter all the time. I wanted to know how I could get her back and how we could start again together. Life felt completely empty. I felt very suicidal all the time and was fighting against the urge to slash myself and overdose. It was the only way I knew how to make myself heard.

I was also very lonely in the flat, as I missed the company of being in the hospital. Also, once Mr Stabard got the news that I was out (they would always give the Stabards my address), he'd be around, ringing the doorbell, following me around. He would try his best to intimidate me because he wanted to keep me quiet. During the summer of 1992, I finally discovered that social services had found new prospective parents for Anna Bella in the faraway city where a family fostered her and that the council were finally getting her adopted, against my wishes. It was going to court to be finalised, even though Dr Brown wrote a powerful report supporting me as

Anna Bella's mother. She thought I was progressing and that taking my child away was the wrong time. I think she knew it would destabilise me further, and I was trying to get myself together then. However, even that couldn't stop the process Margaret Vallelly had started. The law would force me to give my daughter to strangers who lived hundreds of miles away.

On the morning of the court hearing, I was getting ready to go, with a very heavy heart, when a nurse came into me and told me there was some more bad news. She sat me on a chair and told me Mrs Stabard was dead. I couldn't understand what they meant. Dead? The nurse nodded. She had gone to stay with her eldest daughter and suffered from pain in her leg. She had gotten out of bed and collapsed from a heart attack due to thrombosis, a blood clot stuck in her heart. I felt my blood run cold and was very sad indeed. As much as Mrs Stabard had never loved me, I had always hoped she would, and I cared very much for her. I loved her. I sat, and the tears started and I felt desolate. This news pushed me to a new level of desperation and despair. Mrs Stabard was gone - really gone. I couldn't take it in properly.

Meanwhile, they wanted to take Anna Bella that very day, and she had become my only reason for living. She was now five, and we loved each other deeply. She was my little angel, my beauty and the thing I got up for in the morning. All I had done was try to protect her from Mr Stabard, and in the end, everything backfired on me.

Ultimately, the council won their case, and I did attend court and give a statement. And the course of our lives – that of my dear daughter and I – were forever changed. I was soon taken to a 'Goodbye Meeting' where I was to see the new parents – a very nice, if strict, African couple – in the city where Anna Bella now lived. It was heartbreaking, and I could barely breathe as I sat on a train (my first train journey ever) with a social worker. How could I say goodbye to my little angel? I loved and wanted to be with her, but all the forces were against us, so I had to give her up. The social worker kept telling me that it was 'for her own good' and that I was 'selfless and sensible', but my heart was breaking into little pieces the whole way there. How could anyone love my baby as much as I did? I had cared for her, looked after her, loved her, and knew her so well – surely it was best for her to be with me, even though I had my problems to overcome? Dr Brown thought I would manage with the proper support - but no one was willing to give me a chance. That was how the system worked.

Once we arrived, I sat in a cold waiting room for a long time, desperate to see my daughter. The social worker told me they had told Anna Bella not to call me 'mummy' any more. She had to call me 'Jennie' instead. All these rules and regulations! I had a five-year-old whom I loved to pieces and who loved me. I wanted to look after her – I just needed some support to do so. Then a social worker called me into a room. It was a horrible, ugly, grey meeting

room with a table in the middle and chairs all around. Five
council workers were already there, and another came in
carrying my beautiful girl in a new set of clothes I didn't
recognise. I hadn't seen her for over six months, and she'd
already changed a lot. She put her little arms out to me,
calling 'Mummeeee', and I put mine out to her, and we
hugged - it was a long, sweet hug. But as soon as she did
and I could feel her clinging on, the social worker pulled
her away. This was our 'goodbye'. Anna Bella looked
distressed, and I wanted to cry but bit my lip.

The new parents were standing in the doorway; a
black couple dressed very smartly in expensive clothes. I
had been told by my social worker what I could say and
what I couldn't say. They even told me not to cry or hug
her. I had made a little photo album, but they wouldn't
let me give it to Anna Bella because I wouldn't include
a picture of the Stabards. I had to give one small photo
of myself instead. That was all I was allowed. I could see
that Anna Bella was confused and upset by everything
happening. She looked at me for reassurance, and I smiled
and held out my hand. She held her hand out to me, but
the social worker pulled her away, and our fingers didn't
touch again. I felt my heart rip further – I loved her to
pieces, I loved her so much, and I could see her being
carried across the room and handed to the woman in the
dark suit, who now held her firmly in her arms. The black
adoptive parents nodded to me, serious-faced, but never

smiled or spoke. And then they turned, and the whole party was gone.

My daughter was gone. I slumped onto a seat, and tears streamed down my face. I was desolate. Empty. Afraid. The pain was so severe that I thought I'd stopped breathing. Those last little glimpses of her ringlets, her dewy, chocolatey eyes, and her dimpled cheeks were all I would have to sustain me for the next fifteen years. Distraught, I pulled a crumpled photo from my pocket and stroked my little Anna Bella. I clasped the picture to my heart which was breaking into a million shattered fragments. This event was simply the beginning of the end of my whole world.

24

FREEFALL

'You have judged Jennie unfit to care for her child, and I would confirm that her shortcomings in this respect are related to her mental health...'

(Consultant psychiatrist's letter
to the social worker)

'... I believe Jennie would grow into a good mother given the right level of support...she needs another chance to live in the community with her child... both mother and child have a good bond.'

(Dr Brown's report to the social worker)

I stayed in touch with my social workers. Dr Brown never gave up on me, but I gave up on her. It was part of the anger and powerlessness I felt inside.

Over a period of time, I tried to challenge the adoption and constantly fought to see my daughter. The authorities made me feel I was a bad influence on her life and would only upset things. Anna Bella was getting further and further out of my reach like she was drifting out to the open sea on a raft. I felt like I would never see her again, and it killed me inside. Meanwhile, I was encouraged to take a case against my foster father. With the help of Dr Brown, my accusations were finally being taken seriously by at least a couple of people in the system. Although social services had known about it for years, Dr Brown was the only one moving things along, stirring things up. However, I was mostly out of control and unable to cope with life. I didn't have a reason to keep going. I couldn't and didn't know how to live for myself. I've always been a mum unable to function; I was now entirely in the hands of the mental health system, having given up the fight to improve my own life. For so long, I had tried to get away and survive, but I had reached a point where I couldn't deal with all that had happened to me anymore, and I just wanted to lie down and die. I felt broken down: broken on the wheel of my life. I had a phantom pregnancy in which my stomach grew, and I had morning sickness, but it was grief for the loss of my daughter.

A few days later, I was awake late at night in my flat when the doorbell rang. I got up and pushed the button to hear who was down there at that time – it was about three in the morning. I heard a familiar slur, a drunken gravelly voice, and I knew it was him.

'You fuckin' black bitch, you're not gonna beat me. Y'hear, y' bitch?'

I start shaking, hearing his voice. Somehow, he'd already tracked me down. His friend worked in local housing and must have given him my address.

'Go away', I shout. 'Go away, leave me alone.'

He shouts crude, revolting things down the intercom, telling me how he'd kill me and smash my face if I proceeded with the case. After that, it went quiet, and it became apparent that he'd staggered off. But him knowing where I was had shattered my peace.

The next day I phoned Ray, one of my social workers, and eventually, the authorities moved me to another address. But it was all too much. I took another overdose, ended up in the hospital, and the destructive cycle started again. Round and round I went, overdosing, trying to jump off bridges, feeling like there was nowhere to put me in this world where everything was full of pain, and I had nowhere to belong. Then I heard the news. Gus tried to break it to me gently. The authorities would drop the case due to a 'lack of evidence'. He told me they needed other foster children to come forward and corroborate my story. Mr Stabard got the last laugh. I'd let Raj and Prathi down, and now it'd all come full circle – they'd let me down. If only I knew where Hope was. She'd be able to back up my story. But my two dear sisters, who went through it all with me, couldn't endure the pain in the end. One was dead, and nobody cared. The other had gone off the rails, and still, no one cared. We were just dispensable. We, kids, were thrown on the scrap heap, and no one seemed to be able to do anything about it. No one would ever know what our foster father got up to behind his white-painted front door and nice, neat front lounge.

Social services had let Mr Stabard off; he wouldn't face the music or be brought to book. Where is the justice in that? It was too much to bear, and more overdoses followed and more silent screams in the night where I'd rail against the moon. The psychiatric system repeatedly rescued me; a couple of times, I nearly didn't return at all. From the age of twenty-four to thirty-six, I spent most of my time as an inpatient, going in and out of the system. I probably attempted suicide over a hundred times. They sectioned me endlessly, sometimes for months or a whole year. I probably had twenty loads of ECT and enough pills to sink a battleship. I became dependent on the system and on the system's view of me as bad and mad. I never really got over losing my darling daughter or the mess around the adoption. I still think, to this day, that authorities poorly handled it and that the only lone voice in the wilderness was Dr Brown, who kept trying to explain to people that there was more to this case than met the eye. All the time I was in and out of hospitals, I also had Mr Stabard threatening me in person or sending his family to do his job – tracking me down every time I moved, following me, harassing me whenever the hospital let me out into the community. It carried on until the day he died. He was terrified that I would tell on him, and tragically, no one ever held him accountable. As far as I know, he died peacefully in his bed of old age. Indeed, the community believed he was a stalwart citizen, and the church and social services upheld him as a solid family man and great foster parent to the very end. Since every child harmed by him was either black or Asian, their protests simply didn't seem to count. Enoch Powell was right; There were 'rivers of blood', but those rivers were made of the blood of the children who nobody loved and nobody thought had any rights – the black dispossessed, the kids who didn't belong, the lonely, scared and unloved kids who were just like me.

After many years of seeking negative support from people who never cared about me, I knew if I were to go it alone in the frightening wild world, I would have surely died, as I had nobody to encourage me, nobody to give me that needed hug or smile of reassurance. I had to again work with myself and my me's, plotting for some normality. After many years of fighting mental health services and not getting hurt by the organised abuse ring, I was kind of thrown out of the system as I was helping myself. They and I, in many ways, had come to a dead end.

Services found me a group home with the same kind of pattern as a hospital but with more independence - they thought they were teaching me how to cook, yet I was cooking daily from being an infant. Support workers would accompany us into town as they watched us choose the product for cooking. I hated the constant watching; I felt I had to spruce these outings up. I would dart around the corner and lose my support worker as I heard them calling my name, watching them dart back and forth, asking if anyone had seen me. Then I'd sneak off and use some of the money to buy a cake and observe them as I munched through a delicious pastry. When they (I allowed them to find me) found me, I would be humiliated in front of everyone in the supermarket; 'Jennie, you are naughty; we thought you were better than this,' they'd say, spitting as they said it. I stood there without eye contact and switched off into my deeper being; my me's - until I returned to the group home and was told off again by the group home's manager. They'd say I'd let many people down as we wouldn't have time to cook and that we had to order takeaways. I can honestly say nobody felt let down as they actually thanked me as we tucked into our takeaways.

I grew bored of this mundane existence and wanted more after a few months of being in the home. I was allowed five hours of free time to do as I pleased. On one occasion, I saw an advert regarding a cook for £6.75 an hour. I was an expert in cooking; the hours would work within my free time, so I applied. By the Grace of God, I got the job - I wasn't the best at communicating and hadn't any references.

I had been working at this place for a few weeks when I met my son's dad. He was very familiar, but I didn't know why, and he asked me out. I never really knew about dating as such, but I agreed, and we met at his. I remember how I had got pregnant; my head was planning as he sat there talking to me. I could have a baby if it stopped me from being lonely. We slept together. I was physically sick and petrified; I couldn't breathe - the same feeling as when those men hurt me. After it was over, I said I had to go, and three months later, a doctor declared that I was pregnant. I had a life inside me that I wanted. I began to have hope as I spent time silently planning our lives.

I had nothing more to do with Sam's dad as he wasn't a very nice person. The authorities moved me from the group home to a bedsit, and all eyes were on me. I wasn't allowed to handle my money. I had to request everything, like the bigger underwear I needed and go into the local maternity shop with my male social worker to buy my items. They even brought Sam's clothes, and lilac overdosed everything as they believed it was a calming colour. They painted my bedsit this colour and Sam's bedding this colour.

One evening while still heavily pregnant, there was a knock on the door; a doorstep loan person asked if I would be interested in a loan. It appealed as I could go out and choose my own stuff then; all they needed was proof that I had money coming in. Again, I silently planned what I would use this money (gold) for. I had a meeting that week with social workers, family centre staff, health visitors and mental health workers all in my bedsit, so I thought I would paint it the brightest orange I could find. I brought a yellow and grey romper suit for the baby and a little teddy and hid the rest for our needs when and if I wanted to spend again. I loved bright colours, and my room looked lovely. I felt proud of myself. Then I brought a tea set and teapot to give my visitors tea in pretty cups. I even brought a tray, so I could carry the drinks to them as they discussed me, without, as usual, input from me. I was just the subject there.

Then the meeting began. The social walked into my bedsit, and her face turned red like a squashed tomato as I handed her a cup of tea in a beautiful teacup. She was literally shaking; I didn't say a thing but kept an eye on her in case she dropped my teacups. The social worker was still red and shaking as my cup rolled around on the saucer. She didn't even say, 'Jennie, you've done a great job; your place looks lovely.'

Her words were, 'again, you've disappointed us - all the hard work we've put in to make your home nice, and you take it upon yourself to decorate and spend money on needless items. Why Jennie?'

She threw me a question she didn't even allow me to answer. It was another professional who did because she always thought she knew best. Then the cups went down on the tray, and the tea wasn't even drunk, rejected because I chose to spend. I stood near the tiny kitchenette, opened a packet of fancy biscuits, and enjoyed each as they talked about me.

I gave birth to my second living child on a hot July day, with social workers and nurses all waiting, I believe, to see me reject my son. I knew it was a boy due to authority attending appointments with me and wanting to know, regardless of what I wanted. 'Jennie, it's a boy', they'd tell me at meeting after meeting, fearing I would reject him due to being abused by men and by having a boy, I wouldn't cope. Sam's dad saw Sam a few times after he was born and gave us a dog to keep us safe.

Sam as a boy, was funny and always entertaining; he would always find a way of cheering a dark situation up. I taught Sam that regardless of what we went through, we could cry and get angry - but we also had to laugh and joke about something. His little angel-like voice singing yellow bird and his honesty sometimes came at the most embarrassing moments, like when a young lady on the bus had a hair on her chin. Sam just wouldn't let it go 'but mummy, she has a beard.' I tried to distract even telling him not to comment on others as it's sometimes uncomfortable for people to be spoken about with an audience, but no, Sam saw what he saw, and Sam taught me the value of life and the impact of being a mother. The joys and tribulations were like I was the richest woman in the world, yet the scariest.

I took Sam and his friend Alfie to the park to fly a kite wearing this horrendous wig. I thought I looked like the other black people, not realising I had the wig the wrong way as I was suffering from alopecia. The wig kept slipping to the side, and then suddenly, my wig got caught in the kite string; up went the kite with my wig; as I was shouting, 'catch my wig, boys, catch my wig!' All three of us sat on the bench laughing our heads off at what must have looked like to passers-by complete madness. At night I would read him a story, and we would always add a couple of sentences each to end the story the way we wanted. Then tell each other 'love you to the top of the sky and back.'

Sam loved buses, and in each town we lived in, he charmed bus drivers by waving to them. Each time we got on, he would insist on handing the money over and then tell the driver, with a big cheeky smile, he would be a bus driver when he grew up.

Although Mr Stabard had died, the abuse rings lived on and in time, the perpetrators tracked us down. Due to our lifestyle, running away from the torturing abusers, we lost many friends as they didn't understand our lives (how could they if they hadn't lived it), and they slowly disappeared. Especially Christian friends, as some saw me as this mad deluded woman who fantasised about being in danger; even when they saw the bruises, they still didn't want to believe and definitely didn't grasp the risk that we were in as a few people from our local church wanted to invite those who hurt to a meeting to discuss why and welcome them to the fold. There's no way I could allow them to do that. It would put Sam and me in more danger; they weren't friendly people, and although they may pretend they were to deceive others, the consequences for us would be terrible. I'm ninety-nine per cent sure the perpetrators wouldn't dare hurt anyone else; it was us they were after. They continued due to the lack of understanding from the public, so we were at most times on our own. We did have a family who was our rock, a Christian family who allowed us to reside at theirs; even though we never understood fully, they accepted us as part of their family. To this day, we have a strong friendship with the family.

Each morning, and believe me, it was early morning, Sam would wake up, run into my room, jump into my bed and chat away. Sam's bubbly personality began changing as the perpetrators exposed him to these brutal attacks. Each time I tried to protect him - we had to flee. I did go to the police, but they just saw me as a mad person asking me if I had been taking my meds or referring me to mental health services. We needed somebody to take note, see our bruises and help keep us safe. I agreed to mental input twice during these attacks on us; each time, they either sectioned me and put Sam in care or left us to the ring. Sam struggled in care, so I promised my me's that we wouldn't seek help again as we belonged together. He was my son, and I was his mum. I know my pain of having to choose to lie and put my child into care. The pain and guilt every day are too much. All we wanted was for the authorities to protect and believe us. In the many schools Sam had to go to, each time not fitting in broke him. It was too late to find a new home for him. I knew firsthand he wouldn't have been given the right support as a mum, you know, deep down, the right/wrong path for your children. Even though I felt immense guilt, I did the right thing with Sam, as with my daughter. I knew I had to escape each time they found us.

From a very young age to today, if Sam wanted to achieve something like driving lessons, a new job, or passing exams, he would put his all into it. When he turned sixteen, Sam wanted to drive. I worked a minimum wage, and Sam was at music tech college, so money was tight. Sam watched lessons on driving and spent hours reviewing theory and learning how to drive. Within three weeks, Sam booked his driving theory, and on the day of the theory, he came up trumps and passed with two mistakes. Next, he took two driving lessons and went for his test again and passed. That's Sam's character - he knows what he wants and works hard to achieve it.

The sad thing is we hadn't anyone we could phone or tell. It was just between Sam and me... even though we knew people, they saw us as small achievers and always compared other children with their own. I knew this wasn't the right way to encourage our children; Sam was happy with his dream job, and I, as his mum, was as proud as punch.

As a single mum and not having anyone to confide in the ups and downs of being a parent, I made some bad mistakes. One of the biggest was about Sam's dad. I told Sam a massive lie, that Sam's dad and I were in love (I was with him, he wasn't with me) and that he wanted to keep us safe by leaving us. Again, this was true, but when Sam asked to see his dad, I pretended it was someone else as I didn't know where he was. He disappeared, and I wanted Sam to see that there were some good people around. This lie almost destroyed our relationship. Nobody can keep a lie going, as well as the destruction and pain this lie caused Sam. He felt betrayed as he felt so guilty about why his dad left; he thought it was his fault. The biggest thing I learnt from this is that the truth, regardless of how painful it is, is better than a lie that penetrates the person's soul you've lied to. I'm so sorry, Sam, for this, and I can only promise this will never happen again. You are so deserving.

I wanted my babies, yet I had to sacrifice a lot to keep them as safe as possible; most of the time, I never thought things through and acted impulsively. My duty was to look after them or find the best solution, so they were cared for. In that way, I made many mistakes, damaging my children and moving, never realising how this would impact them as adults. The guilt I carry is heartbreaking; literally, it breaks my heart. I messed up as a mother, not deliberately, but that's not good enough because it has damaged them differently. My son is so confused about the meaning of life compared to what he has experienced. No child should have ever gone through what he did. That's when I would say I had no right to have a child until I knew there was safety. The results are devastating otherwise. Don't get me wrong, Sam is my heartbeat, and I wouldn't change having him for the world. But he has endured unmeasurable pain.

You may be asking why these people would still come and hurt you after all these years. It wasn't the same people who hurt me as a child; these were people who joined this evil abuse ring. It's like drug gangs; they continue with a new leader each time. Paedophile rings are no different over time, just new handlers. I really believe they used my son and me to test us for resilience in a kind of experimental way, as why didn't they just kill us the many opportunities they had? The kicking, rapes, beatings over the years and the acid attacks. Why keep it going? If they were scared, I would speak; they could have ended it. Neo-Nazis come to mind.

Also, remembering the Roots programme, they played to us repeatedly and how they whipped us and treated us like dogs. The games they played were all very similar to those played by the power of these rings, running, chasing - in other words, hunting us down for the adrenaline this would give them. Like fox hunting, they were beasts after innocent creatures, and that's the same game they played with us. At the parties, there were the fancy dresses, the liquor and cigars and the money wheel spinning tables. We stood dressed up and plastered with makeup; some wore wigs of their choosing as we stood in corners. The game had massive stakes at play, and the prisoners were us. If someone were to escape, they would be brought back and throttled in front of us just enough for them to pass out.

Meanwhile, they sat with their small glasses of liquor and what looked like salt crystals that they lay on the table and sniffed or burnt in silver foil. Their eyes widened, and their personalities changed as they gambled with us and drank and used drugs. They became the wild beast walking around to us children, groping some of us, hitting and kicking if we were weak and cried or whimpered. At times we could be mistaken that some children had died. I believe this wasn't the case. My fractured memory is emerging together. I remember so much more again about these powerful elites and their workers. The fractured memory can be useful for them because it never makes sense when relaying what happened to you. Parts of me carry different parts of the trauma. If those parts were too scared or didn't know how to say anything, there would be great big holes in what I disclosed, the forgotten bits, missing bits - feeling there is a literal hole in you. There are many holes, as nothing makes sense, but they don't want it to, as they would have to change the course of the game. I dread to think what that would have been like!

When we spoke with professionals, it sounded complete nonsense, fabricated nonsense. Yet you knew it wasn't, and it would cause us so much fear because we would question ourselves how could this happen if there wasn't this, or how could that have come about? It's called

Disassociation DID. Part of you becomes fragmented to be able to survive. We become different parts; some are essential (most caregivers give to their children), but children like us must form our own salvation. The parts of you who went through the trauma and survived it change who you are in personality; some parts of you become scared; some become the leader, the informer, the ones who carry the pain of the trauma, the ones who witness things, the ones who are silent, the one who fights back, the one who manipulates, the one who steals and the one who lies to survive. The ones who have been older than their years, ones who mimic adults, become the parent, the nurse, the teacher, the boss, the lookout. This is necessary for a child to survive the trauma and neglect they suffer at the hands of their caregivers. It then becomes very difficult to change those ways of survival because childhood is our primitive years, and what we learn as children help to steer us into adulthood. Suppose caregivers haven't given us the right tools and only picked up the ones we have had to provide ourselves with; it completely sabotages our growth in the real world. It is like being born on a desert island until adulthood and finding yourself in the city as an adult. It's overwhelmingly fearful, especially if those around you have never believed you. You are like a trapped animal falling over yourself, trying to determine what is going on. Your fragmented parts become more significant as you try to navigate a new life/situation. Getting it totally wrong by misjudging situations and being paranoid of people's motives makes us isolated like we were as children, alienated again because we are different. Professionals are even too scared to help us, so we, at times, can become re-victimised by society.

Those men and women who abused and got involved, whether through ferrying us around or abusing us, had a role to play, and they did it well. Each person was able to break a child so much that the child would become completely dependent on them; we would also accept abuse as a way we thought at the time was their love for us. You starve a child so much from their essentials like love, guidance and acceptance; any ounce of a drop that resembled our needs would be lapped up. Again, it was just how they wanted it. The outside world was happy with them because of their brainwashing us. So how could I have been rescued? It wouldn't have been through escape, as when we got older, there were many opportunities to escape...but if someone could have seen me as worthy and get to know me (it would take time), the trust would be paramount for me to have left and never feel a need to return. I also needed to be told the things they were doing were wrong and had to have it explained why it was wrong by showing me the opposite of their ways. I would have needed a caregiver to give me fun things to do relevant to a child and their age at the time. If someone had prised me away from them, it could possibly have killed me as my brainwashed duty was to be a victim of abuse, or the consequences would be far too great.

25

HANDED AN OLIVE BRANCH

'Jennie shows no sign of mental illness...her symptoms and behaviour is a result of adverse experiences in her foster home...to this end, there are no doubts that Jennie has been sexually abused.'

(Dr Brown's report)

Schizophrenic. Psychotic. Depressive. Paranoid. How often did I hear those labels attached to me? I was mad, crazy, Jennie, always out of control. I was 'difficult' and had temper tantrums, which was proof enough for them. I know now that I owe my life and my gradual recovery to the efforts of Dr Brown. She completely re-examined all my case notes (and helped me get them from the NHS eventually) and who was the only psychiatrist out of the dozens that I saw over the years who finally twigged that my behaviour had something to do with the abuse

I suffered as a child and the other terrible experiences I'd been through as an adult. She was a beacon, a leading light, the only one to believe me. It is to her that I owe everything now that my life is finally turning around.

Firstly, Dr Brown believed I was traumatised by the rape and inhuman, racist treatment I had experienced at the hands of the Stabards. Hence most of my 'symptoms', including the flashbacks where I'd 'hear voices', were down to me having an acute case of post-traumatic stress disorder. All my erratic behaviour, anger, fear and accompanying symptoms were explainable. In Dr Brown's view, I was not mad; I was distressed, not bad; I was traumatised. With the rapes, beatings, racist humiliations, starvation and other obscene punishments being part of my daily life, why was Dr Brown the only psychiatrist to be able to see her way through the maze of other people's dismissive reports? Partly, it was because she came to my case with fresh, unbiased eyes. Also, she saw me as a human being – a woman struggling with a mountain of terrible feelings – rather than someone who was inherently crazy. When Anna Bella was adopted, Dr Brown believed I was on the brink of becoming a good mother. She thought it was a tragedy that social services snatched my child away just as I began improving under her guidance.

In the realms of notes about my case, Dr Brown is a lone voice, arguing against the accepted idea that I am just beyond help. She writes things like *'...I feel she might be able to cope with looking after her daughter provided there is an appropriate backup.'* She also notes that the *'Social Services team is very hostile'.* Most importantly, when Anna Bella is finally wrenched away from me, Dr Brown's notes make it clear that I am experiencing *'reactive depression'* and I am *'bereaved, like any normal mother who has lost her child.'* Of course, I have lost not only my daughter but also my only little bit of family – my sisters and Mrs Stabard (whom I loved, regardless of her faults). There was clearly a lot to feel traumatised and bereaved about.

Dr Brown was brave enough to go against the grain. She was tough; she told me repeatedly to stop overdosing, and I often ran away in protest. But when I returned and asked her to take me under her wing again, she generously agreed. Unlike any other health practitioner I met, she believed the drugs were increasing my aggression and paranoia. She also thought they stopped me from coping rather than helping me cope. Together, we worked on a long-term programme whereby I had to give up the drugs slowly (because there were lots of them at high dosages). Eventually, I learned to live with feeling my feelings properly again. It was as if the doctors had me drugged for so long that I had no idea who I was underneath it all. I had been so 'zombified' that I had to learn to taste things again, to feel and touch and to start smelling and seeing the world as it really was. It was obviously a slow process, and I fell at many hurdles, but I eventually got there. After a long battle, I finally ditched my medication in 2004. I was able to start taking charge of my life for the very first time for myself with a new clear head.

It meant I could start slowly but surely moving into the community. After a period of being in a halfway house, I decided the best thing was to consider moving to another part of the country. Whenever I saw people in my hometown, like Andrea, Rina, or other extended family members, it was always very awkward. The most important step in my move towards having my life back was when I had a brief relationship and got pregnant again – I decided to have the child. This time it was my decision, and I had my wonderful son, Sam.

Since Sam's birth, I gained a lot of strength; I think I needed someone to care for, to keep me carrying on through life. Once I'd moved away, I kept in contact with Dr Brown, who was always encouraging and helpful. I learnt to manage my own life, raising my son and trying to live as normally as possible. I kicked the habit of reaching for the pills when in despair, and I have tried hard to live an ordinary life of a mum who got her child to school on time and paid the bills. It's not been easy, and I have had many false starts, but I feel proud I have gone it alone at last. Everything is down to me, but I have much joy and fun with my son. He did well at school, and I am lucky to have finally established my own little family. Isn't that what life is all about?

Every year I light a candle on Anna Bella's birthday and tell Sam that somewhere he has a lovely sister who is simply gorgeous and that someday we will all be together as a proper family. I have spent many long nights wondering if she is still with her adoptive parents and whether she remembers me at all. I tried to see her, but unfortunately, the adoptive parents cut me off. Perhaps they feared what I might bring to their family life as a 'mad, bad woman'. Oddly, about three years ago, I woke up almost choking and feeling great fear that something had happened to my daughter. My feelings convinced me she was hurt, but I had no way of checking, so I just had to try to forget about it as life went on.

In my darkest hours, I continue to wish for a family, a place to belong, for someone to love me and to have someone to love (apart from my gorgeous son, of course). I have not been able to form romantic relationships very easily, as I have felt it too painful to be vulnerable with someone else. I'm unsure if I know yet what healthy love is – let alone sex. However, I have slowly formed friendships with both men and women. Although it is a painful process for me, as I find it hard to trust and disclose things about myself, I am gradually learning how to do all those social things that I never got a chance to do earlier in life. Luckily, I have a wicked sense of humour, and that takes me a long way. My first job I enjoyed was working for mental health as a support worker. Then I went on to work as a manager at a charity helping those with mental health by setting up discussion groups, working alongside the NHS in setting up a community event revamping an old psychiatric ward and waiting room where I won 'inspirational woman of the year.' I worked for a charity helping deprived communities build healthier neighbourhoods. I set up art groups at weekends and holidays when most people who suffer from mental health are at their lowest.

This is my second book; I wrote the first with very little info regarding organised abuse and dissociation. So again, I felt compelled to write the whole truth for the same reasons as almost ten years ago - highlighting the long-term effects of abuse on children. In relating my own experiences, I might help bring someone else's terrible suffering to an end. We, as a society, have reacted against the threat of child abuse by putting up barriers between people. Today there are so many restrictions on the closeness between children and adults working with young people it can feel like walking across a minefield. I find it devastating that teachers are no longer allowed to cuddle a child in their care, even if they're hurt or upset. What are we saying to children when we make rules like this? Do we believe outlawing caring human contact will stop paedophiles from hurting children? The problem with this sort of legislation is that people come to believe that their children are protected; that the laws mean that nothing bad can happen to them. I know from bitter experience that this is not the case.

It breaks my heart to think that child abuse still occurs in the twenty-first century. Even with all the new technology and communication methods we've developed, children still aren't being heard. Instead of relying too much on legislation, we must work together to create a safe environment for our young people. We must learn to stop and listen to what our children say, see how they behave, and not be too quick to label them as troublemakers without discovering what might be causing their 'bad' behaviour. We must spend time with them – really get to know them – so if they are ever hurt or frightened, they'll know they have someone to talk to, someone they can trust and someone they know cares.

By telling my story, I want to open people's eyes to the suffering of thousands of angry young people who have slipped through the net. Our prisons, secure units, children's homes and psychiatric hospitals have been full of abused and confused people for years. It has got to stop before more troubled people have their lives wasted. Every day, we read in the papers about youngsters killing and killed in our streets. These youths often don't know how to deal with their feelings of hostility and a sense of being on the margins. Some end up in gangs, where they get a sense of respect and belonging – until someone crosses them or looks at them the 'wrong way'. All it takes is a tiny trigger for their insecurities to come flooding back. Then, in a moment of madness, lives are destroyed forever.

Now's the time for us to start asking difficult questions. Who loves these kids? What makes them go wrong? And how can we help them choose a different path? We all have a collective responsibility to provide more for all our young people – especially the angry, confused ones. They desperately need youth centres, walk-in clinics, training and incentive programmes. But they need someone to listen to them and take their problems seriously most of all. We look at our children and worry about the future, wondering if things will improve for their generation. It's up to us all to ensure it does, and no child ever has to suffer in silence. If children live in an atmosphere of praise, stability, love and understanding, they have the chance to grow up into successful adults who have a real feeling of esteem and self-worth. Sadly, without this start, they are much more likely to manifest anger, bitterness, resentment and self-loathing.

We also need to extend the same concern and support towards adults who have been victims of childhood abuse in the past. We need to help them to take back control over their own lives. It means acknowledging that while their memories will always be there, we can try to take away their power to cast a shadow over their lives.

I spent so much of my life being angry – towards my foster parents, Social Services, and mostly myself. I found it hard to let people get close to me, and even when I did, I'd keep testing them to see if they really did care about me. It became a vicious circle where I'd push away anyone trying to help me. When I read reports of young people acting out, I understand what they're going through. Like me, they're just doing their best to survive any way they can. The bottom line is that everyone needs someone

– especially the so-called 'problem kids.' We are all a product of the environment we grew up in, and it's up to all of us to offer encouragement and a sympathetic ear to the next generation.

I hope that this book will make people sit up and think about the society we're living in and their own relationship with their children. I also hope it might contribute to a change in 'the system' for the better. Most importantly, to offer comfort to abuse victims and inspire others who may be suffering in silence to come forward and seek help.

26

SAMUEL

I was around three when I remembered someone breaking into our flat and screaming my mum's name. 'Where is the crazy B?' they would shout. Wherever we moved, Mum would always prepare me for this and find a hiding place I would go to if anything happened, like a perpetrator breaking in and hurting her.

I was too late to hide in the place on this occasion and crawled under the bed. I saw them hurt her by kicking and punching her. I was stuck. I couldn't help as I was stuck with fear. I never understood why this happened each time. We'd take the suitcase, which we never emptied and leave the place, moving to a new home or, at times sleeping on park benches. Mum used to sing to me until she thought I was asleep then I heard her cry; it was a painful cry. The same pattern went on for years. They would find us - either they would follow us from school or shopping and watch us in their cars outside our homes. Mum never told anyone what was really happening, not even me, as she carried this on her own. People used to think she was crazy, a bad mother who just uprooted her child for the sake of it, even having meetings on how they could stop her from moving. As an adult, I can understand why she never asked for help.

Occasionally when there was a threat of me going into care due to them badly beating up mum, she would say it was an uncle or brother of hers who was after her (which we knew, or my mum did as aunts and uncles, and those proclaim they were doing God's work). Aunts and uncles are what the foster family asked mum to call some of the people who abused, as well as brothers from church. After hurting mum, they spat on her like she was rubbish each time. How would the services understand the full story when Mum did call the police or someone felt they needed to? After seeing her injuries, the police mocked my mum again and made out she was crazy, so each time, in each town and school, we carried this secret and were so alone. We moved again; this time, mum knew she had to risk making friends for my sake. We had a few people around us who didn't get us, but cared for us (to be honest, how could someone get our life? It was bizarre.

I went on trips, even camping with the local church. We knew the risk this had, but mum wanted me to be a child and experience good things. We had so many laughs together; mum taught me that regardless of how painful life is, we have to be able to laugh. She would arrange holidays to Butlins in secret names - the laughter there was amazing; we were silly and danced at the nightclubs, we rode the trike bikes - well, I rode while mum pretended to be the queen. One time I was going so fast that I lost control of the bike and nearly knocked over a housekeeper carrying a whole load of laundry; the laundry went up in the air as she dodged the bike. Both my mum and I roared with laughter. Another time at Christmas, a neighbour had lost her husband, and mum wanted to cheer her up. We emptied our big dustbin on wheels. Then mum decorated up and got her music player with Christmas music and a chair with flashing Christmas lights and made me dress up as Father Christmas, and she dressed as a fairy. The neighbour lived up a slope; mum stood on the chair while I held the wheelie bin as she lowered herself in it and told me to push her up the hill; I must add she wasn't a thin mum. She switched on the cassette player, and with the fairy lights on her head, holding her fairy wand, I pushed her. But also with a sack of presents for the neighbour and her disabled son. When we got to her house and knocked on the door, the neighbour rolled around with laughter, and then a few other neighbours came out with their pennies thinking we were from the sally army. When told we weren't, they were not pleased and couldn't see the funny side of it. I got my mum back as I managed to turn the bin on its side with her in it and rolled it down the hill while the lights were flashing, and all you could hear was, 'get me out!' We couldn't stop laughing; that was my mum always cheering up people who were struggling.

The effects of witnessing others hurting my mum began to take its toll on me mentally. I felt angry and lost and blamed myself, and I still do for being unable to stop them. I overeat to comfort myself, as it's my control; everything else is out of my control. When I was an eight-year-old boy, some women forced my mum to give me to them as they said she wasn't a good mum. Those two women abused and raped me. For years, I never told anyone, not even mum, as I felt dirty, ashamed, and blamed myself. I didn't understand what happened but knew it was dirty, shameful, and bloody hurt. I even thought at the time until recently that mum knew somehow, yet she didn't. My mind played tricks on me, even believing I wasn't really her child but possibly her dead sister. I was lost and didn't have anyone to talk to as when we did seek help, people had their own ideas about what help this would be.

I never really fit in at school either and used to truant often. I'd go home to make sure mum was okay. The church told me I was the man of the house and I should look after mum; this was such a heavy burden on me. The church people used to drum into my very being my responsibility, so when I couldn't protect mum, the guilt ate at me. I felt like a failure. I hated my very being because mum got hurt, and I couldn't stop it. People can and have caused so much pain, not purposely, but by wanting to hide the fact we were abuse survivors; they felt so ashamed of us being this that they tried everything to try and cleanse us of our past, even burning mums' files and most photos of my sister because it belongs to a sinful part of our past. Why couldn't they just accept us as us? Then we could have found solace and learned life from the acceptance of others. But no, they never taught; they just controlled us so they could clone us to be like them. Then there was the cheek when they felt upset by us not being the guinea pigs. They wanted to cast out the devil in us because of being abused. They never understood why we didn't pray against abuse, but it was like the word, and those who had gone through it had to be cleansed by man before we could ever resemble what they saw as an equal. I began to loathe church and religious people.

My mind sometimes becomes splintered; other times, it is clear as day about what happened to me. I began to run away from school and couldn't concentrate on schoolwork even though I did well with exams. I helped at the local church with the sound, which helped me sometimes block out my pain. I remember I went on a school trip to a farm for a week. It was the longest I had been away from mum. I was, and I know she was also scared of me going due to the danger this could have for me. It was not because she didn't want me to enjoy myself; it was that the people who had spent years hunting us down could follow me. However, they wouldn't because they were cowards and were secretive and sly about how they hurt us. It was halfway through the week, and everyone except me had a letter from their parents. I felt sick as I thought mum was gone. Had she left me? Didn't she love me anymore? Have they killed her because I wasn't there? Yet I couldn't tell anyone how I felt. When we returned, I was so happy to see her waiting at the school gate for me but also angry about why she didn't write to me like the other parents. She told me that nobody let her know that was the case, which was true because teachers always thought my mum held me back because of our lifestyle, so they thought without discussing it with either of us, mum didn't have to know about letter writing to allow me to have some space from her. The damage that decision has left on me, they will never know.

Many times in my life, people have made decisions for us and completely screwed up our lives. They act like knights in shining armour and want to control our lives or sort it out instead of just accepting us as we are and allowing us to heal how we need to. We don't have many friends because of being hurt so often because people don't understand and try to patch us up how they feel we should be. That makes me feel suffocated, so I rebel, and so does mum; then people chuck us and feel hurt by us.

When you have lived through pain, especially if others have put this pain upon you, you see things clearly and people's motives. The funny thing is, most others believe they have come to help us and improve our lives (and I believe that), but how can you live and organise someone else's life? Why can't they just be friends and accept us as we are? We are strong individuals who, yes, have had a terrible life but are still here, and we still care about others. We laugh and cry just like other people.

I have a lifetime of hurt and control, professionals who didn't want to help us because we are too complex. I have a letter from mental health stating this. I never asked for this life. Surely there must be professionals willing to support us to understand and help us unpack our past to pack in the box it belongs. I'm afraid to seek help now regarding how long in support I will be. Services gave me a psychologist when I was 15. I had five different psychologists in nine months, so I learnt to say what they wanted. I also knew the pattern of the question sheets I had to fill in each session. If added up, the boxes could get you more time, probably with a bunch of different psychologists again, or you could add up enough to be discharged and in their books better. I aimed for the latter as I wasn't getting anywhere and had no consistency, so I wouldn't open up and be raw again, not knowing how to deal with it. Many people hurt me more than the paedos due to how they treated my mum and me.

I have worked since the age of 13 by choice. Mum has taught me to work hard for what I want and give back to society. We lived near the sea when I was younger, and I had my birthday celebrations there. They were great, and mum would make all the sandwiches and drinks and my birthday cake. Money was short as it was only my mum; even though she worked, we didn't have family or friends at the time to help us, but I always felt rich with those parties she held for me. Many people have treated mum as stupid, but I know the real woman and her talents. She is far from stupid, and I'm so proud of her; she is my mum.

All I ever wanted and still do is to belong and be accepted. I've had relationships that I thought were right (I would do everything; looking back, I was over the top), cleaning, looking after the children if these relationships had them, cooking, driving, and then doing everything for their wider family. I became physically unwell, and when asked if I had done something they asked me to, I would say yes because I thought I had and then, knowing I hadn't, felt I had let down the person. But that was my problem, being a people pleaser whom I mirrored off my mum; some of her behaviour patterns I picked up weren't because she was a bad mum but because she was never given a chance to learn and helped to do some things. Then it becomes a merry-go-round.

My mum and I clash, especially when fractured (dissociated). That can happen quite a bit, especially when we are tired or there is a common trigger. We both get affected, and we've had nobody to help us. I've now started proper counselling for the truth of our lives. My mum and I will continue to help others. Mum speaks about abuse, DID and the aftermath that pours out in families if we keep silent about it. But we both agree it is our time to live and grow as individuals. I want to sample the world and have a family, which will happen.

Ever since I was a toddler, I knew my dream job was to drive a coach, ferrying people across the UK, experiencing places, and meeting different people. It helps me to be part of the community. But more importantly, working provides the money I've worked hard for, giving me pride and an excuse to get up every day.

27

THE TRUTH

Why didn't I tell the world about all the abuse I suffered from and the people who drugged and raped me?

How many of us find it easy to disclose everything about ourselves to those we love? Let alone to the world... but about something as secretive and intrusive as rape by men in power.

How can someone who was not believed as a child, when speaking about the Stabards and a few others, put themselves forward again?

I was punished by trying to reveal what they were doing to us as children. They also punished me by sending me to a mental institution for adults when just a child, giving me so many labels that I lost my identity. The perpetrators punished me, and the most damning of rape and torture by powerful deathly individuals was allowed to continue. I knew I could never tell due to the fear of the internal tattoo; the constant reminders of what they would do if I did tell of the men and women who had something to do with capturing my body and exploiting it to all they could to earn themselves pockets loads of money. There was immense fear if we ever spoke out, yet we would sometimes reveal bits, in some ways deliberately. Who knows why? Maybe it was to show those who hurt us that we could still tell if we wanted to, or was it because we were testing whether it was safe to tell? I don't know, to be honest. Different parts of me would drop different clues about those in power to look after us children; if they wanted to pick up the signs of what was happening to us, they would have done.

I had an opportunity to speak out while away from my foster home, but I only spoke about the Stabards. She was dead by then, and my psychiatrist had already sussed something was up by adding two and two and coming closest to four - more than anyone else. Even though what they all did to us was beyond evil, it was easier to tell of my foster parents as people began to see that these people weren't who they portrayed themselves as. But in no way did that open the doors for the reveal of the more significant powerful abusers - who on earth would believe a stupid crazy person like me? Others lavished them with protection and security; even a stupid child like me could see that. To cross these people would be to give up your life.

When I heard one of the powerful abusers had passed away, it very much validated my fears. I cried and couldn't stop, not because he died but because I wasn't the only person he had abused. I thought this was it. I could now open the prison doors and free my family and myself by allowing myself to share some more truth. Those who had come forward regarding some of the influential people who abused me, too, seemed to be believed, so it was my time to tell the whole story. I was petrified, yet I thought I could smell the freedom of peace and life. It was going to be when I could finally let go of some more of my heavy burden, which may, in turn, help my physical health. I had an opportunity to speak, revealing the other people who raped me. I talked to the police and how the police treated my son and me; during disclosure, I knew I had done wrong. Not only had I put my son and me in even more danger, but also my daughter and her family, which meant I couldn't again have anything more to do with her. This broke my sons and my heart.

For speaking out, the perpetrators raped and beat me; humiliation was even greater as an independent organisation set up for survivors called me a liar, and I was jumping on other people's bandwagon. Why, if it happened to me, I didn't disclose it when I spoke about my foster parents? I tried to explain why, but they wouldn't support that. They'll never know its impact on my well-being; it was like the uttermost betrayal of all time. I have never once lied about my past; trauma prevents my memory from not being fully formed of dates, places, times, and names but people's faces, smells and buildings I remember. I can recall the marks on someone's body; I remember teeth, voices and noises.

When things become too much, I've learnt to shut down and push things to the back with devastating effects on my mental and physical well-being as it becomes like a dam ready to burst. You put things mentally around the traumatic memories to try and keep them from bursting, but it becomes too heavy. You are not just fighting with the memories; you are also fighting against your fractured mind. You have many pieces of yourself (I call them 'my me's') from different stages of abuse and neglect. There are the various stages of revealing and not revealing stuff - the frightened bits of me, the bold, outspoken me. Wounded, hurt, baby me, young child, teenager, mother, carer, cleaner, and slave me. Manipulating, mad, bad, coping me - please those who label me, which pleases my abusers. Silent me, funny me, coward me and many other parts of me. All are trying to hide the sickening secrets of the past, and the longer I have had to hide the truth more parts of me become fractured.

Many times while talking to the police about what happened to me, I wrestled with the parts of me that didn't feel safe to disclose. It was all for our safety, I was putting us at risk, and I was responsible for us all. Yet at times, I also heard my parts telling me bits they remember, parts fighting with each other, and those who needed me to comfort them as they became scared. Yet I was terrified the police would think I was mad as I tried to scratch out the noise of my parts. I wanted comfort, yet no police officer offered care or a kind word. They even allowed me to travel fifty miles from the interview to where I was staying alone. The memories triggered me on the train, and I blacked out a few times due to the memories being too overwhelming. Once I started to speak to the police, memories formed and kind of slotted into place. I didn't let anyone know immediately as I needed to make sure what I remembered was right. Once I knew they were, I contacted the police to say I remembered more and we could do another interview. This happened three times, and they told me that because I didn't disclose everything at once, it added doubt to what I was saying.

28

MY ME'S

Which one of us is going to be heard?
'Me, me, shh, the other two give away secrets you mustn't tell or else...'

One is bold, using their voice to speak about the perpetrator's lies.

'You are telling lies; nobody will believe you. You're evil; you are nobody.'

'Stop, don't tell, we will get into trouble; you know they will kill us.'

She really wants to free some of her burdens. Giving bits out and closing the lid to other bits as she learnt to as a hurt child. She switched off her emotions so that when others abused her, it didn't hurt, by screwing up her inner being and drifting off into semi-consciousness. But when someone gives her an opportunity to tell the truth, to reveal the dark secrets of the past, the fragmented parts of her aren't allowing her to let go of it all. Her head gets in a tangle trying to tell without affecting the others. Hanging on to the truth as if it is treasure, to keep under lock and key.

In the police interview room, we are arguing, but nobody sees this as it's silent. Not one of my me's is in agreement. Some wanted to speak but knew if they did, a doctor would section them as the police would see it as a mental health issue. Some of my me's have different voices; some pretend to be boys as they feel others will hear them better than as girls. The others are scared they'll get into trouble, so again, I'm protecting them... but nobody is protecting me. I'm trying to block out those of me who think I am betraying them as they call me stupid, mad, evil, and they trust others ...but if they knew me, I don't either.

As I talk to the police, I become fractured by my me's enemy. I hear my parts shouting, crying, and fearing, but the vocal ones tell me not to tell. Telling me I know what will happen, and that I must say that. I whimper because I'm scared and tortured by the betrayal of my inners. But those interviewing me don't care as it's not the done thing to offer comfort or kind words like 'are you okay?' I try to keep it together, as interviewers will just see a mad black woman sitting there going on about some stupid stuff. 'Shut up, shut up, my head tells my me's. I will tell you what I need to say.'

Even the interviewing officer isn't really interested in what I am saying. She won't even notice I'm wrestling with my inners as she picks her nails and looks at the floor. Pick,

pick on my jeans, but I managed as I told what I safely could. I knew I had to stop as I was beginning to feel sick.

'I need to stop', I told the officer.

She jumps up, and I presume the person recording has now switched off the camera.

'I need to go to the loo.'

I told the officer I didn't feel well and would be sick.

'Okay, she mumbles, I'll show you where the toilets are.'

I don't hear much more; it feels like I betrayed the whole world. I'm ashamed, sick and dizzy. I go to the loo and chuck up as I used to when small, chucking up all that was ugly about me. I learnt to empty the filth by being sick when I was about five. I think it's like clearing a water system.

Later, my mind remembers more I could have said without getting us into trouble, which is probably true. Nobody came to the door and took me away this time to section me. I began to think it was safe to have said what I did. My inners weren't speaking to me, just about me. I couldn't sleep for days remembering stuff and making sense of the paedophile ring and the threats and drugs they forced me to take. And the many times I'd end up in another town or another psychiatric hospital, confused about how I got there.

I remembered the threats made regarding my daughter and putting her into care near where the abuse happened as a way to shut me up. As I became scared that my daughter would get hurt by them, too, I tried to behave when they told me to take an overdose, and when to say I was ill, I did. I became such a controlled being that there was nothing about me that I had control over. So many people messed with my head and body. Was it deliberately done so I could not untangle the truth? Except it was my fault because it was too difficult, too confusing for anyone to understand the programming the abusers had on me.

I'm at fault for not telling the whole situation in one go, but honestly, I knew I couldn't even when the doors opened, I knew it wasn't safe either. When I finally told the complete facts of my life, I knew there was still stuff I didn't remember. I'm trying to allow memories to emerge freely from the fragmented parts. It's funny because people say we have false memories. We have false programming making us so fearful to tell the truth which is so muddled by fear embedded into us by the perpetrators. I am aware there may be a few people who lie (I'm not going to say I understand why this is) but to allow yourself to be publicly humiliated time and time again for trying to speak the truth deserves the right justice and validation that it wasn't your fault and for the truth to release you from the death sentence. I was wrong to believe it was safe to speak the truth to the police and other organisations.

They called me a liar for jumping on the bandwagon of other people's stories. Do they really think that was the case for me? It was the hardest thing ever to speak about my truths of organised abuse by powerful people.

I took a massive chance to talk about the truth. I have always been ashamed of being a victim of abuse, afraid of what the world thought of me. Too scared to seek a proper relationship because of what they would think of me. Many still don't want to believe child sexual abuse happens. It doesn't matter if you are rich or poor; there are rapists, sex traffickers and paedophiles.

With the belief - services would adequately support victims, and trained professionals could help us through our recovery. There would be schools sufficiently adapted to support those abused within their care. There would be the right support and provision for the police and the criminal system on why rape as children is still so silenced, especially if the child does not receive the support needed in the first stage of revealing. We can touch on the subject but never fully, as it scares people. They don't want to see this happens, but this is saying that they also don't want to help protect their young or others on how to safeguard themselves and seek the right support.

It allows an epidemic of systematic child abuse to continue with eyes closed and ears blocked. Well, wake up, nation, as we can no longer avoid this. Take it from me, and I would say this for most survivors: we need support, guidance, and to know how to live without fear and constant redemption when we speak out. We can't just accept that not talking, supporting, educating and not listening is the way forward. But more importantly, we can become more visible and be communities that watch and protect our children.

Sadly, it's not a happy ever after for most of us. It's how we cope with everyday living with the invasion of child abuse. My son and I both have DID dissociative disorder; let me explain how that developed for me, who I was, and my me's. I split into different parts to cope with the constant abnormal way of life. I ended up with about twenty me's by the time I was eight. Not all were a blessing; some were a hindrance.

I wanted love, so I developed a me who loved and gave love. I wanted revenge, so I became revengeful. I wanted others to see me, so I became visible. I wanted to hide, so I hid. I wanted to read, so I learnt to read. I wanted to eat, so I stole food. I wanted to play, so I became a child who made up stories and games in the shed that entertained us. I wanted to feel clean, so I tidied up. I wanted to feel loved, so I became sick. I wanted to be listened to, so I became loud and defiant about being split in ways that I had to cope with living. There was crazy me, bad me, and evil me. Parts of me split into what they labelled me; parts did the opposite, so I had a lot of conflict within me and in the outside world.

We never hurt anyone; that was not what we needed to do. We also became best allies when needed but argued, especially when scared. As we got older, a part of me became so scared of authority and still is. She turned into this scared child, so fearful that if professionals saw it they'd think I was mad; of course, there couldn't be another reason.

Giving birth as a sufferer of DID is so complicated. I found my me's more vocal than ever. The fear of each carried memories of past pregnancies and what happened; after a few hours in labour, the midwife said I needed a caesarean, again something I didn't know about; an alien word. I thought I would hurt as I did as a little girl having an abortion. Even after those many years (still to this very day), people tell me bits of info, and I discreetly do what they want, thinking I don't need to know. It makes me so ill as I can always pick up the signs when someone holds back...which is what they did when giving birth to Sam. I remember a nurse telling me to sit up but not to move as the injection could paralyse me. I thought they would hurt my baby and me, and I didn't have a say, so I switched as I couldn't cope with the unknown.

When I had my son, he was so poorly in and out of the hospital with his breathing. The staff automatically deemed me the incapable mother who couldn't put my son's needs above mine. Even the paediatrician said my son would have special needs, writing him off too. We all need to remember that what we say to our children repeatedly is what they believe, whether negative or not. Every child is not their parents or siblings; they are individuals, but they need love from a caregiver, guidance, warmth, positive boundaries, food and a home to feel safe. Perpetrators indoctrinate grooming, so many people still believe if you're an abuse victim, you will go on to abuse; that is not true. Some who abuse children have an illness (addiction). Most of our abusers are egoistic people who love control and, sadly, choose the weakest of us to feel powerful. Once they have that and see that we jump to their beck and call, the higher the stakes become and that's where you get organised abuse. Remember, it is not a title that abuses; it's a person who chooses to. It's a few people in different authorities and organisations. Don't blame everyone and miss the opportunity of good people. That's, sadly, a lesson I had to learn the hard way.

29

SUPPORT

We all need some support at some time in our life, especially those of us who suffer from historical child abuse. It is very hard to get the proper help. Sometimes it's a patch-up job that causes more trauma, as most therapy is not speaking about our trauma but about finding ways to live in the here and now. This is all well and good, and there will be a need for that once we have opened up our pain to understand and end the shame and self-blame. To deny this adds to what the abusers did to make us feel dirty and worthless. We can't just put a plaster over us and hope the pain and trauma will disappear and heal.

Many have told me, 'it's the past; you are choosing to live in the past - FORGET.'

'The devil is in you because of your trauma; you need delivering.'

'Burn all that is to do with the past, and then you can move on.'

'How old are you - and you're still allowing your past to affect you.'

'Don't mention anything about your past, as it will put me off my food tonight.'

These are just a few comments that have completely floored my son and me. Then you get people who want to direct you to healers and different potions that will heal us. I want to scream at them, 'accept us; that's it unless we've asked for help.'

I have been on the road for many years seeking the proper support for my son and me. It's extremely difficult to find for my son, don't get me wrong; there were offers for a community group for young black boys who had drug and alcohol dependencies. My son never did - but their view was due to his past, he would, in the end, go down that road. He was nine, now twenty-three, and has never taken drugs, and cannot stand alcohol.

At age twenty-three, we found my son's support due to Nancy Borret helping us; she listened to and offered us support where she worked at the Clinic of Dissociation Studies in London. Nancy heard and saw us and the need for Sam to get the proper authorisation; she reached out to a therapist who dealt with trauma. Sam is now in therapy. I'm getting help too from Nancy, who listens to me. She never tells me what to say or how to think. She listens and remembers what I've said for the following sessions as she helps to clear the debris of the past to make a more transparent future. That's part of how our growth is the essential essence of being able to stand in this world. Don't get me wrong; I've had therapy previously, which was very useful, but as the therapist said, there will be times throughout my life I will need to go back into treatment to deal with other things that may prevent me from taking steps forward. Words and judgemental comments hurt so much; if only we could use the same energy to support.

I'm not saying we would talk about our past. Most of us keep the shame so deeply hidden that it does cause us physical issues. Our needs include wanting to be allowed to feel the way we do so we can come to terms with it. We want friends from all walks of life. People with the best intentions try to pair us up with other survivors; that baffles me why they feel this need. If we've met people who have walked the same path and feel we have a friendship, that's fine, but we can't automatically assume that because we've been through similar, we will be friends. I want friends from all walks of life. I want to learn from others and be inspired by our ability to build regardless of our past.

Since my son's birth, I have been helping others through my life experiences. I've worked for local charities as peer support. As a psychiatric hospital patient's user council, I set up art groups on wards and opened a weekend art group for people with mental health issues. I also set up one of the first community revamps in an old mental health hospital, gathering people from the community, families of patients and staff from the hospital to update the ward's sitting room and garden area. I've worked as manager of a charity helping deprived communities build safer, stronger relationships, revamping their area and working with local schools and councils. Each job had its own gifts. I was privileged to be able to work with some amazing people. I thank my past (not saying what happened to us was right, as in no form was it). Still, the fact I can use it to support, educate and challenge the system for the better makes my being here now an exciting time. I will never give up on supporting others as it helps me use my life positively.

AFTERWORD

I first met Jennie when she approached CDS UK (the Clinic for Dissociative Studies) for help and support with the aftermath of her trauma. She has consistently moved me with her courage, openness and personal warmth.

CDS UK is a London-based clinic and charity working with survivors of extreme trauma and abuse all over the UK. We offer specialist assessment, psychotherapy and support to people with dissociative disorders, most typically Dissociative Identity Disorder (DID). All funding comes through the NHS and is considered individually on a case-by-case basis.

Sadly, the vast majority of people with histories of extreme abuse do not receive the kind of therapeutic support and care they need. Most mental health training in the UK does not teach dissociative disorders in any depth, if at all, meaning that recognition and understanding of the impact of extreme trauma are sparse. It seems that as a profession, we have dissociated dissociation itself, and its associated severe trauma, from our accepted 'knowledge'. Sadly, the unbearability at the heart of this topic often elicits denial and disbelief in us, leading to repetitions of neglect and the potential re-traumatisation of survivors.

DID develops as a result of repeated trauma that starts in the earliest childhood, in conjunction with the absence of a safe and protective attachment relationship. The mind fragments into multiple discrete identities or personality parts to enable the person to survive circumstances that would otherwise be unbearable. Different parts of the person hold and remember various aspects of the overall experience – some typically being present to manage daily life and others containing elements of trauma. The parts may have limited awareness or memory of each other, or none at all, which can lead to sudden fluctuations in behaviour and emotional expression. It can be very confusing for professionals if the fragmentation - also known as structural dissociation of the personality – has not been identified and understood. Unfortunately, although DID is evidence of extreme and overwhelming trauma experiences, how it manifests can often lead to others not believing, discrediting or dismissing survivors' testimonies as 'unreliable'.

Although the contents of Jennie's book are painful and uncomfortable to read, it is important for us to hear and listen to her. It is horrific and terrifying to consider that adults, including groups of perpetrators, work together in an organised manner to torture and abuse small children. However, assuming that such things do not happen simply because they take us outside our comfort zone only helps to continue facilitating these kinds of crimes.

Nancy Borret,
Consultant psychotherapist and Clinical Manager
CDS UK (clinic of dissociation Studies)
London

CONNECT WITH ME

If you have been inspired by this book and would love to connect and/or leave me a review on Amazon you can find me here:

Website: www.giftsmadewithzazzle.store
Email: Handsthatcreate@icloud.com
Facebook: Jennie Grace
Etsy: Giftsmadewithadazzle
Instagram: Giftsmadewithzazzle-Jen
Twitter: @Jennie76180258